State and Class
A Sociology of
International
Affairs

Ralph Pettman

ST. MARTIN'S PRESS   NEW YORK

Library of Congress Cataloging in Publication Data

Pettman, Ralph,
    State and class.

    Includes index.
    1. International relations. 2. State, The.
3. Social classes. 4. Social structure.
I. Title
JX1251.P47   301.5'92   79-19109
ISBN 0-312-75602-X

CONTENTS

They complained in the East,
They are paying too high.
They say that your ore ain't worth digging.
That it's much cheaper down
In the South American towns
Where the miners work almost for nothing.

Bob Dylan
'North Country Blues'
(Reproduced by kind permission of Warner
 Bros. Music Ltd)

for my father,
gone to his long home

INTRODUCTION

The subtitle to this work — 'a sociology of international affairs' — is a shorthand hoarding over a very extensive subject indeed. The most obvious problem is the sheer scope and scale of what I have set out to describe and explain. The parameters are far from clear and in touring the horizon one tends to neglect the sort of empirically precise performance that a more circumscribed study might permit. New 'facts' are less likely to emerge, and in many places one treads familiar country trading in concepts worn smooth and slippery with much use, searching for the patterns and dispositions that those closer to events might have missed.

The enterprise is still worth while. One feels like the philosopher that J.D. Mabbott depicts in his book, *The State and the Citizen*; like someone climbing the tower of a great cathedral. Up the spiral stairway he goes, and as he does so

> the common and particular details of life . . . shrink to invisibility and the big landmarks shake themselves clear. Little windows open at his elbow with widening views. There is *conscience*; over there is *duty*; there is *conscience* again looking quite different from this new level; now he is high enough to see law and liberty from one window. And ever there haunts him the vision of the summit, where there is a little room with windows all round, where he may recover his breath and see the view as a whole . . . and where that gargoyle (determinism, was it?) which loomed in on him so menacingly at one stage in his ascent shall have shrunk to the speck that it is.
>
> We shall be told that no one reaches the top. A philosopher who ceases to climb does so because he gets tired; and he remains crouched against some staircase window, commanding but a dusty and one-sided view at best, obstinately proclaiming to the crowds below, who do not listen, that he is at the summit and can see the whole city. That may be so. Yet the climb itself is not without merit . . . and even at the lowest windows one is above the smoke and can see proportions more clearly so that men and tramcars never look quite the same again.[1]

International relations is most commonly construed in terms of the

political interactions apparent between the diverse states and state-like
entities we find in the present-day world. This is clearly indicated by
the synonym 'world politics'. This construction has been assailed on
the one hand by those who attempt a broader 'behaviouralist' definition
of 'politics' and who seek to bring diverse transdisciplinary insights
before the more traditional scholars who have fostered their neglect,
and on the other by those, particularly development theorists, who
apply neo-Marxist/neo-Leninist paradigms to their understanding of
world affairs.

Partly because of the latter there is now an emergent *political economy* of international affairs. There are few ready references to a *political
sociology* of the subject, however. The sociological approach is a curiously neglected one, and sociological theories, concepts and research methods
are rarely identified as such, either because they are simply not recognised for what they are, or because theorists and practitioners have
chosen to ignore the source of what are really 'sociological' ideas. Sociologists themselves scarcely acknowledge the structure of international
relations as a determinant of social affairs, while students of world politics neglect the importance of a sociological view.

And yet such a perspective is a seminal one. The present work
is an attempt to locate this component of the discipline, to give it
explicit recognition, and to explore further aspects of the approach
that may not have been fully developed so far. Indeed, I am convinced
that the study of global politics proceeds the wrong way around. Its
current impetus mainly comes from its attempt to understand the flow
of diplomatic traffic and to trace the well-springs of foreign policy and
the way such policies interact. General principles – political, economic
and strategic – are adduced to explain the international events that move
over and around us. Comparatively little attempt is ever made, however,
and it is one source of a growing sense of dissatisfaction in the field and a
feeling that the discipline is less than 'relevant', to reach for arguments in
terms of the overall social structure of the contemporary world and the
fundamental social forces at work there. If the discipline has substance it
must derive in the end from whatever account we can give of these forces
and their manifold political and economic effects – the general pattern and
shape, that is, of global social change.

It is to sociology that we turn for a sympathetic understanding of
that human collectivity we now call 'society' – its social configuration;
its constituent and compulsive 'forces' and manifest 'structure'. We invite
thus a comprehensive description of the interrelations of the smaller
groups of which any 'society' is composed, of the influences that fashion

society, and the way its patterns of interaction are revised. An intellectual product of nineteenth-century Europe, sociology betrays its origins
in a continuing preoccupation with the methodology of science and the
distinctive characteristics of industrialised life. We happen to have inherited a most dynamic world and though the process of change, global
in extent, is explicit and profound, there is I think one key touchstone:

> In the twentieth century, the essence of man is not that he is a ration-
> al, or a political, or a sinful, or a thinking animal, but that he is an
> industrial animal . . . The interesting thing about this essence of man
> is that, as usual, it exists both in actuality and in potentiality. One
> part of the world consists of societies which are industrial; the other
> of becoming such.[2]

There is much more to it than this, of course. The advent after World
War Two of a large number of new states in Asia and Africa altered the shape
of global affairs. How significant this alteration has been is still a moot point
but decolonisation and the subsequent process, much debated, of neo-colon-
isation did see a rapid expansion in the compass of sociological concerns. It
was necessary to account for the presence of these new political units and
to describe and explain in a global context their politico-economic 'underdevelopment', their emergent modes of urban growth and civil administration,
the ideology of modernisation which has been pervasive throughout, and the
changes this ideology has wrought in both the local and the international configurations of socio-economic class. The often militant mood of South
world spokesmen, marked in the global North by scholars of diverse
political persuasion, has reinforced the fact that contemporary sociology should also be 'critical', that it cannot take social forces and structures for granted but ought to attempt an overt study of their ideological
proclivities and their capacity to persist.

A project of this kind is obviously predicated upon the assumption
that a *world* society does indeed exist in something more than a nominal
sense. I shall elaborate this assumption in Chapter 2, and Chapters 4 and
5 of Section B will attempt to convey my understanding of the complex
contours the said society displays. Initially, however, I shall try to locate
the notion of *society* with respect to the larger concept of *culture*, and
the larger question again of the character of human consciousness. Siev-
ing these contextual concerns before moving on towards my core concern with *state* and *class* should help in defining the configurations of
the topic to hand; it will also help to establish some of my working
assumptions and identify those rather more nebulous philosophic

premisses which characterise our age and which permeate where they do not already pre-empt our appreciation of the phenomenal world. My central question: what are 'world affairs' that we may know them? is therefore predicated upon a prior interrogative: what are 'we' that we may know world affairs?

Notes

1. J.D. Mabbot, *The State and the Citizen* (Arrow Books, London, 1958), pp. 9-10.
2. Ernest Gellner, *Thought and Change* (Weidenfeld and Nicolson, London, 1964), p. 35.

Part I: SOCIAL CONSCIOUSNESS

1 CULTURE AND CONSCIOUSNESS

'Society' and 'Culture'

'Society' is a notional fiction. The concept is meant to correspond to various perceived facts about human relationships, to particular aspects of human behaviour, to a collection of people in some sense autonomous and internally organised with a place and history of their own, a common sense of their identity (the 'we' feeling sociologists refer to),[1] and a shared style of life. In practice,

> the idea of society can be elaborated as an abstract model, or series of models, applicable with varying complexity, differing implications, and a high degree of approximation to a wide range of human groups. The essential criterion of applicability is that the group concerned manifest some set of orderly social relations. Thus small experimental groups, a classroom, a political organisation, a village, a metropolis, a nation, and the population of the world at a given time, or for a defined period, may each be analysed as a society, if the analysis concentrates on the relational aspects of the relevant behaviour.[2]

Though it comes perilously close to defining a 'system' rather than a 'society', the concept of 'orderly social relations' does suggest more than mere interaction, while demonstrating how diffuse the idea can be.

'Society' is the mental arrangement, however, of only part of what we understand as human experience. If we stand back from the concept for a moment, if we stand back from the traffic between individuals and groups of individuals which animate social institutions, we find an envelope of ideas, values, and symbolically significant meaning systems that shape behaviour, and shape the 'artifacts, mentifacts and socifacts'[3] such behaviour is pleased to produce. This is the part of the definition that refers to a common way of living and indeed, *social* systems cannot be understood without reference to *cultural* systems since individual members of the one usually act in the light of meanings established in the other. As such, culture is a species-specific phenomenon. We seem to be genetically obliged to live in groups and to use complex linguistic symbols and tools if we are, purely physically, to persist.

The distinction is not as clear-cut as the concepts would suggest, since they refer to sets of phenomena, often the same set, that are neither very concrete nor empirically precise. Unlike toads and tables they exist as analytical abstractions; they do not appear before us as common objects we can readily taste or touch. None the less the distinction is important, and to talk of the one wholly in terms of the other is a reductionist ploy that robs us of many of the riches that an anthropological or sociological perspective now allows. 'To speak of a "member of a culture"', then, 'should be understood as an ellipsis meaning a "member of the society of culture X"',[4] and it is the way these notions complement each other rather than compete for our intellectual attention that is of interest here.

Human cultures represent, among other things, the historical accumulation of human values. Any understanding of them will rest upon prior premises about the methodological propriety of the historical method and the nature of human consciousness. I would argue the superiority of the historical perspective since it allows a broad approach to the topic while retaining as much as possible of the feel of the subject-matter. In studying the material world our knowledge is furthered by that which can be verified experimentally and, if at all possible, expressed in the universal language of mathematics. When we confront the social world, however, and human culture at large, tracing causal chains is seldom simple. It is often less productive than a sense of context and of the complexities of what is a very dense and rich subject-matter indeed.[5] Social scientists are pattern-seekers and patterns are assembled, and are usually most apparent, over time. Given its synoptic diversity one would assume a less than automatic sequence to the process of cultural change, and a historical approach seems to elucidate this best.

Consciousness

The further fact that cultural systems carry forward from generation to generation what a society considers right and due prompts one to ask how effective people are in general as value-creating, value-bearing beings, and what the source and strength of their evaluative capacities might be. Here we confront the fact of human consciousness and the individual's sense of volition and will. Personal awareness and the individual's sense of the group predisposes a propensity to choose and knowingly to avoid otherwise ineluctable ends. On the evidence of contemporary brain research Roger Sperry argues (and while aware that the point is controversial, I cite his position alone since it is so clear and extreme) that consciousness is not simply the intrinsic effect of neural function but a synergistic motive force of its own. Thus:

mental events are . . . not merely *correlates* of brain activity, but
also *causes* . . . Conscious mental experience in our present interpretation is conceived to be a holistic emergent of brain activity, different
from and more than the neural events of which it is composed . . .
As dynamic emergent properties of cerebral excitation, conscious
mental phenomena are given a working role in brain function and a
pragmatic reason for being and for having been evolved.[6]

Though a precise physiological formulation of the process is not yet
forthcoming and perhaps may never be, if Sperry is correct we have cor-
roborating evidence for an important philosophic stance, namely, that
human beings possess an unbridled *physical* capacity at least to exercise
their free will. Sperry goes on to assert that contemporary neuro-science
must now account for subjective mind states in any comprehensive description of the way the brain works. Moods, moral assessments and so
on are independent variables, with independent influence over any decision we take.

The freedom thereby introduced into the causal brain sequence leading to a volitional choice far surpasses, in both degree and kind, the
notions envisaged in the more mechanistic and atomistic forms of
determinism that have excluded mental events . . . Our new approach
to mind-brain theory thus goes far to restore to human nature some
of the personal dignity, freedom, inner creativity, and responsibility
of which it has long been deprived by behaviourism and by materialist science generally.[7]

As a philosophic position this is very familiar stuff. It bears modest if
somewhat elliptical rehearsal here, however, since it is a particularly
significant position that conditions all consequent debate. It is also, we
must remember, only one point of view. In totally detaching values and
feelings from their physical and biochemical substrates Sperry discounts
the conditioning influence of the needs, drives, perhaps even instincts that
seem to have at least some part to play in the overall outcome of human
behaviour. The evidence is contentious, but psychological and ethological
research, as well as aspects of the neuro-sciences themselves, would suggest that a model of the mind as an autonomous monitor is incomplete.[8]
Some account must be taken of the individual capacity —rather erratic
and difficult to locate but evident none the less —for aggression for
example, or for the urge to identify with a group or cause. To the extent
that species-specific needs and drives do obtain we are less than free,

which is not to suggest that what we do is somehow ultimately determined and beyond our comprehension and control. Conditioning processes may be very subtle, but by becoming aware of them we may accommodate them; we can exercise the voluntaristic power that Sperry would applaud to scrutinise our subjective mental experiences and to account and allow for those that might have a phylogenetic root.

Culture

Much turns upon our capacity for making choices. In choosing we define values. These only too readily become reified in turn. Human cultures themselves are 'essentially value systems . . . complex sets of alternatives which, having been chosen at some time in the past, have become fixed and repetitive in their form'.[9] Choices become habits, and socially sanctioned are granted customary status. Like any habit, however, they can be good or bad. The question remains: in what respect might they be assessed so? We know, and any reading of history amply documents it, that the range of what we have chosen as a species to value and to do is very wide indeed. We have been benevolent and we have been conspicuously cruel; we can be well-meaning and generous, or dishonest and greedy.

Given such a diversity of choice, of value systems and cultures, can we talk of a universal moral code that pertains to a world society, and how might it be realised in the present day?[10] In the same paper I have already quoted, Professor Sperry not only cites values as independent variables and hence of compelling professional concern. He sees science itself, after the exclusion of diverse 'metaphysical and mystic alternatives including "other-world" mythologies', as 'man's most important means for determining ultimate value and meaning', as the

> source and arbiter of values and belief systems at the highest level . . .
> the final determinant of what is right and true, and the best authority
> available to the human brain for finding ultimate axioms and guide-
> line beliefs to live by.[11]

Not all would share the unquestioning faith manifest here in the ability of those who practise as scientists to legislate the highest principles of human conduct. Even allowing a scientific basis for free will, we are no nearer in fact to a definite understanding of how that will might best be exercised. 'Science', while aspiring to a cultural objectivity, is still the product of a particular philosophical environment and the bearer of its own value-laden preconceptions. Despite its extraordinary success in generating new knowledge and hence its rapid acceptance around the world as a fruitful way to understand and hence to manipulate the material world, it is one culture among many, and not, despite its manifest advantages and its halo of achievements, *a priori* superior to the rest. Even within its own milieu it cannot in any ultimate way resolve questions of value choice.

On the global level anthropologists have documented a wide array of such value systems. None would appear to possess a monopoly on what is authoritative or humane. This does not preclude our making judgements as to comparative worth, though assessments of this kind cannot be established by majority lot alone, nor can they hope to stand unrevised forever, and there will be more than one of them. It would be cultural chauvinism in disguise, no doubt, to anticipate one particular such value system that was more or less flawed than the rest. Our task, then, would appear to be a serious and detailed attempt to compare them all. To do otherwise would require opting for one above others in advance, and without the benefit of sustained comparison, to lapse into ethnocentric certainties decked out as an objective choice.[12]

We are much better placed, then, if we advance with caution; if we remain aware of the plurality of human beliefs, but do not retreat into relativism. We must look for those cultural patterns that emerge from the synergy of more limited individual intentions, those aggregate behaviours that we label in retrospect as an 'Industrial Revolution' or the 'Global State System' or 'Imperialism' or the like. We have to account for social structures that may never have been meant as such or that may have little to do with the limited actions or thoughts of their individual protagonists. We have to account for systems of values and ideas that prove on inspection to be truly pervasive, but that very few people seem explicitly to own. Foreign-policy-makers, though in practice often appearing to lack a very abstract understanding of the diplomatic process to which they contribute, are always the more or less unwitting purveyors of ideological doctrines which are tangible in their effects and of which they may be quite unaware. In a general fashion most of us live like this, inheriting a culture that in certain fundamental respects is very widely shared, a culture that we practise and pass on, and yet one that remains largely subliminal. We forward its distinctive features while remaining on the whole oblivious to them.

Where Western values prevail, the world has been Europeanised, which is the most recent and the most significant episode in an age-old process whereby cultures, or rather the peoples who bear them, meet and are changed by what they are told and see, or are told to see. A European veneer has been drawn across a world that once consisted of comparatively remote groups whose influence upon each other was usually spasmodic and took place over long periods of time. Diffusion and borrowing now occur at a very rapid pace and the traffic in economic and political ideas and cultural forms in general is truly international and much more immediate and profound in its effects. In a process originally initiated by the imperial powers of the West, the last four hundred years have witnessed major readjustments to the ethnic map of the world, the disarray of competing cultures, and the widespread accommodation to European capitalism and technology and its attendant values and norms on the part of the diverse communities this process has paused to co-opt. The indigenous response has been a prominent feature of the modern world. Many groups have managed to throw over direct European rule and to install governments of their own that have attempted to articulate a sense of local identity and difference. Where there has not been an active policy of post-colonial subversion on the part of the former metropolitan power or another one like it, the example of the West has usually proven so powerful that its diverse forms of economic, political, military and cultural control have found widespread acceptance anyway. The social consequences have been extensive.

Johan Galtung gives a provocative, if partial, description of one aspect of the cultural dynamic operating here. The world consists, he says, of Centre and Periphery nations (each of which has a centre and a periphery in turn), and

> [i] f the Center always provides the teachers and the definition of that worthy of being taught (from the gospels of Christianity to the gospels of Technology), and the Periphery always provides the learners, then there is a pattern which smacks of imperialism. The satellite nation in the Periphery will also know that nothing flatters the Center quite so much as being encouraged to teach, and being seen as a model, and that the Periphery can get much in return from a humble, culture-seeking strategy . . . For in accepting cultural transmission the Periphery also, implicitly, validates for the Center the culture developed in the Center, whether that center is intra- or inter-national. This serves to reinforce the Center as a center, for it will then continue to develop culture along with transmitting it, thus creating lasting demand for the latest innovations.[13]

Local demand for the intellectual products of the Centre, however selective, can only expand as peripheral populations seek access to the material affluence so visible in metropolitan powers. One seemingly self-evident way to secure an enhanced share of what national product there may be is to replicate in the Periphery the forms and content of the knowledge reproduced in the Centre. This demand is further fostered by the import of books and journals, and by those who have been trained themselves in Centre states.

This process can be a personally disorientating one. The psycho-pathological consequences have been widely discussed,[14] and those who have studied them document in different ways the feeling of inferiority that can pervade an indigenous population of a colony prior to its nominal independence, and which persists in subtle ways after that date. The effects will vary widely, however, depending upon the indigenous peoples themselves, and the way they come personally to terms with the stress inherent in their life situations. The relationship between the coloniser and the colonised, once come to an end, has often been resolved not in the realisation of a new freedom but in the search for alternative modes of dependence to fill the gap the loss of an imperial presence has left. The erosion of an 'old' world view with its customs and its reasons for why things are so; the difficulties of visualising a secure and satisfactory future in the 'new'; the daily demonstration of the ways of the West and the comparisons it invites with the quality of local life; these things can produce an ambivalent attraction for and aversion to the goods and influences of that extensive culture that now flows around the globe. One notable response has been the complete and uncritical adoption of 'new' forms (though we might note such various and complex consequences as cargo cults, millenarian movements and diverse culturally self-conscious attempts to reaffirm local values and to reject the sorts of social relationships the capitalist world economy and industrial modernisation tend to produce in favour of more communitarian ways and the reinforcing web of social kin).

The process generates what have been termed 'marginal men'.[15] All in such a predicament directly experience the clash of different ways of life, and must either decree a preference for one or the other, or compartmentalise them, or evolve some sort of mental compromise between or synthesis of the two. They look to those who can translate the meaning of an alien set of shared symbols into something that makes sense in terms of their own. The meaning of important concepts can be changed in the process (where they are not actively manipulated for personal gain); new groups of ideological entrepreneurs arise, actually ruling or serving rulers, oiling the mental links that run from each state capital to the outside world, and from there back into the countryside behind. Such individuals can pay their own psychological price for the privilege.

The Marxist Response

'Modernised' groups at the centre of non-Westernised states are uniquely placed, then, to mediate the process of cultural penetration. This idea is familiar from the argument, particularly strong in the Marxist tradition, that the social reality of the world is that reality defined as such by its ruling class. Among its other attributes such a class controls the means of communication, of education and religious faith, and hence the immediate way in which, for most people, 'reality' is defined. The most important aspect of this 'reality' is the common understanding it engenders of the 'new' world and what it means. Such a definition will inevitably be one that serves ruling-class interests, and those of any other group that dissents will tend to be construed as unreal or meaningless. The most telling way to maintain effective control of a community, in fact, is to ensure that mental alternatives to the prevailing order simply do not occur; that they are literally not thought of, at least on a general scale. The attempt to institute such control is perennial, though it is never wholly achieved, since it is impossible to locate, co-opt, ostracise, kill or otherwise constrain all dissidents who think for themselves. In a general sense, however:

> The ideas of the ruling class are in every epoch the ruling ideas: i.e., the class which is the ruling material force of society is at the same time its ruling *intellectual* force. The class which has the means of material production at its disposal, has control at the same time over the means of mental production, so that thereby generally speaking, the ideas of those who lack the means of mental production are subject to it.[16]

If we construe Galtung's global division of the world into Centre and Periphery in class terms, then this argument applies on a world scale too. It also pertains to the traffic between the centre and periphery *within* Peripheral states, and within those of the Centre itself.

There are difficulties with the Marxist concept of culture, though the theory is more subtle and a lot less mechanistic than is popularly supposed. Shlomo Avineri locates Marx's epistemology half-way between classical materialism and classical idealism, a somewhat precarious position and one that 'never fully denies the validity of traditional mechanistic modes of consciousness as expressions of alienated life in existing society'.[17] In Marxist parlance social structures and the relationships from which they are derived are radically conditioned by existing modes of production, and 'culture' in general, and a putative 'world culture' in particular can only be understood effectively in terms of society's material base. The Marxist model of a substructure of productive forces and a superstructure of social situations erected upon it does allow of reciprocal influence, but it tends to depict a society's economic underpinnings as the ultimate determinant. Thus Marx argued:

> We set out from real, active men, and on the basis of their real life-process we demonstrate the development of the ideological reflexes and echoes of the life-process. The phantoms formed in the human brain are also, necessarily, sublimates of their material life-process, which is empirically verifiable and bound to material premises. Morality, religion, metaphysics, all the rest of ideology and their corresponding forms of consciousness, thus no longer retain the semblance of independence. They have no history, no development; but men, developing their material production and their material intercourse, alter, along with this their real existence, their thinking and the products of their thinking. Life is not determined by consciousness, but consciousness by life.[18]

And in more general terms:

> In the social production which men carry on they enter into definite relations that are indispensable and independent of their will; these relations of production correspond to a definite stage of development of their material powers of production. The totality of these relations of production constitutes the economic structure of society – the real foundation, on which legal and political superstructures arise and to which definite forms of social consciousness correspond. The mode of production of material life determines the general character of the social, political, and spiritual processes of life. It is not the consciousness of men that determines their being, but on the contrary, their social being that determines their consciousness.[19]

I do not intend to argue the issues raised here. Even if we accept the dichotomy of substructure and superstructure as a practical distinction, however, they do not appear in historical sequence. They evolve together and neither substructural nor superstructural factors appear on their own. The changes that occur in the economic base do not proceed against a static socio-political backdrop. They take place as part of the total process of cultural evolution and the industrial capitalism which Marx so clearly locates in its historical context is no less a general cultural artifact because he was able to trace it out in abstract material terms.[20] We can, of course, put one aspect notionally before the other, and the influence of forms of economic organisation and the changes in those forms upon social relationships is abundantly evident on a world scale. Marx was only one of a number of important thinkers who attempted to capture for our collective understanding the significance of 'industry', which has proved such a truly radical phenomenon, and to trace its origins and the influence it continues to have on each and every social and political edifice. Perhaps in its global form industrial culture really will appear in the end as 'finally determining', explaining much about social and political behaviour that would otherwise remain obscure. But the larger pattern will continue to assert itself none the less. 'America' and 'Japan', for example, though eminently successful capitalist societies and sharing similar traits, do not *feel* like the same place, and in describing the workings of each one their individual and unique histories must bear some weight at least of the explanatory load.

World Culture: 'Traditional' *v.* Scientific Consciousness

This said, there *are* important continuities and parallels. Whether merely borrowed, or the result of some innate logic that the industrial process will reproduce wherever it is applied, it is the correspondence that constitutes world culture. Modern industrial civilisation is unique, we may safely assert.[21] It is also — and to document this would require a résumé of contemporary world history — in the process of becoming universal. What is the salient feature that industrial societies share? What is the temper of the sort of mind that the complex character of such society helps to realise and comes to reflect? 'Some have sought the crucial distinguishing mark in the division of labour, some in rationality, in democracy or the equalisation of conditions, in economic organisation,' and yet whether cause or effect, or both in a complex way that defies reduction, the single most striking feature it seems to me is the mode of thought itself. To what extent does a 'modern' human being possess the sort of consciousness that permeates the age, and is it qualitatively different from that of our forebears or that of peoples not yet engaged in a modern milieu? What is the crucial change in awareness as one moves from a 'traditional' society to an industrial, technologically complex and science-oriented one?

At the risk of appearing facile, I shall attempt a brief discussion of the characteristics that seem critical here. And the best place to begin, I would guess, is with the mode of scientific cognition that antedates industrial culture and yet informs it at every point. What difference do we discern between this and a non-scientific understanding of reality and the world? We must abstract and dichotomise, since there are many cases one could cite of groups, leisured and literate, who could hardly be called 'traditionalist' and yet who bear little resemblance in their attitudes of mind to those who live in the technologically complex civilisations extant today. Indeed every human society can offer evidence of creative intellectual endeavour on the part of some of its members at least. The dichotomy itself is easily overdone since the way individuals accept what they are told about the world can be very much the same whether they be peasants living in the Periphery or newspaper boys in New York. And though what the newspaper boy believes may appear contemporary, this can obscure a personal mental aspect every bit as unscientific and as 'unenlightened' as any Fourth World farmer's, if not more so.[22]

Modern means of communication and indoctrination have ensured a comparatively general appreciation of Western concepts and analytical forms, and there do appear to be real differences between a modern and a non-modern world-view. First, however, we should consider what seems to be the same. Robin Horton, in his discussion of 'African Traditional Thought and Western Science', has nominated a number of important similarities between these two mental arenas, similarities that seem to characterise any attempt at abstract thought at all. Regardless of whether the context be Molepolole or London, to explain an event in general terms involves, he argues, the same species-specific responses. It is to look, for example, for 'unity underlying apparent diversity; for simplicity underlying apparent complexity; for order underlying apparent disorder; [and] for regularity underlying apparent anomaly'.[23] Any reflective individual will seek causal patterns that transcend those we discern with our common sense, though he or she will tend to appeal to such patterns only when common sense fails to provide a useful cognitive return. Theories will vary in their scope and explanatory power, and will move, whether scientific or religious, through a similar process of 'abstraction, analysis and reintegration'.[24] Furthermore: 'In evolving a theoretical scheme, the human mind seems constrained to draw inspiration from analogy between the puzzling observations to be explained and certain already familiar phenomena.'[25] The analogy

seldom involves more than a limited aspect of such phenomena . . .
[I]t is only this limited aspect which is taken over and used to build

up the theoretical scheme ... [and] once built is developed in ways
which sometimes obscure the analogy on which it was founded.[26]

Though the above does hopefully tell us something about the way we
think—in this particular case, that the religious reasoning of tribal
Africans is in important respects the same as the cognitive mode of contemporary science—it fails to describe the 'closed' character of the non-
modern mind, the complete acceptance of prevailing ideas, and the
ostensible failure to work out new methods of understanding the world
by questioning the old. There is psychic comfort in the certainty such
sacrosanct beliefs can bring, since to relinquish them means to court
the void. The modern mind has become used, Horton concludes, to con-
templating this mental space without feeling faint. Those who think in
this way can more readily conceive of other theoretical options. No one
notion can lay claim to absolute truth and to challenge the established
order is no longer to risk the collapse of reason itself.

All of which is rather too harsh, I feel, on those intellectual members
of non-modern cultures who *have* evinced a capacity to keep an 'open'
mind, while being altogether too generous towards those contemporary
folk who seem no better than primitive stereotypists at surrendering their
preferred and tenaciously defended cosmic views. Science itself proceeds,
to some extent at least, by rigidly enforcing learned 'paradigms' and
solving the 'puzzles' they set rather than by seeking separate sorts of
understanding altogether.[27] The point is well put by Gellner:

> consider the implications of accepting this as a general criterion of
> traditional mentality: it means that within it there can be no syncret-
> ism, no doctrinal pluralism, no deep treason, no dramatic conversion
> or doctrinal oscillation, no holding of alternative belief-systems up
> one's sleeve, ready for the opportune moment of betrayal.[28]

The key factor lies, it seems to me, further down, and again I quote
Karl Marx: 'Reason', he said, 'has always existed, but not always in
rational form.'[29] A traditional world-view, in other words, is fundamentally a *subjectivist* one that rests on a sense of personal and immediate
continuity with the universe; an intimate connection that objective
scrutiny can only elaborate and confirm and does not deny. The modern-
ist mind, drawing in the West on the legacy of the ancient philosophers
of the Hellenic world, has breached this link, and posits an objective
reality that exists outside the individual, that we observe and that we
try to describe and explain; a reality that, because of our imperfect

faculties, we no doubt fail to perceive as it 'is', perhaps will never be able to perceive as it 'is', but lies 'out there' none the less. We can subvert the discontinuity by claiming a mystic appreciation of absolute truth, but this is not good enough; the knowledge must be demonstrable, teachable and public. I would not confuse all modernism with positivism, but the risk of self-deception and of fraud does require no less at least.

In the same vein Edmund Husserl distinguishes the 'universal attitude' (a religious-mythical one founded in the 'natural sphere') from the 'theoretical' perspective which arose, he argues, historically and uniquely in Greece:

> [W]ith the appearance of Greek philosophy and its first formulation, through consistent idealisation of the new sense of infinity, there is accomplished . . . a thoroughgoing transformation which finally draws all finite ideas and with them all spiritual culture and its [concept of] mankind into its sphere . . . Scientific culture under the guidance of ideas of infinity means, then, a revolutionisation . . . of the whole culture, a revolutionisation of the whole manner in which mankind creates culture.[30]

While the mythic notion is an intensely subjective and practical one, the scientific/theoretical perspective aspires to something quite different, that is 'pure theoria'. Anyone who subscribes to the latter becomes a 'nonparticipating spectator, [a] surveyor of the world . . . a philosopher'; he or she becomes *objective*.[31]

Once the mental break is made the issue does not rest there, however. A new continuity may be established, whereby human-kind is seen as part of the natural order of things, but an order that is a materialist and not a mystical one. Or the notion is advanced that continuity can never be re-established; that we can only endorse the difference between matter and mind. In this view

> man is discontinuous with the thing world and an understanding of what he is like needs a basically different approach . . . [he] intuitively grasps himself as different from the world of things and it is through his intentional and intuitive capacities that a shared world of experience comes to have the kind of significance that this world has for [him].[32]

To adopt what is identified these days as an existentialist view is not to retreat into the non-modern and mystical one. It is not a return to a religious and subjectivist perspective. It is 'scientific' still, but it is intensely introspective.

Once established, the effects of a radical objectivity are quite striking. The act of naming, for example, becomes one of labelling only; it no longer serves to secure a potential means of environmental control, and words lose their assumed power as instruments of magic. It is not that the non-modern mind fails to perceive any other way of understanding the link between language and the world, but in the 'mystic' mode man and the world are continuous and the linguistic description of the environment not only defines an external nature but establishes something intrinsically relevant to the individual too. Conversation with 'natural' objects takes on the sort of importance one associates with verbal commerce with other human beings. In scientific terms such a conversation has nothing to say. To 'science' the enchanted use of words is 'intolerable' since it implies that a change of mind is a change in fact and we are well advised, if we are to make sense of it in objective terms, not to accept that the world shuffles about to accommodate human fancies. Horton sees this as evidence of the modern capacity to countenance radical alternatives to any preferred perspective.[33] We need not strain so hard, however, for a reason for what is a real difference in what we expect of language. It is sufficient to indicate that in detaching our appreciation of reality from reality itself the words we use to articulate what we perceive become detached too. They become arbitrary human sounds that by mutual and learned consent signify things. The link thus established allows only this limited traffic. There is no capacity for working magic effects and no human purpose to be derived from what is seen to be an unheeding universe. Not just words but general ideas and concepts can be taken out of the 'real' world in this way. We do not need to posit the additional ability to conceive of alternative possibilities to appreciate that if we feel ourselves to be as one with our environment, then we are also likely to experience difficulty in dissociating what we think about our surroundings from the environment itself. Once we can lift ourselves out of our context, however, that signal effort of the imagination allows us to link ideas directly to each other in systematic constructs that can then be held apart from reality as models of it, and susceptible to manipulation in their own right. Profound *reflection* becomes possible, rather than explanation and prediction alone. It becomes much easier to divest the environment of emotional and aesthetic properties, and just because it *has* been externalised we can view reality as a depersonalised realm 'without', that is oblivious to and does not partake of the human qualities we bear 'within'. It allows of scepticism towards the natural order without a sense of personal threat, a posture of disbelief that may upset our *theories* but not so directly and immediately *ourselves*.

In holding back from the world we can judge more readily, then, the distance of one thing from another. We become relativists, more aware of philosophic fallibilities, and knowledge itself takes on something less of the quality of what we are as people and of our sense of society and place. Should we remain mystics and mentally at the centre of everything we must refer all phenomena back to ourselves, and objective referents are more difficult to apply. If we appeal to subjective agencies of one kind or another — animal spirits, for example, ghosts or gods — we can explain away anomalies in what we believe, but it is a sleight of mind. An objective thinker would not have it.

This 'modern' point of view is much more conducive to the idea of the experimental method, to the notion of coincidence, probability and chance, and the sort of outlook that is receptive rather than fearful or dismissive or complacent when confronted with a new issue or event. Time itself becomes a less personal phenomenon, and less human; a flowing stream that carries all before it rather than a circle that returns and brings the familiar and the expected back again. All of which has its price — the loss, for example, of an 'intensely poetic quality in everyday life and thought, and a vivid enjoyment of the passing moment — both driven out of sophisticated Western life by the quest for purity of motive and the faith in progress'.[34] In viewing reality minus ourselves we sharpen our analytic senses, but we tend to lose some of the qualities we would otherwise appreciate about ourselves as human beings.

When we ask where a 'scientific' outlook comes from in *socio-cultural* terms, the same analysis applies. What would tend to break down an abiding sense of personal continuity with the environment, with the phenomenal world? The first thing one thinks of is sheer human curiosity, which would presuppose a rudimentary sense of objectivity at least, and an interest in generalising about what one sees and thinks.

In this attitude, man views first of all the multiplicity of nations, his own and others, each with its own surrounding world which is valid for it, is taken for granted, with its traditions, its gods, its demons, its mystical power, simply as the actual world. Through this astonishing contrast there appears the distinction between world representation and actual world, and the new question of truth arises; not tradition-bound, every-day truth, but an identical truth which is valid for all who are no longer blinded by traditions, a truth in itself.[35]

In the traditions of the West, beginning with a 'few Greek eccentrics', there grows a 'new humanity: men who [live] the philosophical life, who create philosophy in the manner of a vocation as a new sort of cultural configuration'.[36] This group grows and others learn of it and unlike its rival cultural artifacts the scientific mode is accessible to any who adopt a universalist, sceptical stance as their own. Objective truth rather than the naïve experience and traditions of daily life becomes the critical arbiter; and what was once valid in the old view is either 'completely discarded, or its content is taken over philosophically and thereby formed anew in the spirit of philosophical ideality'.[37]

In defending his own thesis that the 'modern' mind is also essentially an 'open' one, Horton cites at this point the development of the written transmission of beliefs. I have rejected his thesis in general, and indeed, in this particular case, the historical record abounds with examples of attempts to falsify and destroy the written record to prevent comparison that might be adverse to the interests of those in authority. Hence it seems to me that the *written* word can be used to sustain a 'closed' perspective just as readily as *orally* transmitted beliefs might do. The process of comparing contemporary ideas against those laid up on paper or stone by previous generations is nowhere near as simple as might be assumed, and is not of itself enough to challenge theories felt to be timeless and absolute. Similarly, I can see no reason why a written as opposed to an oral culture should be more likely to develop a sense of itself as outside or beside nature in the way that I have argued is decisive, except that the written word makes language more concrete and in doing so makes it easier to see what we say as separate physically from what we are actually talking about. The human capacity to objectify the phenomenal environment might well be enhanced in this way, but not necessarily so.[38]

The development of cultural heterogeneity is another matter altogether, however. If groups of people meet each other, and if the nature of that contact is sufficiently profound to counterpose different world-views, then one side can either reject the other's rival belief systems or co-opt them or it can begin to appreciate the derivative and external character of *all* belief systems including its own. To those curious as to the range of human response, it is tempting to try to establish empirically just what that range might be and then to think behind it for patterns of an objective kind. The notion of 'culture' itself is part of the attempt to establish such a pattern.

It is an act of considerable intellectual courage to try and stand apart from the world in this fashion. It is in many respects an impoverished place to be, though what can be achieved there has given it demonstrable material advantages. Because of the costs, perhaps, it is no surprise to find what seems to be a long-term need to close the gap again between the human enterprise and its context, to re-establish the individual as a member once more not only of society but of the material world. This has been attempted in recent times in a very interesting way; namely by enhancing subjectivity to the point where it makes the very notion of what is 'object' an extension of ourselves. In apprehending any 'object' we attempt to see the truth of it, and yet to establish the truth beyond dispute we must effectively eliminate all human bias, any trace of the human status as observer, which would mean in the end effectively eliminating ourselves. The fear that lurks behind all abstracted thought is that, in the end, we can explain nothing, and that our pottering dialogue with the unknown is not a dialogue at all but a soliloquy, a windy presumption, with no final prospect of finding the truth. How are we to respond? There are a number of technical points that we can make, more or less cogent.[39] They hinge, however, on looking harder not just at things, but at the validity of what we *know* about things:

> Thus, the foundation-stone of our conceptual and moral edifice, and quite literally, of our world and our identity . . . is shifted inwards to our cognitive equipment, to out criteria of sound knowledge, of the recognition of truth.[40] First of all, examine how you know things, the criteria you have for assessing the validity, the legitimacy of cognitive claims. If these criteria themselves be sound and legitimate, they will transmit their own validity to the substantive knowledge which has been authenticated by them; but if not, then the whole edifice is worthless. This is the Copernican Revolution in philosophy as conceived and heralded by Kant . . . the shift of the ultimate seat of legitimacy to knowledge.

And, of course, it is a shift that restores man's role as arbiter and as a part of the whole.

> The silence of the infinite spaces out there need no longer frighten us. Their emptiness is irrelevant, if what confers meaning on life and validates our procedures is no longer expected to be out there, but is right here, in our cognitive and other competences.[41]

To place the ultimate emphasis on how we know what we know is to re-establish the link between subjective experience and the outside world, to reconnect subject and object, to link once more consciousness and cosmos in one concept of reality. A human reality this time, however. One that can in principle abstract the human quotient, but not one fastened on some awesome or fallible agency that legislates the whole. We can move at will now, in the way non-modern thought does not, from an 'objective' world-view where we are separate from our reality, where we can look across at it for the purposes of understanding and control, and a 'subjective' world-view that asserts that we are never divorced from what we see because the act of observation is always to some extent an act of participation too. To manufacture 'science' we remove as much of ourselves as possible from the picture; to recover our shaky self-esteem we argue that all 'science' is, in the end, colonised by the mind.

World Culture: Rationality and Alienation

From the 'objectivist' perspective I have just described flow the other features we recognise as characteristic of contemporary world culture. We can discriminate a scientific from a religio-mythic perspective as far back as the Greeks. With the advent of industrialisation, however, we get the dramatic acceleration of effects, and the technological/scientific world-view comes into its own as the most potent single sociological force. It bears directly upon more and more of that community of labouring men and women who are detached from primary production; it prompts a growing range of specialised jobs which require a standardised performance, which generates in turn a demand for higher standards of mass education and a mobile populace eager not only for material and social advancement but prepared to move house to achieve it.[42]

The search for scientific rules in *nature* can be turned to that of *social change.* As an efficient way of ordering knowledge about the material environment, a scientific perspective can then be applied where rules as such are hard to find. They can be nominated regardless, however, and used in a consistent way to regulate the social environment. It is this process that one generally terms 'rationalisation'; it is the essence of bureaucracy and it expresses a profound preference for regular means that proceed to planned ends, for rules and predictable administrative results.

Max Weber introduced the concept of 'rationality' in order to define the form of capitalist economic activity, bourgeois private law, and bureaucratic authority. Rationalisation means, first of all, the extension of the areas of society subject to the criteria of rational decision. Second, social labor is industrialised, with the result that criteria of instrumental action also penetrate into other areas of life (urbanisation of the mode of life, technification of transport and communication) . . . The progressive 'rationalisation' of society is linked to the institutionalisation of scientific and technical development. To the extent that technology and science permeate social institutions and thus transform them, old legitimations are destroyed.[43]

What are the consequences of such a process? In the pursuit of regular means a sense of their original purpose can be quickly lost and this has become a common complaint. Bureaucracy, it is claimed, renders human beings progressively more alienated and anonymous, the victims of elaborate administrative structures that have surrendered their sense of service, or find it submerged by administrative forms. Though there seems to be no other way to organise the large societies that the contemporary modes of industrial production can physically sustain, there is less of a feeling of social immediacy and the 'effective mutuality' that prevails in smaller social systems.[44] Confronting this problem and the way human beings ultimately become the victims of the industrial economy and the bureaucratic polity they so eagerly build is an academic task of its own. 'Science', it is said, breeds a mechanistic ethos that presupposes as final fact 'an irreducible . . . material, spread throughout space . . . senseless, valueless, purposeless . . . following a fixed routine imposed by external relations which do not spring from the nature of its being'.[45] An ethos that has generated spectacular insights while at the same time moving further and further away from common human comprehension. Applied to social affairs the objectivist/materialist outlook becomes a seductive attempt to render highly complex entities amenable to more precise analysis and control.

Thus Herbert Marcuse has described 'rationalisation' as yet another device for establishing and legitimising comprehensive political power. He says:

The scientific method which led to the ever more effective domination of nature thus came to provide the pure concepts as well as the instrumentalities for the ever more effective domination of man by man *through* the domination of nature. Theoretical reason, remaining pure and neutral, entered into the service of practical reason. The merger proved beneficial to both. Today, domination perpetuates and extends itself not only through technology but *as* technology, and the latter provides the great legitimation of the expanding political power, which absorbs all spheres of culture . . . unfreedom appears neither as irrational nor as political but rather as submission to the technical apparatus which enlarges the comforts of life and increases the productivity of labour . . . and the instrumentalist horizon of reason opens on a traditionally totalitarian society.[46]

Jürgen Habermas has taken up the same idea,[47] positing one mode of rationalisation that operates from 'below' as it were, in terms of the consequence of capitalist enterprise, and one from 'above' as traditional belief systems are replaced by codes of formal law. Whatever else it may be, this argument is a trenchant one, and it draws our attention to the way 'science' can become a technocratic *ideology*, a critical part of the attempt, whether witting or no, to represent reality from the viewpoint of that fraction of society that can successfully generalise its own particular values as valid for the whole; a device which lifts decision-making out of the realm of moral debate into the hands of technical decision-makers who then use their powers to school and repress. 'Reasoned debate' becomes 'deferential adaptation', a 'totalised world view which produces a fatalism on one hand, and amenability to technological manipulation on the other'.[48]

All thinking occurs in a social and political context and scientific thought, like any other cognitive system, will help shape but will also convey something of the context in which it occurs. Even a scientist as seemingly remote in his professional understandings from human society as a contemporary physicist must choose his projects, and he will often have such choices made on his behalf with extra-scientific criteria in mind. The question of choice leads the discussion back to the earlier question of consciousness, of the nature of 'human nature', and we appreciate with greater force the fact that our concepts about such things have profound social, political and economic implications. Rescuing the right to define our human nature by struggling to transcend what we perceive to be our limitations is not a simple matter. Nor does the fight end there.

Though it is a difficult concept there is much that is covered in the above by the concept of 'alienation'. When human beings come to consider what they make or think or do as something apart from themselves, something estranged, then they can be said to feel 'alienated'. As a psycho logical and sociological phenomenon this sense of distance and loss is a perennial and a universal one. The Marxist analysis of it, however, locates a quite concrete cause: the industrial division of labour and particularly that division typical of contemporary capitalism. Workers produce goods but they remain unsatisfied because, while they might otherwise realise themselves through their labour, what they produce are objects that have little meaning for them, in which they fail on the whole to find anything of themselves. In those parts of the human environment that have become more mechanised and specialised it has become progressively more difficult for people to relate to what is in effect an inhumane world (whatever a humane one might look like), though this would seem in fact a general consequence of technologically complex societies and not a feature of capitalist ones alone.

This subtle consequence may not be apparent to those communities concerned to modernise and industrialise as quickly as possible because of the promise of rapid material rewards. If the phenomenon is a real one, though, it will be increasingly manifest as traditional attitudes and ways of life are changed, and 'rationalisation' takes effect.

On the one hand, then, we find those who would celebrate technocracy convinced that knowledge *is* science and can be acquired in no other way. On the other there are those who view such 'objectivism' as a life-denying force. Separating knowledge and interest, description and prescription, value and fact, emotion and cognition leads, they would argue, to a concept of 'theory' without a meaning of its own for human existence.[49] There are also those who would ride the scientific legacy like a long wave; who would see it as a vehicle of tidal power destined perhaps to dissipate for lack of a sense of the human dimension, but bearing on its back the most comprehensive civilisation the world has yet seen. And there are those who shuffle from one foot to another, not knowing where it will all end, believing it

> a waste of breath . . . to debate which is true, the religious or the scientific outlook on life, when the psychological fact is that all men . . . find both outlooks true; the deep and still unsolved problem is to harmonise the contradictions of the two outlooks . . . If we know with our selves and our feelings, we inhabit a personal timeless universe; if we restrict ourselves to the operational 'I', there are only atoms and a void.[50]

The discussion so far should help to some extent to establish the profile of a modern cultural milieu that becomes progressively more pervasive in our age. If there is a temper to the contemporary mind, a set of intellectual qualities that characterise how many of us think, then it lies, I would suggest, in the domain sketched above. And these attributes have received a universal distribution. They delimit attitudes, values and conceptual forms that help define a society now global in breadth, if very uneven and varying considerably from place to place in depth. For growing numbers of people they express common attitudes to new experience, revised social relationships and different notions of time; they constitute the whole complex of ideas conveyed through a 'modern' education. But this expression does not occur in a vacuum. It is part product, part inspiration of a paired process that practically no individual has been able to escape – the emergence of the twin phenomena of the 'nation' and the 'state'.

World Culture: the Nation-State

The fact of 'nation-states' (and the attendant ideology of 'nationalism') has been one of Europe's most important political exports. The doctrine of sovereignty on which the European concept of statehood rests has found near-global favour, and for an obvious reason. Any group that can demonstrate its physical control over a designated capital city is, by the mutual accord of other ruling elites, 'sovereign' and hence to that extent 'legitimate'. Any regime that receives this international sanction will tend to support the theory upon which such ready recognition and endorsement rests. There are often quite immediate challenges and threats to its power – pretenders to the throne, neo-colonising corporations, regional power competitors – and any and every shred of support is used as reinforcement, to be passed on elsewhere.

> Legitimacy is, indeed, the crux. For, in the end, what did the Euro-
> pean theory of the state amount to but the assertion of an authority,
> supreme by virtue of its power, uncluttered by any mythological
> explanations of its mandate and beyond which there could be no
> appeal. Because it extracted from European history an abstract
> theory of authority, state theory was necessarily scornful of 'culture',
> and so, for the same reason, capable of universal application. The
> theory seems ideally suited for export. In any event, its success in
> non-European markets has been overwhelming.[51]

More complex conceptions of how to divide authority on a world scale have, for the moment at least, been conspicuously trumped by a doctrine so ruthless and so easy to apply. Those who would conceive of other networks in terms of shared culture, religion, class and so on must account for them in the context of a global congress of states.

'Nation-building' is a more difficult business than asserting sovereignty and it takes place over an extended period of time. It has on the whole been a highly contrived and self-conscious undertaking, and the social and political preconditions have been very varied indeed. An important aspect of the Westernisation of the world, it has given rise to the most visible of political cultural forms, prompting and sustaining the global development of industrial societies and seized upon by political elites, or active elements within them, as a powerful instrument for pushing their peripheral populations into what is judged to be the historical mainstream. In so doing it has also worked to some extent against the advent of a uniform world, helping to secure social and traditional diversities in the face of the homogenising effects of technological change. But the root and substance of the notion is Western, and only limited contributions have been made to it by the new clientele that have emerged elsewhere.

The 'nationalist' preference for boundaries that coincide with ethnic or linguistic frontiers has not been easy to satisfy—the dissolution of the European empires, for example, bequeathed an often quite arbitrary set of state borders, the legacy of geopolitical and military agreements rather than socio-economic ones. The underlying doctrine was, in its earlier forms, an elitist one, but in its later development became associated with ideas of mass social revolution, of self-determination, of representative government, and the assertion of independence from imperial political and economic controls. Ethnic contiguity, or rather the lack of it, a less relevant factor when the primary object is the fight for freedom from a common foreign foe, becomes subversive of political unity once those who win the state attempt to secure their long-term political future. The notion of 'nationalism' can be and has been used by social groups all over the world to justify their claims for a political and economic autonomy that is territorially discrete, and issues of rival jurisdiction may only in the last resort be resolved by force. Where resolution does not occur we tend to get long-term incipient and more or less violent insurrection. Among other things (like the simple pursuit of power), such groups are often defending some sense of a distinctive meaning system that they value, and it is ironic that one of the most important components of what we recognise as global cultural property should be exploited to protect and preserve local and regional idiosyncracies. 'Nationalism' has an inturned and rather murky aspect that corresponds to an expanded concept of 'tribe', and it is curious to see this welded to the more secular, universalist and outgoing version of the doctrine that has emerged in the present day.

The phenomenon is diffuse and I shall return to it later. It is no simple matter discriminating nationalist from religious or other ideolog-

ical impulses with socially consolidatory effects, or from complementary feelings of diverse kinds like patriotism and xenophobia. The social
circumstances from which they derive are unclear, and there is no typ-
ology that adequately covers the forms of nationalism historically manifest around the world. Whatever its roots, however, whatever common
properties the notion does describe, it draws heavily now upon the
social transformations that industrialisation and modernisation bring.
Here we encounter a related political irony, since nationalist movements
in post-colonial states, a conspicuous part of the global response to
European expansion, often tend to reject European influence in principle
while embracing its philosophy and its social systems in practice. When
Third and Fourth World spokesmen press claims for distributive economic justice, or for an end to neo-colonial structures of dependency
and exploitation, they do so in the language either of their erstwhile
imperial mentors or of the radical critics indigenous there, rather than
elaborating cultural concepts of their own. As often as not Marxist categories prevail, for the insidious process of perpetuating or establishing
neo-imperial control as they see it is one that Marxist theorists have
been much concerned to chart and change.

Marx himself gave the phenomenon of nationalism only passing consideration. He saw in it one instrument whereby the rising bourgeoisie
might be able to overthrow the feudalist or other outmoded and backward societies they found about them. The advent of a global capitalist
market and a global division of labour were, he recognised, supranational-
ist and homogenising processes. The conscious recognition of their common plight on the part of the proletariat would, he believed, eventually
lead this underclass to reject their exploitation, to overthrow the capitalist system and to institute one cosmopolitan world. Contrary to such
expectations, the world has coalesced not at the bottom but at the top,
as bourgeois elements in many parts of the globe, products of the capitalist system and beneficiaries of it, seek to ensure that it persists.

If a world society does exist, the culture that informs it is still largely
an elite one, a culture of the privileged and the aspiring rather than the
dispossessed. It is an urban culture of 'modernised' or 'modernising'
individuals who have bought the package of values implicit in contemporary science and technology. The aspiration to industrialise, and
the ethos of political and economic contemporaneity that accompanies
it, are very widespread, and none of the various divisive forces at work
in the world has prevailed against it. The explicit commitment to 'modernisation' constitutes in many a case the ultimate rationalisation of the
right to rule. The critique of modern techniques in terms of their ecol-

ogical degradation of the environment has found little purchase in the Third World, except where it has something practical to offer by way of appropriate alternatives. It is abundantly apparent that

> modernisation is everywhere a necessary, if not a sufficient, justification for the exercise of political power. Even where traditional authority survives . . . it does so by monopolising the modernising role and commanding the loyalty of those who possess the new (scientific and technological) knowledge . . . it is the old, culturally exclusive order that is under attack, the objectives and values of modern secularism that are upheld.[52]

Which is not to say that the old cultural orders have not fought back, and that the right to rule has never been denied. 'Nationalism' is widely used to disguise the alien and external nature of the modernising process, and its role as such and as the ideology of domination is repeatedly pointed up by repressed groups. A plethora of pre-capitalist cultures have demonstrated their capacity to persist, and their attachment to their own communal structures and to the human values inherent in subsistence production has been fed by the feeling that industrialisation may prove not only perverse but pernicious as well.[53] On the whole, however, it is those who possess the new universalistic knowledge we find wielding political power. 'Modernisation' is the hard currency of their culture. And the self-consciously secular, rationalistic and materialistic values on which their concept of a 'modern' world is based are its bright and shining coin.

Notes

1. E.g. Talcott Parsons, 'Culture and Social System Revisited' in L. Schneider and C. Bonjean (eds.), *The Idea of Culture in the Social Sciences* (Cambridge University Press, London, 1973), p. 33.

2. C. Belshaw, *The Conditions of Social Performance* (Routledge and Kegan Paul, London, 1970), p. 1.

3. artifacts — material objects created for carrying out material functions; socifacts — institutions and organisations for providing the framework of a social or political unit or for maintaining social relations between its members; . . . mentifacts — mental constructions which provide the psychological framework of a culture and carry out intellectual, aesthetic, spiritual, ethical or other psychological functions.

The categories overlap . . . all artifacts have been shaped by mind, all mentifacts have a material basis or vehicle, and all cultures are embodied in societies. Thus a piece of pottery may be both a useful artifact and a beautiful mentifact;

socifacts like codes of law and morals incorporate much of spiritual and ethical mentifacts; and the intellectual mentifacts we call scientific theories and laws become transposed into technological artifacts (J.S. Huxley, 'Evolution, Cultural and Biological' in William Thomas (ed.), *Current Anthropology* (University of Chicago Press, Chicago, 1956), pp. 16-17).

4. A.L. Kroeber and T. Parsons, 'The Concepts of Culture and of Social System', *American Sociological Review*, vol. 23, no. 5 (October 1958), p. 583.

5. A.L. Kroeber, *The Nature of Culture* (University of Chicago Press, Chicago, 1952), p. 24.

6. Roger Sperry, 'In Search of Psyche' in F.G. Worden *et al.* (eds.), *The Neurosciences* (MIT Press, Cambridge, Mass., 1975), p. 430.

7. Ibid., p. 431.

8. These points are developed further in R. Pettman, *Human Behaviour and World Politics* (Macmillan, London, 1975), Ch. 7. But see also G. Globus *et al.* (eds.), *Consciousness and the Brain: a Scientific and Philosophical Inquiry* (Plenum Press, New York, 1976).

9. J.D. Freeman, 'Choices, Values and the Solution of Human Problems' in J. Calhoun (ed.), *Adaptation, Environment and Population* (forthcoming).

10. See Chapter 3.

11. Sperry, 'In Search of Psyche', pp. 432-3.

12. Kroeber, *The Nature of Culture*, p. 6.

13. J. Galtung, 'A Structural Theory of Imperialism', *Journal of Peace Research*, vol. 8, no. 2 (1971), p. 93.

14. F. Fanon, *The Wretched of the Earth* (Penguin, Harmondsworth, 1967) and *Black Skin, White Masks* (Penguin, Harmondsworth, 1967); O. Mannoni, *Prospero and Caliban, the Psychology of Colonisation* (Methuen, London, 1956); A. Memmi, *The Coloniser and the Colonised* (Orion Press, New York, 1965); G. Balandier, *The Sociology of Black Africa* (Andre Deutsch, London, 1970).

15. E. Stonequist, *The Marginal Man: a Study in Personality and Culture Conflict* (Charles Scribners' Sons, New York, 1957). Also R. Taft, 'Coping with Unfamiliar Cultures' in N. Warren (ed.), *Studies in Cross Cultural Psychology*, vol. 1 (Academic Press, London, 1977), Ch. 4.4.

16. K. Marx and F. Engels, *The German Ideology*, C.J. Arthur (ed.) (Lawrence and Wishart, London, 1977), p. 64.

17. S. Avineri, *The Social and Political Thought of Karl Marx* (Cambridge University Press, London, 1968), p. 69.

18. Marx and Engels, *The German Ideology*, p. 47.

19. Preface to the *Critique of Political Economy* in *K. Marx: Selected Writings in Sociology and Social Philosophy* translated and edited by T.B. Bottomore (Penguin, Harmondsworth, 1963), p. 67.

20. R. Williams, *Culture and Society: 1780-1950* (Chatto and Windus, London, 1958), p. 281.

21. Ernest Gellner, *Legitimation of Belief* (Cambridge University Press, London, 1974), p. 149.

22. Jack Goody has expressed strong doubts, and fairly so, about dichotomising cognitive developments in human culture and characteristic modes of thought in this way. He sees it as based on a 'we/they division which is binary and ethnocentric' (*The Domestication of the Savage Mind* (Cambridge University Press, London, 1977)). 'We speak', he says, 'in terms of primitive and advanced almost as if human minds themselves differed in their structure like machines of an earlier and later design' (p. 1). Rather than counterposing magic and science, myth and history, status and contract, concrete and abstract, collectivist and individualistic, 'cold' and 'hot', pre-logical and logical, mythopoeic and empirical, ritual and rational, closed and open, and so on, we might be better placed to talk in terms

of a complex and polarised field. Dichotomy fails, he argues, (1) to explain such differences (2) to give any indication of how and why change occurs from one state to the other. Furthermore, a sense of subjective difference (between 'ourselves' and the 'rest') all too readily becomes a judgement on 'their' failure to 'progress'. In his own work in the field, Goody declares that he has

> never experienced the kinds of hiatus in communication that would be the case if I and they were approaching the physical world from opposite ends (p. 8) . . . modern man is emerging every day . . . without . . . the total, transformation of processes of 'thought' or attributes of 'mind' that theories imply (p. 16).

We need to maintain a balance between bland analysis and a blank indifference to those distinctions that do exist. And yet, Goody himself is at pains not to deny that there are real and significant differences between 'us' and 'them' in terms of our thinking patterns and prevailing cognitive modes (p. 8).

23. R. Horton, 'African Traditional Thought and Western Science' in M. Young (ed.), *Knowledge and Control* (Collier-Macmillan, London, 1971), p. 209.

24. Ibid., p. 222.

25. Ibid., p. 223.

26. Ibid., pp. 224-5.

27. T. Kuhn, *The Structure of Scientific Revolutions*, 2nd edn (University of Chicago Press, Chicago, 1970).

28. Gellner, *Legitimation of Belief*, p. 156.

29. *Werke*, I, p. 345, cited in Avineri, *Social and Political Thought of Karl Marx*, p. 44.

30. E. Husserl, *The Crisis of European Sciences and Transcendental Phenomenology* (North Western University Press, Evanston, Illinois, 1970), p. 279.

31. Ibid., p. 284. One should note here Mircea Eliade's argument in *The Sacred and the Profane* (Harper & Row, New York, p. 28) that 'what characterises traditional societies is the implicit opposition which they see between their inhabited territory and the unknown and undetermined space which surrounds it . . .'; between an ordered love-space, or cosmos, and an 'other world' that is chaotic, alien and unknown. Eliade's observation would, on first glance, suggest a conflict with my notion of the traditional world-view as one resting on a sense of personal and immediate continuity with the universe. However, it is the very intimacy of this link, I would answer, that prompts the attempt to secure a spiritual centre that is then expressed in terms of the physical defence of territory, particular house and village designs, cultural ethnocentrism and so on.

32. Pratima Bowes, *Consciousness and Freedom* (Methuen, London, 1971), p. 222.

33. Horton, 'African Traditional Thought', pp. 234-5.

34. Ibid., p. 255.

35. Husserl, *Crisis of European Sciences*, pp. 285-6.

36. Ibid., p. 206.

37. Ibid., p. 208.

38. I am in direct disagreement here with Jack Goody (*The Domestication of the Savage Mind*) who sees the influence of the advent of writing on human cognitive structures as critical. There is no sense of history, he argues, without archives, documents that contradict each other, and the mental discipline involved in writing itself. And science derives from the distance so established between 'man and his verbal acts. He can now examine what he says in a more objective manner. He can stand aside, comment upon, even correct his own creation' (p. 150). Writing 'encourages special forms of linguistic activity associated with developments in

particular kinds of problem-raising and problem-solving in which the list, the formula and the table played a seminal part' (p. 162).

39. In the first place, our organisation – that is, our mental apparatus – has been developed precisely in the attempt to explore the external world, and it must therefore have realised in its structure some degree of expediency; in the second place, it is itself a constituent part of the world which we set out to investigate, and it readily admits of such an investigation; thirdly, the task of science is fully covered if we limit it to showing how the world must appear to us in consequence of the particular character of our organisation; fourthly, the ultimate findings of science, precisely because of the way in which they are acquired, are determined not only by our organisation but by the things which have affected that organisation; finally, the problem of the nature of the world without regard to our percipient mental apparatus is an empty abstraction, devoid of practical interest (S. Freud, 'The Future of an Illusion', *The Standard Edition of the Complete Psychological Works*, vol. 21 (The Hogarth Press, London, 1961), p. 55.

40. 'If we imagine the philosophical discussion of the modern period reconstructed as a judicial hearing, it would be deciding a single question: how is reliable knowledge possible?' (J. Habermas, *Knowledge and Human Interests* (Heinemann, London, 1972), p. 3).

41. Gellner, *Legitimation of Belief*, pp. 28, 29.

42. Gellner, *Contemporary Thought and Politics* (Routledge and Kegan Paul, London, 1974), pp. 146-7.

43. Jürgen Habermas, 'Technology and Science as "Ideology"' in *Toward a Rational Society* (Beacon Press, Boston, 1970), p. 81.

44. C. Turnbull, 'Human Nature and Primal Man', *Social Research*, vol. 4, no. 3 (Autumn 1973), p. 524.

45. A.N. Whitehead, *Science and the Modern World* (Oxford University Press, London, 1946), p. 20.

46. H. Marcuse, *One-Dimensional Man: the Ideology of Industrial Society* (Sphere, London, 1968), p. 130.

47. Habermas, 'Technology and Science as "Ideology"'.

48. J. Benthall (ed.), *The Limits of Human Nature* (Allen Lane, London, 1973), pp. 262, 263.

49. Ibid., p. 263.

50. A. Schultz, *A Theory of Consciousness* (Philosophical Library, New York, 1973), p. 425.

51. J. Mayall, 'International Society and International Theory' in M. Donelan (ed.), *Reason of States* (George Allen and Unwin, London, 1978), p. 131.

52. Ibid., p. 133.

53. For an interesting discussion about such phenomena see N. Sharp, 'Nationalism and Cultural Politics', *Arena*, no. 43 (1976), pp. 58-77. Also my article on 'The Solomon Islands: a Developing Neo-colony', *Australian Outlook* (August 1977), vol. 31, no. 2, pp. 268-78, a country where the dilemmas are very clearly displayed.

2   WORLD SOCIETY

If we can establish, as I have argued we can, a common body of ideas characteristic of a contemporary 'world' culture – an elite phenomenon certainly, but global none the less – we have the conditioning ground for the prime figure in this study, that of *world society*. World society is predicated, upon the processes of 'modernisation' and of 'industrialisation' – their requirements and consequences – and I have cast these complex sets of factors in abstract and very general terms, though the particular debate about them remains in many ways an inconclusive one.

'Industrialisation' and 'Modernisation'

What do they mean precisely? 'Industrialisation' and the wider term 'modernisation' are broad concepts and their effects are not as readily determined as my rather broad assertions might suggest. It would be useful to pause to qualify and refine the picture drawn so far.

As more than one analyst has noted, industrialisation and modernisation may not even be cognate, since what we know of them would suggest that they are separable and sometimes in fact opposed[1] and if we do still choose to dichotomise modern and traditional orders[2] in such terms, then we must also remain alert to any propensity to denigrate the old and to endorse the new just because social change is disturbing or we happen to approve the extension of our own contemporary norms and forms, and vice versa. There is an insidious and often implicit preference, too, for an evolutionist philosophy of history 'according to which the *total* future of mankind is subject to a law of increasing rationality and morality',[3] a philosophy which, among other things, demonstrates a rather ethnocentric and optimistic faith in our human progress rather than regression.[4] This preference is commonly associated with structural/functional premises. In sociology, Talcott Parsons' 'pattern variables' are the most conspicuous reference point here.[5] As a description of what is happening to the structure of society, variables like the ones he offers provide us with little in the way of an explanation of social change and how and why it comes about, and what explanation we do find is usually in terms of the teleological assumption that system components must cohere if the society as a system is to persist. Structural/functional notions of modernisation which see it in terms

45

of the spread of Western modes of production and thought also obscure the key neo-Marxist insight that the incapacity to modernise may be a consequence of the very process of diffusion itself[6] and that traditional orders are now in important ways the historically conditioned creatures of modern ones rather than different from them and intrinsically retarded. Again, we must be wary of dressing up normative or revisionist instincts in terms of abstract analytic generalisations, and the too ready assumption that one and the same way of producing societal wealth results in all places in like changes in systems of social class and political structure, as the neo-Marxists tend to suppose.[7]

Industrialisation is none the less the most obvious aspect of the modernising process, and it does reproduce common social effects that we can, at least partially, try to specify. The 'industrial society' as this entity has developed over the last two hundred years is seen to be

an urbanised society of nuclear families and mass culture. Its division of labour is increasingly determined by its technology, as also is its accumulation of capital and its search for a calculus of rational choice. The ownership of the means of production is less politically critical than the actual control of those means. Although politically pluralised because of its need for specialisation, aggregate associations such as unions or corporations may have great leverage, and in any case find their true counterpart in a large, centralised, meritocratic bureaucracy.[8]

We can expect these features to be reproduced around the world as industrialisation proceeds apace. But it does not necessarily proceed in one way, nor has it received uniform accommodation by affected groups.[9] Many social changes derive from social influences other than that of industrialisation, though they may accompany it. Such changes can be realised in practice in many different ways, and the 'traditional' orders upon which they impinge are often dynamic, culturally complex and heterogeneous entities, quite different one from another and quite selective about the industrialising process.[10] Modernising forces do not necessarily *supplant* the old; in fact they can permeate and strengthen them. They not only conflict with but can also reinforce existing values and social forms; and the intervention of intellectuals and state government office-holders can directly affect how this comes about.

'Industrialisation' and 'modernisation' are generally construed in terms of specific changes in particular social structures or in some more personal set of attributes. As to the former, we can list factors like those cited above, or we can refer more broadly to the sort of social change, prevalent for the last two hundred years, which has produced the economic or political predominance of 'pioneering' societies, to pervasive effect on 'follower' ones.[11] In the latter case we are dealing with individual traits, with an 'industrial' or 'modern' person, who is receptive to innovation and change and is willing to form opinions on matters beyond his or her immediate range, who demonstrates considerable faith in science and technology, who values achievement as a criterion of status and the notion of individual initiative and mobility,[12] and so on.

Empirical attempts to test for changes in personal attitude have come to differing conclusions. One study argues:

> Basically, the commonality in workers' values runs along country lines, and . . . national value differences are not being systematically eroded by industrialism . . . Traditional values are being altered by industrialism, but not in the direction of a greater degree of global consensus.

The Westernisation of human culture, in other words, has simply failed to occur.[13] Another asserts, however, that there *is* a 'general modernity syndrome'[14] and that as developing nations build contemporary institutions and these are further diffused their peoples come to include a growing proportion of 'modern' individuals. Though not ultimately incompatible, these two points do lead in different directions—one towards divergence, and the other towards convergence in terms of global intellectual values.

Whatever its conceptual efficacy, the attempt to measure how individuals change as their societies become more modern, to quantify a discrete body of modern mental attributes that universally obtain, has largely failed.[15] Even where modernity has been given empirical referents that work, its effects remain paradoxical and do not necessarily proceed in one way. The result in the West of a protracted and complex process, it has often been superimposed elsewhere in such a fashion as to positively impede modern development and hence the further diffusion of Western values.[16]

It would seem well nigh impossible to establish a conclusive proposition either way, but my own impression of the social forces at work in the world sees them moving us towards more similar social experiences, not less, at least as these concern the nature of employment and education and the pattern of rural/urban residence.[17] Dependence upon expanded systems for the manufacture and distribution of increasingly diverse products and services continues to grow, and though this phenomenon is clearly compatible with more than one type of polity, it has had one very important social consequence in the advent of a global bourgeoisie that shares Western values and co-opts local positions of command.[18] National differences remain pervasive but so, it seems, does the process of class formation, as I shall attempt to establish in a moment. We must begin with the one, but we cannot end without due consideration of the other, too.

World Society as a 'System'

What is this world society that the cultural consequences of industrialisation and modernisation help us define? What are its conceptual competitors?

The most conspicuous and the most widely noted unit in global affairs is that of the 'state'. The contemporary complement of diverse bodies we collect together under this label make up in their manifold interrelations the 'state system' so called. Though opinion differs about their significance and their desirability we may also note now many non-state actors with quasi-autonomous global interconnections of their own. When we add in these so-called 'transnationals'[19] we discern a more general social cosmos that surrounds the central network of states; we expand our understanding of the ways in which human society seems to be arranged.

It is useful to think at first in terms of a continuum, of a scale along which increasingly more intimate social relationships occur; to picture the world initially as a 'system', growing progressively more 'social' as we examine in greater detail the various qualities that global interactions display. A *system* of states, their representatives in touch with each other on a more or less regular basis who feel they must not only account for the behaviour of some at least of their confrères but also accommodate the fact of the system as a whole, is one fundamental facet of world affairs. The concept of a 'system' is used here in its technical sense to mean a number of units alike enough to form a set and sufficiently independent for a change in the state of one unit to cause repercussions for others. They operate within a boundary that marks the major discontinuities in the transactions and traffic between them and their environment. As such, the *inter-state* system is 'closed' since the interactions fall entirely within the system boundaries, which are the world. One can still discriminate between a global set of countries as an *energy* system or as an *economic* system for example, and these separate systems can be seen as part of each other's environment. In this sense the system of states is not closed but 'open'.

Depicting the world in terms of a collection of discrete bodies whose only point of contact is some generalised idea of 'interaction' does not carry us very far, however. Certain 'behaviouralist' analyses of the 1950s and 1960s attempted to move beyond the concept of a 'states' system and to confront human-kind as a single mass of four or five thousand million people, organised for some purposes into states but for others into interrelated economic, scientific, cultural, ideological and religious sets that might not be so apparent but are still real. Less explicit regularities and less formalised non-state collectivities were seen to emerge that might well be concentrated into territorial and administrative conclaves called 'states', but were also dispersed beyond them. The world was made up, in this view, of universal networks covering many parts of it, plus regional interactions and those of more local-ised entities such as the family — the whole being infinitely complex and confused.

A set of relationships, a system that is, can be abstracted from the human totality by analytic means, but the persons involved in one set are often involved in others. An oil magnate, for example, a member of a sectional trading and resource network, may also belong to a regional set of an ethnic or cultural kind. Separating out a system becomes a process of reduction. Rather than identifying people as such as they interact with each other, we highlight for the purpose of the enquiry the set of relevant roles particular individuals play under specified circumstances. The world then appears

> like millions of cobwebs superimposed one upon another, covering the whole globe ... Each separate cobweb ... represent[ing] a sep-arate system — trade flows, letters exchanged, tourist movements, air-craft flights, population movements and transactions in ideas, cultures, languages and religions, traffic flows within towns and social interactions within village communities.[20]

Systems are linked, sharing their constituent units, and linked systems cluster in specific geographic areas that we then identify as societies and states.

This particular use of the systems concept to describe world affairs is rather easy to criticise.[21] It does serve, though, as a first attempt to develop the notion of human society as a whole. How interesting this might be depends upon the heuristic insights it can confer. If one has already decided that it is appropriate to complement the traditional state-centric picture of the world with other perspectives then such a point of view arrives as no surprise, and though it offers suggestions on how to locate global social networks in detail, it does not tell us what they mean.

George Modelski has adopted a similar idea, arguing that the main merit of such an approach has been to establish a 'viable characterization for phenomena of global interdependence, and to signal the need for a greater understanding of particular interdependencies'. In the history of the discipline it has served, he says, as a corrective to the 'unsubstantiated images of chaos, if not anarchy, that were frequently associated with perceptions of international politics' and it has helped to organise analysis around the premises of 'coherence, regularity and persistence that underlie the concept of a system', and of society as well.[22]

Modelski has gone on to depict world politics in terms of a 'layer-cake', and he has identified three levels of analysis – global, national and local – that correspond to three separate clusters of interactions and three sorts of spatial organisation. The model does not cover all possible levels; it does not account, for example, for national networks or regional state groupings, and there are problems of differential development at each level too. Thus social systems in the 'less developed' part of the world, growing into their nation-state containers, may develop quite different preoccupations from the more 'developed' societies which are rather growing out of theirs.[23]

He is aware, however, that the world as we know it has a history, and that our picture of the past is highly pertinent to out understanding of the present. The world today is unique, he asserts, because of its 'globality'. It is the 'first society that, through a process of globalization lasting a few centuries, has come to satisfy such criteria as global awareness, global interaction, and some degree of worldwide value commonality'.[24] The process of globalisation can be identified as one of Westernisation as well, and in this respect may be seen as one prolonged attempt to incorporate external domains into the 'ongoing fabric of Western-centred world politics'. To the extent that this process has become a two-way one we find Western-style modes of living being adapted to what the rest of the world may need, which means that 'globalisation' as such 'could yet be carried to completion in unsuspected ways'.[25]

It is Kenneth Waltz, however, who has taken the final logical step and detached altogether the structural arrangements of the world political system from the attributes of individual states and the way they interact.[26] He has advanced a system-level explanation of world international affairs in terms, that is, of the balance of power that will tend to emerge whenever social entities under ungoverned circumstances seek to survive. Structure in this sense refers to the constraints and dispositions that determine state behaviour by simple virtue of the competitive positions they bear, each to each, under conditions of global anarchy. These conditions will be dynamic ones and they will apply regardless of how different the separate states may be in themselves, regardless indeed of any other sort of interrelationship. They will limit what states do, generating similar and predictable kinds of political processes and political outcomes. The analogy with the relationship between micro- and macro-economics, between market behaviour and that of the firm, is purportedly exact. Individual social groups attempt to help themselves, and in doing so define collective standards of performance that no one of them intended as such, but all will observe if they want to persist. Thus order prevails, though no one specifically orders it. Thus there is organisation of a crude kind, though no 'organisation' is obvious as such to the analytic eye.

That this involves a radical simplification of what takes place in the real world, Waltz does not deny. Loss of descriptive detail is justified if it generates explanatory power. And indeed, in casting the structure of world affairs as independent of individual motive, Waltz has gone a good way to clarifying why pluralist systems converge upon like patterns of inter-play. The particularities remain, however. Statesmen do not always engage in balancing behaviour, as he would have us believe, whether they are aware or unaware of the balancing act itself. Many historical systems show no strain towards balance, and many examples exist of competition not breeding imitative responses or socialisation to the system. In his holist fashion Waltz goes too far, and the majority of pluralist observers would still endorse the traditional view that looks to the attributes of states, and the way they interact, more often than systemic/structural constraints. Which is not to say the latter do not exist, but they are commonly held to be less important than Waltz would have us believe.

World Society as a 'Society'

Except for the notion of 'value commonality' none of the analyses above conveys much of a sense of the moral concepts, social origins, educated outlooks and interests that statesmen share and which are made manifest in mutually observed codes of conduct and common institutions. By moving along the continuum we find the idea of a *society* of states, with

more in common than just their characteristics as states and the fact of
their secular intercourse.

> The element of international society has always been present in the
> modern international system because at no stage can it be said that
> the conception of the common interests of states, of common rules
> accepted and common institutions worked by them, has ceased to
> exert an influence. Most states at most times pay some respect to the
> basic rules of coexistence in international society, such as mutual
> respect of sovereignty, the rule that agreements should be kept, and
> rules limiting resort to violence.[27]

When we add in the transnational entities that share some at least of
these defining values and interests, we can begin to talk in terms of a
universal pattern, of a 'world society' as such.

The picture is still incomplete, however. 'World society' is structured
not only in terms of states and trans-state entities but also in terms of
socio-economic classes. Which is not to assert that the process of global
integration has proceeded at different depths, with one or the other
phenomenon historically prime. We are simply dealing with two aspects
of one extraordinary event, that is, the rise and dissemination of the
industrial mode of production by both capitalist and collectivist means.
State formation and class formation are the competing and the complementary social consequences of this process on a world scale. We have
two dimensions to account for, both of which detail the singular development of a sense of coalescence, and of conflict too.

The vision implicit here is not new. Those with an interest in the process of law have frequently been led to extend their feeling for the network of rules that knit societies together to global society as a whole.
Though the advent of nation-states has made this generalising feeling
more difficult to sustain, the Grotian notion of one human grouping
under 'natural' edicts of some kind has been restated in a modernised
form many times. Grotius himself transmitted a tradition that reached
back to the Stoics; to the Platonic idea of an overarching body of
ultimate values that all might apprehend if they could only be brought
to recognise them. These values were considered to be a phenomenon
apart, an 'impersonal system of pure ideas',[28] and for two millennia the
concept of such a system has remained an emergent principle of world
affairs. In its differing European modes it has helped sustain the expectation, entirely unreasonable perhaps, but a powerful picture none the
less, that there must ultimately arise one cultural framework to which all

people can refer, and maybe a single political system along with it. The rulers of the Roman Empire drew heavily on just such a sense of unification, of that part of the world at least that lay within their ken, and Cicero in particular was concerned to advance and defend very general notions of justice and peace. The Church that won the patronage of Rome adopted the same imperial outlook, though the attempt to establish a spiritual cosmos of Christian citizens failed finally to stall the process of schism, or to contain more secular conflicts, or indeed, to carry the day against the equally potent universalising force of Islam. Non-religious philosophers, generalising from their diverse understanding of the history of the human enterprise, came to locate the potential for global coalescence in other places, but the urge to define a fundamental set of ideas for all persons everywhere and for the world society immanent in that concept has remained much the same.

We can move toward this vision, as I have mentioned already, from the idea of separate interacting states, or from our image of a plethora of pre-capitalist social formations and the growth of a world capitalist economy and within it a global class system, in particular, a global bourgeoisie. Different methodological paradigms have been evolved to interpret these two perceived processes, and any theory of world society can be classified in terms of one or the other arena of analytic discourse and its shifting and fashionable concerns. I refer in fact to what I call the 'pluralist' and the 'structuralist' approaches, though I do not mean to suggest that these are the only ways of approaching the abiding issues in world affairs or that there has been no traffic in ideas from one arena to the other. On the contrary, throughout the history of the study of the subject we find a confused and contentious debate between the two. Within each approach, furthermore, there are important differences of emphasis and argument. But the distinctions stand, and I would maintain that they draw our attention to the major divisions of analytic interest in the social field.

A *pluralist* view of the world grants the groups—most obviously the states—of which the world is composed a quite distinctive status. Such groups are seen to be the ultimate and preferred source of self-identification and command. 'Pluralism' depicts a world divided into a multitude of states of unequal size but equally dedicated to the pragmatic pursuit of their interests and moral desires, joined in strategic alliance, the balance of power forming and reforming, and the conflicts between blocs of states potentially domesticated in the shared interests of all.[29] A *structuralist* perspective confronts global politics in terms of the horizontally arranged hierarchies that run across geographic boundaries, throwing into high relief the pattern whereby 'overdeveloped' states reproduce characteristic socio-economic and political forms within 'underdeveloped' ones in terms of the uneven spread of the industrial mode of production, the uneven and complex character of the class systems that have grown up in its wake, and the current global division of labour.[30]

My reading of these two paradigms is based on the central concern of the present study — my attempt to describe the social structure of the contemporary world. Here I discern two fundamental historical processes at work, in some respects parallel and in others opposed. One is the familiar story of the evolution of the present-day system of nation-states which the traditional understanding of the subjects accords central significance. The other is more a Marxist/Leninist view, depicting global class divisions as the pre-ordinate fact, and the place of state institutions as subordinate to them if not finally irrelevant altogether. For myself, I see them both as equally important in historical perspective, though obviously their significance is different in different contexts for different issues at different times. One's notion of world history, of the motive forces at work there, and of the most pertinent periodisation to be made of it, varies markedly depending upon whichever picture one seeks to support.

One effect is to highlight the fact that the same term or concept may mean quite different things depending upon one's analytic point of view. The notion of the 'state' itself, for example, probably the most common term in the world political vocabulary, immediately suggests a political history of the concept from the Peace of Westphalia, through the Congress of Vienna, to the present-day collection of sovereign, territorially discrete constructs which, competing and co-operating, are what most people expect to find abroad. With the exception of the Waltz's of this world, this is very much a state-centric, a 'pluralist' perspective. To the 'structuralist', however, the picture is a radically different one. Each set of political forms is the contemporary expression of a much broader historical movement whose touchstones in this case tend to be the age of mercantilism, the Industrial Revolution and so on, and a finance and monopoly capitalism that is now global in its reach. A preoccupation with legislatures and diplomacy can only serve to obscure the fact that global centres of production, distribution and exchange reach into the global periphery to profound effect and 'states' are only one expression of a political-economic dynamic that carves out competing classes at the cost of fundamental social change. The same thing, incidentally, happens to the notion of 'class', which structuralists consider prime and are apt to invest with very particular meaning, and pluralists variously render as a phenomenon of the 'group'.

What of the concept of 'world society'? *Pluralist* scholars, confronted by analytic attempts to accommodate the actors other than 'states' which now tread the global stage, are apt to proclaim a return to the notion already introduced and common to the history of Western political thought of one potential political entity embracing all humankind. In doing so they tend to underplay the advent of more novel events. They embrace the sort of analysis that identifies the twentieth century with the seventeenth century, for example, without due consideration for the fact that the Industrial Revolution has intervened, an event of paramount significance which marks, in one analyst's words, 'the most fundamental transformation of human life in the history of the world recorded in written documents'.[31]

This point can be applied to our understanding of the state. Thus it has been argued that: 'The modern highly complex large-group society is . . . only possible upon the basis of modern technology, and any comparison with social groups like the states of the 19th century is in reality entirely misleading.'[32] Though such things as the balance of power can be found wherever systematic circumstances allow them, whoever selects to see the notion of 'world society' as a *revival*, as a return to an earlier set of conceptions, will still have to account for the much changed circumstances of an industrialised world. Whether in the end he or she decides to retain the label or call what is happening by a different name, such identity as exists must be established in detail—it cannot be assumed.

'Structuralist' contributors can be equally one-eyed. Preoccupied with the patterns of global class, they tend to downplay the fact of the state and the independent force the notion of nationalism and its proliferating ideological progeny exert upon world affairs. The contemporary approach is a universalist one and the state system, in Marxist/Leninist terms in particular, is seen as the political product of and vehicle for a pervasive process of socio-economic 'exploitation'. One should add, however, that this is a caricature, and that structuralist theorists have also been led to more sophisticated attempts to accommodate the fact of states and of statehood. Many scholars from peripheral countries are hostile not so much towards Western claims that (in 'pluralist' terms) an integrated world society of states may be seen to be developing or ought to be doing so, but rather towards the fact that to them, in 'structuralist' terms, it already exists. They then attack the process of rationalisation, common in the West, which portrays the contemporary world hierarchy as beneficial or inevitable or fit to be defended for other reasons. Which has led them in turn to define development strategies as often as not in terms of self-reliance, and to advocate the attempt to rescue a modicum of economic and political sovereignty from their penetrated or neo-colonised plight by neo-mercantilist or other such means.

Soviet theorists of international relations, another group of structuralist scholars, attempt to 'diagonalise' the two basic social vectors, the 'vertical' one of class and the 'horizontal' dimension of the state,[33] and though the analytical products of the Soviet academies and their satellite schools and the sort of institutionalised Marxism manufactured there is not what I would choose to accept as a rendition of world affairs, it seems in its attempt to accommodate a contemporary class analysis a more realistic performance than the one a strictly pluralist view provides.

World Society: the Pluralist Perspective

These categories are fundamental, and I would like to consider each one at greater length. *Pluralism*, as I have said, invests human groups with fundamental political import. They are seen as the most significant purveyors of political acts, capable at best of satisfying the individual's communal urge while still reserving to him or her residual responsibilities and rights. The conflict of social groups should be, in theory, a manageable and regular one because it occurs in the main in a co-operative context where the clash of interests can be resolved by compromise. Conflict is regularised (which is not to say that relations do not periodically break down) and a co-operative milieu is meant to maximise personal freedom while minimising the tyranny of determined men or the undiscriminating oppression of the 'mass'. The individual can be politically involved without having to surrender to the dictates of some distant oligarch or reified regime.[34]

First mooted in this form as a description of domestic state affairs, and then as part of the Western liberal prescription of how such affairs should proceed, the pluralist ethic found a close fit in the doctrine of state sovereignty and it has lent the latter, which goes back a considerable historical distance in fact, added analytical support. It began, to be sure, as a reaction *against* the sort of monolithic and absolute power that the modern age has made possible, placing human groups in opposition to the 'state' as the individual's final protection from it. But the 'group' theory it attempts to articulate has transferred without much fuss to a world of discretely bounded national bodies, ostensibly serving each one's needs while bargaining with and balancing out competing claims. In the ideal-type pluralist *state* there is no centre of authority sufficiently pervasive to pre-empt the interests of the whole, which can then be severally defined. In the ideal pluralist *world*, where the groups are states themselves, no ring-holding referee can co-opt their primary authority despite the fact that co-option might well serve, as it would today, a number of notions of a 'world interest'. States and state-like entities ostensibly seek to secure the needs and interests of the individual without the price of a global sovereign. In the end this has served only to reinforce the paradigm since state boundaries, bolstered by exclusivist nationalist sentiments, reinforce the barriers against extended hierarchies of a cultural, political, social and economic kind.

The paradigm was somewhat confused by the advent, after World War Two, of many new states that were not cohesive groups in the preferred sense but consisted of rather rudimentary political machines in control of their urban capitals and laying claims for recognition strident enough to be met by other ruling regimes that were not on the whole much interested in the relevance of such claims to the peoples they purported to represent. Most of the tenets of pluralist theory have been fulfilled, however. 'States' as 'groups' are of a dimension within which individual claims might realistically be met. The emergence of overarching units, too gross to represent individuals adequately or to fulfil these needs, has been forestalled. The empirical fact of human diversity has been accommodated while the practical necessity for widespread co-operation is preserved. Inter-state policies can arise through reciprocal actions that are not always coerced, and any centralised organisation like the United Nations can only speak to the world and perform its function with the common consent of those who belong. The only criterion of 'pluralism' that this sort of 'statism' does not seem to meet is the requirement that membership of the group be voluntary. The very definition of the state covers the idea that individuals are born into it, and that affiliation is thereby compulsory. Despite this, multiple loyalties do exist – to a profession, tribe, company, religion, revolutionary group, class interest and so on – and states cannot be construed as wholly inclusive and commanding all of an individual's loyalty, which meets the pluralist preference quite well. As such, it is the modern manifestation of a very traditional view of international affairs.

Pluralists have found it much easier to accommodate transnational entities since the self-interested motivation of most of them, and the relentless pursuit of advantage or profit on the part of the commercial ones, comes much closer to the pressure-group philosophy than pluralist concepts sustain. Even on the most cursory review, however, the general description of the world in 'pluralist' terms is incomplete. Only a minority of regimes can adequately claim to represent individuals in such a way as to fulfil their needs (which does not hinder them from asserting that they do so). Weaker states need not, except in particular cases, be readily advantaged by alliance among themselves, and as often as not the system works to ignore the dispersed, the inarticulate, and those not organised in their own defence. It fails to account for the concept of 'class' (which it can only render as a phenomenon of the 'group') and the advent of a global hierarchy that favours the industrialised parts of the world, to the diverse disadvantage of much of the rest.

Pluralist doctrine proceeds in terms of rudimentary group likeness, and in the global arena this is provided by the idea, nominal but pervasive, of state sovereignty. It is further bolstered by the feeling that the industrialisation process is one that has distinctly 'pluralistic' consequences. 'Industrialisation' is a complex business, but evidence of the growth of local industries has been employed to argue that the links between core powers and peripheral ones are loosening, and that the pattern of global politico-economic clout is becoming less uneven and more diverse as a result.[35] Many peripheral states have demonstrated a capacity for sustained growth in real terms, servicing their own markets and those of rich countries abroad. Bill Warren, for example, argues that 'the post-war period has witnessed not merely a change in the character of . . . inegalitarian relationships but a significant and continuing reduction in inequality as well';[36] that the diversity and range of peripheral manufactures is considerable; and that the hold of core monopilies is starting to fail. Formal political autonomy *has* made a difference, he would say. 'The historical evidence unambiguously shows that since their independence underdeveloped countries are steadily improving their bargaining positions and their ability to control foreign firms operating in their territories,' and the process of 'independent industrialisation' is producing, under circumstances of enhanced interdependence, growing equality between groups previously very ill-matched indeed.[37]

Against this we may put evidence of the macro-movements of capital on a world scale. On balance, this seems to be out from rather in to the global periphery. Furthermore: 'Apart from raw materials and certain agricultural products which have to be sought where they can be found, the movement of capital is not an increasing but a decreasing function of difference in incomes.'[38] Core states are quite capable of using the capital they generate, and investment opportunities on the periphery remain comparatively limited,[39] which reinforces the divide between the two rather than promoting pluralism. The divide is also likely to persist, since the quality of life taken for granted in the centre is not shared

by more than enclave elites in the periphery, and the fact that few
people surrender privilege willingly would seem to exclude the possibility of radical changes in redistribution or greater growth. Those ill-
served by the contemporary hierarchy are ill-placed to perceive the
principal contradictions that reinforce their plight, and remain mostly
quiescent as a result.

World Society: the Structuralist Perspective

Industrialisation, whether capitalist or collectivist, has served to reinforce
the historically evolved class structure of the global social system, in turn
the result of the establishment of a capitalist world economy. The conventional line between 'national' control over foreign influence and the
sort of world where state action primarily secures the interests of transnational decision-makers in their pursuit of particular advantage and
global profit, seems less and less important. A world where mass living
standards are *absolutely* on the decline,[40] of economic denationalisation
and structured political violence, is not one conducive to plural concourse. It is at this point that the *structuralist* paradigm serves to identify
social continuities that bind in common concern those who for pluralist
purposes should be prised apart. The social configuration of the globe,
in structuralist parlance, is highly unrepresentative in character, its mass
clientele apathetic where it is not positively oppressed, its distribution
of military and economic power highly uneven where not demonstrably
unjust. The concept of a global 'common good' of some social or ecological kind, confused though it might be, is unlikely to emerge from
any group confrontation that does prevail. Its realisation would require
a redistribution of wealth and it might be beyond the scope of the pluralist doctrine to recommend an outlook that only reluctantly anticipates
the radical reconstruction of the global system as a whole. The way the
economic power of 'developed' states reaches into 'underdeveloping'
ones repeats a pattern of imperialism, structuralists assert, that is a
fundamental aspect of our socially asymmetric world. The economic inequalities that result have military, cultural and political concomitants.
'Developed' states will remain, in their own interests, committed to
global stability and the material advantages such stability provides,
employing many means to reinforce class distinctions (except where
exaggerated discrepancies become a manifest threat to their preponderance and call forth ameliorative measures of some kind).

The simplified form of this picture, that of a global 'core' and a
'periphery' linked by indigenous bourgeois and petty bourgeois elites,
is hardly adequate to represent a world 'class' structure, however. It fails,

for example, to represent the key role played by 'semi-peripheral' (or 'semi-core') countries in defusing what is seen to be a polarised socio-political situation, and it fails to account for the uneven spread of the industrial estate and the complex social effects this has brought about. Peripheral states with an advanced industrialised sector, for example, tend to display there a class structure typically Marxist, a sector that is tied to one or more of the metropolitan powers, that is an integral part of the 'internationalisation of production'. Numerically small in population terms, such a sector constitutes an important political force in countries which are still largely organised along traditional lines. There are other such states, however, that have declined as appendices to metropolitan powers, and where the local bourgeoisie or modernising-technocratic military junta is trying to build a national system that consolidates its socio-political base, generates capital, and generally attempts to shift traditional components of the economy on to a more dynamic footing. There are yet others that have remained comparatively untouched by industrialisation and the capitalist world economy, where a semi-colonial mode of capitalist accumulation still prevails and the restructuring of the society along class lines has scarcely begun except in marginal ways in the traditional sectors.[41] Hassad Riad has charted the social structure of Egypt in terms of a rural/urban dichotomy and his outline gives some indication of the complexities involved.[42] Under the 'urban' category he lists servants, a 'subproletariat', wage-earners in traditional sectors, a proletariat proper, 'lower-level employers', traditional entrepreneurs, 'intermediate-level employees/civil servants etc.', a bourgeoisie and an aristocracy. Under the 'rural' category come 'the common people', among whom he distinguishes those without land from 'poor peasants' and 'intermediate strata', a 'privileged strata' of rich peasants, and agrarian capitalists. This plethora of possible groupings gives some indication of how mixed an aspect a particular social scene can present. While attempting to identify more general global configurations, we do not exhaust the richness and diversity of the patterns that prevail in any one place. Furthermore, much of the proletariat in core countries may well stand in an exploitative relationship to that on the periphery. Once heavily penalised by the capitalist mode of production, they have become accessories to it. In terms of social differentiation and social stratification, the consequences of industrialisation have been and continue to be diverse in the extreme, and this regardless of the capitalist, socialist or Fascist predilections of the industrialising regime.

Meanwhile, the opportunities for global industrialisation have proceeded apace, not only under the state-directed aegis of the governments of China and the USSR, not only for the countries in Europe and for those outside this 'developed' sector who have been 'invited' to apply,[43] but among peripheral countries, too. And in market terms at least, the world is no longer a divided one but a single entity. Regimes that control the means of production to collectivist ends still act abroad on world markets as capitalists, whatever criteria they use to distribute their profits at home. *Economically* the world is one formation. Thus: 'the only system in the modern world that can be said to have a mode of production is the world system . . . and this system currently [but not eternally] is capitalist.'[44] Indeed:

> Even if *every* nation in the world were to permit only state ownership of the means of production, the world system would still be a capitalist system, although doubtless the political parameters would be very different from what they presently are.[45]

The occurrence of a number of socialist states that have nationalised or otherwise socialised their productive processes does not of itself give rise to a 'socialist system' over and against a 'capitalist' one, since they continue to operate in profit-maximising terms rather than manufacturing for 'rational' use or allocating and consuming goods and services with direct reference to what might, on a world scale, 'optimally' benefit all (however we determine what 'rational' or 'optimal' might be).

Politically, the situation may be depicted in terms of the

> peculiarity of the capitalist world economy . . . [where] the boundaries of the economic and political structures are different. While the world-economy is defined as a system having a single division of labour, in a capitalist world-system, the political units are states . . . This results in the following situation: while a group's social activities are in some ultimate sense determined by their role in the world-economy, the object of their political activity is directed at the state of which they are a member.[46]

The historical legacy and contemporary reality of industrialisation has had distinct *social* consequences too. The transcultural psychology of profit maximisation[47] facilitates these, though there is no conclusive way to establish a single causal factor, and the connections between economy, polity and society are also ultimately elusive. Immanuel Wallerstein, whom I quote above, sees the world economy as 'in some sense' the final determinant, but the 'state' remains an important independent idea, subject to its own, though related, logic of formation. Pluralists expand on this fact, preferring to refute the structuralist perspective by elaborating the notion of 'power' and pressing the divergence between 'politico-economic' as opposed to purely 'political' affairs. The growing significance, they say, of statist loyalties has led to a 'far more complicated world . . . a safer world . . . for the triumph of pluralism is, in essence, the triumph of nationalism'.[48] And indeed, any notion of a global class structure must contend with the pre-ordinate potency of state boundaries and the fact that global peoples as part of their socialisation process tend to identify themselves in terms of states, or are coerced into doing so. Despite tacit agreement on the rules of the game, important differences also remain between regimes at different stages of development and the growth of transnational interactions and of class structures does not will these differences away. There is also evidence on the part of some states of developing economic independence, as well as cases of poor countries where radical groups have displaced self-serving elites and attempted some revisionist development strategy of a more populist kind. Local elites in general may generate a far more independent sense of their place and wants and needs than structuralists tend to suppose, and a state of 'dependency' may only be recognisable in the end as an idea that disgruntled regimes employ to describe felt limits upon their use of state power.[49] Furthermore, the differences that exist between the metropolitan powers — the United States, Japan, the Soviet Union and the nation-states of Western Europe — are scarcely insignificant. And as a group they grow marginally more vulnerable to boycotts by peripheral states and their unionised demands.

The debate, implicit here, between 'economic' and 'political' determinism is never likely to be resolved. And there are good reasons why it need not. In the meantime these two foci provide us with alternative versions of the concept of 'world society'. As an ideal type the pluralist, as we have seen, will approach the notion in terms of a society of states. States and state-like entities, as they become progressively more interdependent or feel themselves to be so (a process that occurs both by regions and across the globe), are presumed to approach something like a 'society'. The level of *absolute* interdependence between states, though not all analysts accept this, has been rising in the world,[50] and we can cite such factors as technological changes in communications, transport and strategic weapons, the broadening of human perceptions and expectations, and the appearance of a plethora of transnational entities in this regard. In *relative* terms, however, it is not so clear whether the level of autonomy of state self-consciousness has risen faster or not so fast as this, or whether it is that both interdependence as well as state self-consciousness are paradoxically being enhanced in complex and related ways.

It is thus that Evan Luard, for example, in pursuit of an effective sociological approach to international relations, construes the subject. It is theoretically possible, he argues, to treat the world as 'one single, immensely complex, variegated, sub-divided, yet at the same time interconnected society, of vast size and many-sided character'. However, the 'essential units', the 'important initiators of action and wielders of power', remain states, and it is the intricate congress of these with their institutions, rules, traditions and expectations that he considers to be international society proper: 'For this society of states can be studied as a factor distinct from, though itself a part of, the world society of individuals.'[51] The difference between a society like this and a domestic one is more apparent than real, he maintains; more a matter of degree rather than kind. In support of his conceptualisation he then argues that: 'Stratification among nations, for example — the class structure dividing nations according to wealth, power, influence and status — is a factor largely independent of stratification among the human populations in the world as a whole.'[52]

Now, to a dogmatic structuralist, as I have indicated, this point of view fundamentally misconstrues the history of the state system. Much of the point of the hierarchy among nations is the relationship this bears to the stratification patterns created by the processes of industrialisation and modernisation across state lines.

Johan Galtung's 'rank-disequilibrium' framework locates states according to their comparative status by various means: by industrialisation, income *per capita*, military power, educational levels, and where states do not stand on the same level across the scales there will tend, he argues, to be instability in the world system as a whole. But a simplistic sociological statement like this one is a crude structural snapshot compared to the detailed portrait of the global hierarchy that is possible in terms of imperialism and dependence, and the matter in which the politico-economic power of rich states is brought to bear on poor ones in their common context, that is, the uneven development of world industrialisation and the world capitalist system.

The lack of uniformity of this system is an important part of the paradigm's explanatory power. In general we observe mutual dependence among core powers, which is a critical part of their capacity to preserve what happens to be mutually beneficial for them. And as far as the periphery is concerned, dependence operates largely as 'exploitation'. The process of domination has often been quite unsystematic,

however, and we need to remain aware of the wide variety of local political and social forms that prevail and the way these have affected the
transfer of Western political and economic forms. Social integration is
not something distributed evenly across the globe; the process is much
more various and intricate than that.

When we look for the boundary of 'world society' we can trace in
retrospect its extraordinary historic expansion. The European powers,
with all the understandings and conventions they evolved to facilitate
their own dealings with each other, established empires that almost in-
advertently brought these principles and rules to bear upon a wider
world. They missionised and plundered, feeling as often as not scant
need to accommodate the groups they encountered in ways found accept-
able among themselves. Where they did meet state-like entities, to exped-
ite political and economic control they sometimes established a system
of indirect rule which did mean the implicit recognition of some sort of
equivalence between the subject regime and their own. By the time,
however, that the dissolution of the imperial systems occurred key
members of the under-dog populations had learned Western ways, which
they turned to their own advantage in the arguments for liberation. There
has ensued in turn the progressive extension of the legal notions and
diplomatic concepts of the West. No significant groups have been left
outside this boundary; nearly everyone, at least nominally, has been con-
signed to some country or another. There are few people now beyond
the pale.

In its most general sense, then, 'society' refers to the meshed fabric
of social relationships. Since there are important networks of human
relationships which are global in extent, though they may not, except
in a rather remote way, include all Earth's people, we can, I think, fairly
go on to speak of a *world* society and not just an international one.

As we apply more precise definitions the concept quickly becomes
strained. In describing a society, in delimiting the extent of some particular set of social structures, it is justifiable to think in terms of a 'relatively independent or self-sufficient population characterised by
internal organisation, territoriality, cultural distinctiveness, and sexual
recruitment'.[53] And as T.B. Bottomore maintains, 'where we find political independence along with distinct economic, religious and familial
institutions we can safely regard the group constituting a separate society.'[54]

There are objections to each of the criteria Bottomore gives – 'political
independence', for example, excludes those groups which are part of
some other entity that we could fairly call a 'society' too. 'Territoriality',

and the idea that a society will be centred on a discrete geographic locale, obscures the fact of social collectivities that cut across frontiers. Each index is inadequate in some way. But the syndrome of them does suggest something quite concrete. Does it define a 'world' entity of this sort?

Societies vary considerably in their coherence and organisation, and the definitions above do not account sufficiently for the fact of rather more diffuse groups delimited in terms of shared cultural attributes alone. 'World society' is defined in this way. Its personnel may share their attributes with other both general and more local societies, but they can also be observed doing those things that are both necessary and sufficient for any society to exist, that is, communicating, producing and distributing goods, socialising new members and recruits, distributing power, and observing the ritual forms that service a sense of cohesion and mark significant social events.[55]

This society can be viewed in more than one way. To repeat: contemporary scholars move towards the concept from one of two particular standpoints, from that of the *polity* (as the 'pluralists' tend to do) and from that of the *economy* (which is more the 'structuralist' starting-point). We arrive in the global arena at a different idea of the social structure in each case: the *pluralist* conceives of a society of states, competing for power but sharing values and institutions, that is, constrained and disposed by a balance of power; the *structuralist* fastens upon the fact of global classes derivative of modern modes of industrial production, distribution and exchange and the universal dissemination of industrial culture. These two standpoints are not necessarily compatible ones, and each case has made sustained attempts to reduce the one to the other — pluralists to describe the consequences of industrialisation in 'statist' terms; structuralists to describe 'states' as an excrescence upon 'class'. And yet, state formation and class formation within world society seem to me to be separable and equally significant processes. Both the one *and* the other provide valuable ways of understanding global social structures, and the most useful image of world affairs will only emerge from a composite discussion of the way they interrelate: the compromises that have been effected between them and their manifold contradictions.

There is, in fact, a more fundamental difference again — between a *molecular* notion of 'society' as the interaction of rational individuals reckoning their self-interests and relating in utilitarian ways so as to secure their life chances, and a *holistic* approach to the idea, as an integrated unit predicated upon common assumptions about human nature and an emergent moral order that social institutions then reproduce. To redress an imbalance that still prevails in the literature I have leaned here towards the latter perspective.[56] I have emphasised cultural qualities in the first chapter, and society as a social structure that inherits and transmits a fundamental set of cultural ideas, not for any ideological reason that I consciously favour, nor because I believe in the immanent expression of a historical 'Geist', but because that is what I happen to see when I analyse the way in which contemporary social forms have emerged. Though the history of the concept has struggled back and forth between these poles, it is enough for my present purpose to point out that a complex set of human relations and interdependencies, regardless of its derivation, will signify a society, and that a common intellectual consciousness and a common moral code will be integral features of it.

The human relations I am concerned with derive in large part from the material impact of industrialisation and the emergence of 'modern' human beings. I would argue that a common *intellectual* consciousness, growing and still very unevenly dispersed but evident withall, does now exist, born of the experience of these contemporary processes. I have not discussed the attempt to secure a common *moral* code, however. 'We may say', Hedley Bull maintains,

> that in . . . world international society there is at least a diplomatic or elite culture, comprising the common intellectual culture of modernity . . . However, it is doubtful whether, even at the diplomatic level, it embraces what was called a common moral culture or set of common values.[57]

From the pluralist standpoint this is a debatable conclusion. From the structuralist perspective, however, it is quite inadequate, and to make this clear I shall turn now to discuss the advent of global norms.

Notes

1. I.L. Horowitz, 'Personality and Structural Dimensions in Comparative International Development', *Social Science Quarterly*, vol. 51, no. 3 (December 1970), p. 513.

2. The least compromised statement of the dichotomy (of which I am aware) is in R. Bendix, 'Tradition and Modernity Reconsidered', *Comparative Studies in Society and History*, vol. 9 (1966/7), pp. 318-23. See also the critique by D. Tipps, 'Modernisation Theory and the Comparative Study of Societies: a critical perspective', *Comparative Studies in Society and History*, vol. 15, no. 2 (March, 1973), pp. 199-226.

3. R. Aron, *The Industrial Society* (Frederick A. Praeger, New York, 1967), p. 2.

4. For Aron's critique see *The Industrial Society*, Part II, 'Development Theory and Evolutionist Philosophy'. Also S. Huntingdon, 'Political Development and Political Decay', *World Politics*, vol. 17, no. 3 (April 1965), pp. 386-430; A. Mazrui, 'From Social Darwinism to Current Theories of Modernization', *World Politics*, vol. 21, no. 1 (October 1968), pp. 69-83.

5. T. Parsons, *The Social System* (Free Press, Illinois, 1951). His pattern variables describe 'modern' social role relationships as functionally specific, achievement-orientated, universalistic and affectively neutral. Under primitive or peasant orders the same roles are seen to be more functionally diffuse, ascriptive, particularistic and affectively rewarding. For the application of these action patterns to social structures see A. Hoogvelt, *The Sociology of Development* (Macmillan, London, 1976), Ch. 3, 'Neo-evolutionary Theory, Structural Functionalism and Modernisation Theories'. Abstract conceptions like these can in fact be very misleading. For a critique of the universalism/particularism dichotomy, for example, see Bendix, 'Tradition and Modernity', pp. 313-14.

6. A point clearly supported by R. Skinner, 'Technological Determinism: a critique of convergence theory', *Comparative Studies in Society and History*, vol. 18 (1976), pp. 1-24. Cf. the classical Marxist-Leninist doctrine that saw modernisation and the demise of capitalism as the result of this process of diffusion.

7. Bendix, 'Tradition and Modernity', p. 308.

8. R. Williams, *Politics and Technology* (Macmillan, London, 1971), p. 12. See W. Faunce and W. Form (eds.), *Comparative Perspectives on Industrial Society* (Little, Brown and Company, Boston, 1969) and W. Moore and N. Smelser (eds.), *The Impact of Industry* (Prentice-Hall, New Jersey, 1965). Also R. Aron, *18 Lectures on Industrial Society* (Weidenfeld and Nicolson, London, 1961), pp. 73-5 where he describes an industrial society as one in which large-scale industry is the characteristic form of production. Its features include (1) the separation of industrial enterprise from the family; (2) the technological division of labour within the firm; (3) an accumulation of capital; (4) the idea of rational calculation (economic not technical; on the ethno-determinant nature of rationality see Skinner, 'Technological Determinism', pp. 5-6); and (5) the concentration of labour in the workplace. 'Modern societies' generally, he asserts, 'are defined first and foremost by their organisation of labor; that is, by their relationship to the external world, their use of machinery, the application of scientific methods, and the social and economic consequences of the rationalization of production' (*The Industrial Society*, p. 15). They are *industrialised*, and basically,

industrialized societies may be called scientific, in that both mechanization and productivity are the fruit of the scientific spirit and are the ultimate causes of both industrialization and the progressive nature of the economy . . . The scientific society is far from being universal, but it is potentially so, in the sense that it has now become a *sine qua non* of power and prosperity. Nations that deliberately reject scientific development are choosing to leave the path of history and to stagnate. They would appear doomed, unwittingly, to final annihilation (pp. 57, 67).

Whether this last point is true or not, where it is assumed to be so it has very potent effects. There is a good brief summary in R. Scase (ed.), *Industrial Society: Class Cleavage and Control* (George Allen and Unwin, London, 1977), Intro.

9. A. Feldman and W. Moore, 'Are Industrial Societies becoming Alike?' in A. Gouldner and S. Miller (eds.), *Applied Sociology* (Free Press, New York, 1965); H. Blumer, 'Industrialization and the Traditional Order', *Sociology and Social*

Research, vol. 48, no. 2 (January 1964), pp. 138-9.

10. J. Gusfield, 'Tradition and Modernity: Misplaced Polarities in the Study of Social Change', *American Journal of Sociology*, vol. 72, no. 4 (January 1967), pp. 351-62. Blumer ('Industrialization and the Traditional Order') lists five significantly different ways in which a pre-industrial society may respond: rejective, disjunctive, assimilative, supportive and disruptive.

11. Bendix, 'Tradition and Modernity', p. 331.

12. Indices like these are developed by L. Doob, *Becoming More Civilised* (Yale University Press, New Haven, 1960) and his 'Scales for Assaying Psychological Modernization in Africa', *Public Opinion Quarterly*, vol. 31 (Fall 1967), pp. 414-21; J. Kahl, *The Measurement of Modernism* (University of Texas Press, Austin, Texas, 1968); A. Inkeles and D. Smith, *Becoming Modern* (Heinemann, London, 1974) for Inkeles' OM scale; also his 'Industrial Man: the Relation of Status to Experience, Perception and Value', *The American Journal of Sociology*, vol. 64, no. 1 (July 1960), pp. 1-31, which includes my favourite Table 3: 'Laughing and Crying in England by Class and Sex'; J. Stephenson, 'Is Everyone Going Modern? A Critique and Suggestion for Measuring Modernism', *American Journal of Sociology*, vol. 74 (November 1968), pp. 265-75.

13. F. Fliegel, 'The Comparative Analysis of the Impact of Industrialization on Traditional Values', *Rural Sociology*, vol. 41, no. 4 (Winter 1976), pp. 44-67.

14. Inkeles and Smith, *Becoming Modern*, p. 295.

15. M. Armer and A. Schnaiberg, 'Measuring Individual Modernity: a near myth', *American Sociological Review*, vol. 37, no. 3 (June 1972), pp. 301-15; C. Coughenour and J. Stephenson, 'Measures of Individual Modernity: Review and Commentary', *International Journal of Comparative Sociology*, vol. 13 (1972), pp. 81-98.

16. A. Portes, 'The Factorial Structure of Modernity: Empirical Replications and a Critique', *American Journal of Sociology*, vol. 79, no. 1 (November 1973), esp. pp. 32-6, 44.

17. Cf. C. Kerr *et al.*, *Industrialism and Industrial Man* (Harvard University Press, Cambridge, Mass., 1960).

18. Skinner, 'Technological Determinism', p. 20.

19. The usual list includes multinational business corporations, international trade unions, professional bodies, educational, religious and cultural organisations, and political parties.

20. J. Burton, *Systems, States, Diplomacy and Rules* (Cambridge University Press, London, 1968), p. 8. Also *World Society* (Cambridge University Press, London, 1972), pp. 35-45.

21. See, for example, W.J.M. Mackenzie, *Politics and Social Science* (Penguin, Harmondsworth, 1967), p. 340.

22. G. Modelski, *Principles of World Politics* (Free Press, New York, 1972), pp. 6-7.

23. J. Galtung, 'On the Future of the International System' in R. Jungk and J. Galtung (eds.), *Mankind 2000* (Universitets-Forlaget, Oslo, 1969).

24. Modelski, *Principles of World Politics*, p. 10.

25. Ibid., pp. 55-6. Cf. W. McNeill, *The Rise of the West* (University of Chicago Press, Chicago, 1963). Also J. Field, 'Transnationalism and the new tribe', *International Organisation*, vol. 25, no. 3 (Summer 1971), pp. 353-72. At this point we arrive again at the question of world culture, which I shall not develop any further here except to point to the prescriptions of 'world order' scholars who find the seeds of centralism and the potential growth of a world community in the moral or ideological 'universalism' of the major global cultures, in the managerial potential of contemporary communications and transport technology, and in our response to the threat that nuclear weapons and the collapse of the world's ecosystems

might pose.

There is, incidentally, no such thing as 'world order' as such. There are *forms* of 'world order', more or less creative, more or less exploitative, and even that Order with a capital 'O' that represents the minimal level of social consensus and control deemed necessary to prevent the holocaust and the end of the human race will nurture some members of the world society at the expense of others. I cannot conceive of a social 'order' that does not convey, even if it does not actively defend, the preferred values of one group or another. Positing some goals as 'primary' or 'elemental' does not solve the problem since life goes on regardless of the fact that fundamental values are daily abused – by political leaders, criminals, by anybody really who resorts to violence, breaks promises, or appropriates the possessions of other people. Society only disintegrates if a significant group decides to reject a particular 'order', and transgression becomes a majority enterprise rather than a minority one. Most members of a society may actively endorse or passively acquiesce in a disposition of affairs because it appears preferable to no order at all, but this can only be characterised as Order, as a reified value in itself, by neglecting the distribution of values implicit therein. We are justified, therefore, in scrutinising with care the *status quo* that exponents of a 'minimal order' explicitly or implicitly endorse, and the likely material and moral consequences of any *new* order that we find recommended, or we see as emerging in the future from contemporary trends.

26. K. Waltz, *Theory of International Politics* (Addison-Wesley, Reading, 1979).

27. H. Bull, *The Anarchical Society* (Macmillan, London, 1977), p. 4. For a brief history of the idea of a society of states, see pp. 24-39.

28. F. Znaniecki, *Modern Nationalities: a Sociological Study* (University of Illinois Press, Urbana, Illinois, 1952), p. 174.

29. 'Pluralism' subsumes under one heading both the 'realist' idea of each state against the others and the 'internationalist' notion that world affairs are predicated upon an international society. These are the 'Hobbesian' and the 'Grotian' traditions respectively, so-called by M. Wight in 'Western Values in International Relations' in H. Butterfield and M. Wight (eds.), *Diplomatic Investigations* (Allen and Unwin, London, 1967), and developed by H. Bull, *The Anarchical Society* (Macmillan, London, 1976), pp. 24-6; 'Martin Wight and the Theory of International Relations', *British Journal of International Studies*, vol. 2, no. 2 (1976). See also R. Wesson, *State Systems*: international pluralism, politics and culture (The Free Press, New York, 1978), pp. 5-10, 'pluralism'.

30. This falls within the European tradition of 'universalist' doctrines; the 'Kantian' construct of Wight and Bull. In using this term, I might add, I do not deliberately allude to that anthropological school of 'structuralism' associated particularly with the works of Levi-Strauss. There is, however, a parallel in that anthropological structuralists look for underlying phenomena, for basic 'structures' that explain external occurrences, rather than confining themselves to a description of 'surface particulars' alone or explaining such structures in turn in terms of social functions, as one prominent school of sociological analysis is wont to do. In attempting to uncover the social logic of global industrialisation, to see how this is reflected in the surface practice and appearance of world affairs, we witness the same instinct at work. See A. Giddens, *Studies in Social and Political Theory* (Hutchinson, London, 1977). Also R. Alford, 'Paradigms of Relations between State and Society' in L. Lindberg *et al.* (eds.), *Stress and Contradiction in Modern Capitalism* (D.C. Heath, Mass., 1975).

31. E. Hobsbawm, *Industry and Empire* (Weidenfeld and Nicolson, London, 1968), p. 1.

32. B. Landheer, *On the Sociology of International Law and International*

Society (Martinus Nijhoff, The Hague, 1966), p. 7.

33. V. Kubálková and A. Cruikshank, 'A Double Omission', *British Journal of International Studies*, vol. 2, no. 3 (October 1977), p. 295.

34. There are a number of pluralist positions. The view I have sketched is not universally shared in all its features by pluralist theorists. There are, furthermore, important differences between the American and Continental schools. This difference is not discussed here, but see the works of the English pluralists in particular – J.N. Figgis, F. Maitland, H. Laski and G.D. Cole. Also K.G. Hsaio, *Political Pluralism* (Kegan Paul, Trubner & Co., London, 1957); H.M. Magid, *English Political Pluralism* (Columbia University Press, New York, 1941); David Nicholls, *The Pluralist State* (Macmillan, London, 1975); W.E. Connolly (ed.), *The Bias of Pluralism* (Atherton Press, New York, 1969).

35. See, for example, Bill Warren, 'Imperialism and Capitalist Industrialisation', *New Left Review*, no. 81 (Sept./Oct. 1973), p. 4, for a particularly clear statement of this position.

36. Ibid., p. 10.

37. Ibid., pp. 20, 35. For a list of the devices conferred by formal political independence which 'must' in the end sustain economic advance (undifferentiated), see p. 12.

38. A. Emmanuel, 'Myths of Development versus Myths of Underdevelopment' *New Left Review*, no. 85 (May/June 1974), p. 77.

39. Loc. cit. Also K. Griffin, *International Inequality and National Poverty* (Macmillan, London, 1978).

40. I. Adelman and C.T. Morris, *Economic Growth and Social Equity in Developing Countries* (Stanford University Press, California, 1973). Also K. Griffin, *International Inequality*, particularly Ch. 6.

41. E. Krippendorff, 'Towards a Class Analysis of the International System', *Acta Politica*, vol. 10 (January 1975), pp. 7-8. For Wallerstein's tripartite picture, see his 'The Rise and Future Demise of the World Capitalist System: Concepts for Comparative Analysis', *Comparative Studies in Society and History*, vol. 16 (1974).

42. Hassad Riad, *L'Egypte Nasserienne* (Paris, 1964), p. 41.

43. On the concept of 'promotion by invitation' see I. Wallerstein, 'Dependence in an interdependent world; the limited possibilities of transformation within the capitalist world economy', *African Studies Review*, vol. 17, no. 1 (April 1974), pp. 14-15.

44. Ibid., p. 6. Its essential features include

the creation of a single world division of labor, production for profit in this world market, capital accumulation for expanded reproduction as a key mode of maximizing profit in the long run, emergence of three zones of economic activity (core, semi-periphery, and periphery) with not merely unequal exchange between them but also persistent merchandise trade imbalances, a multiplicity of state structures (strongest in the core, weakest in the periphery) and the development over time of two principal class formations (a bourgeoisie and a proletariat) whose concrete manifestations are however complicated by the constant formation and reformation of a host of ethnic-national groupings (I. Wallerstein, 'The Three Stages of African Involvement in the World-Economy' in P. Gutkind and I. Wallerstein (eds.), *The Political Economy of Contemporary Africa* (Sage, Beverly Hills, 1976), pp. 30-1). On the advent of a world market economy (and the hierarchy of 'capitalism', 'market', and 'material life' see F. Braudel, *Afterthoughts on Material Civilization and Capitalism* (John Hopkins University Press, Baltimore, 1977). Also A. Walker, *Marx: his theory and his context* (Longman, London, 1978) who construes this seminal sociologist in this very light, e.g. p. xi, 'while Marx attributed the development of the modern world to the rise of capitalism, his notion of capitalism can be rendered as the predominance of the market relations in society'.

45. I. Wallerstein, 'Dependence in an Interdependent World', *The Political Economy of Contemporary Africa*, p. 7.

46. I. Wallerstein, 'Class and Class Conflict in Africa', *Monthly Review*, vol. 26, no. 9 (February 1975), p. 37.

47. A. Mazrui, 'Modernization and Reform in Africa' in J. Bhagwati (ed.), *Economics and World Order* (Macmillan, New York, 1972), p. 294. See further A. Hirschman, *The Passions and the Interests: political arguments for capitalism before its triumph* (Princeton University Press, New Jersey, 1977).

48. R. Tucker, *Nation or Empire?* (Johns Hopkins Press, Baltimore, 1968), p. 123; see also *The Radical Left and American Foreign Policy* (Johns Hopkins Press, Baltimore, 1971) and B.J. Cohen, *The Question of Imperialism* (Basic Books, New York, 1973).

49. Sione Tupouniua, 'The State in Post-Colonial Societies: Some Theoretical Notes', unpublished manuscript, p. 30.

50. R. Rosecrance and M. Stein, 'Interdependence: Myth or Reality?', *World Politics*, vol. 26, no. 1 (October 1973), pp. 1-27; O. Young, 'Interdependencies in World Politics', *International Journal*, vol. 24, no. 4 (Autumn 1969), esp. pp. '730-4; K. Deutsch, 'The Impact of Communications upon International Relations Theory' in A. Said (ed.), *Theory of International Relations* (Prentice-Hall, New Jersey, 1968); K. Waltz, 'The Myth of National Interdependence' in C. Kindleberger (ed.), *The International Corporation: a symposium* (MIT Press, Mass., 1970).

51. E. Luard, *Types of International Society* (Free Press, New York, 1976), p. 50. Choosing a number of such societies that have occurred in history – in ancient China, ancient Greece, the European age of dynasties, of religions, of sovereignty, of nationalism – he compares them from the point of view of a number of defining sociological features, that is, the nature of their elites, elite motivation and political methods, the pattern of stratification, the structure of their interactions, the roles performed by individual unit members, their styles of social control, their institutions and basic ideologies.

52. Ibid., p. 50.

53. L. Mayhew, 'Society' in David Sills (ed.), *International Encyclopedia of the Social Sciences* (Macmillan and the Free Press, 1968), vol. 14, p. 577.

54. T.B. Bottomore, *Sociology*, rev. edn (George Allen and Unwin, London, 1971), p. 116.

55. Ibid., p. 116.

56. This is, in terms of the history of the concept, closer to the traditional view of Comte, Durkheim and the nineteenth-century German school of philosophic 'idealists'.

57. Bull, *The Anarchical Society*, p. 317.

THE ADVENT OF GLOBAL NORMS

Those who share the ethos of an industrialised society and the personal attributes of a 'modern' milieu subscribe to more than the *intellectual* values implicit in their cosmopolitan creed. The dissemination of a Western (now generally understood as a Northern) way of life bears with it an attachment, more and less hypocritical, to certain *moral* standards too. Accompanying elite commitments to 'development' and 'technology' and the cognitive shift to a 'scientific' frame of reference has been the pandemic acceptance, in form at least, of characteristic moral concepts and normative aspirations. This is partly because the processes involved are so pervasive. Fundamental changes in modes of production will tend, as they make their presence felt, to be reflected in correlative revisions in moral premises as well. It is also, I suspect, because the latter can be construed as more than characteristic of one way of life: that there is something potentially universal about such values too.

I am aware of the ethnocentrism of this sort of statement, and I would guess that the emergence, should it ever occur, of a truly pervasive global culture will involve many more ingredients in it of a non-Western kind. There is no room here for local prejudice writ large. Nevertheless in the attempt, however conditioned, to arrive at universal moral predicates from first principles, the Western tradition does speak to Everyman. How this voice is heard is another matter, but the argument, where it aspires to anything approaching 'truth', declines to accept that local differences in what people believe necessarily denotes the relativity of all and any value response.

Moral Pluralism

A generation ago Hans Morgenthau described the dissipation of European international society. Within this society, from the Treaty of Westphalia to World War One, national leaders had been wont to declaim one body of like beliefs. The potential for effective diplomacy such a shared culture allowed had progressively declined, he said, until the stage had been set for the clash of total and mutually exclusive world views and an ethical reversion on a world scale to the 'politics and morality of tribalism, of the Crusades, and of the religious wars'.[1] The diplomatic mores shared by this regional ruling class for three hundred years had been effectively displaced by the advent of nationalistic ideologies, plus the more diverse values that foreign-policy-makers recruited from outside the ranks of the aristocratic elite, seemed to espouse.

Even as these words were written, however, and the events of the ensuing Cold War came close more than once to vindicating them, other patterns were coming to complement the stark conclusions he chose to draw. Foreign-policy-makers, for example, were emerging as a more uniform group again, their family context the 'world's great middle class—professional, business, and public service, with only a sprinkling of artisan or peasant background, and without any great wealth'.[2] Those who responded to the study from which this quotation comes considered educational experience a significant influence over their subsequent policy performance, and George Modelski for one has claimed that: 'The university is the major educational institution of the world system and it is an institution which shapes the outlooks and the career, of most of the world's elites.' Furthermore: 'It provides the major element of cohesion, not only for the global political system but for the entire world society,'[3] which is an interesting, if contentious claim. Occupational experience was construed as the other major factor shaping such careers, an experience that typically tended to immerse the prospective Foreign Minister in matters of national concern.

Along with the re-emergence of some sort of cohesion among foreign-policy-makers, this time on the global and not just the European stage, went growing reservations about a morality specifically attached to nation-states. Obviously states, or at least those who lead them, have continued to possess a pre-ordinate capacity to compel moral compliance, and human loyalty will still attach considerable importance to national identity over universal creeds. It is also obvious that this is not something that equally obtains in all places, and as a reaction to the particular state-based doctrines that precipitated World War Two, as well as in response to the presence of the global poor whose common plight has become daily more evident, there has been a shift towards the recognition of the individual as the ultimate source and recipient of duties and rights.[4]

Morgenthau's perspective is very much what I term a 'pluralist' one. While he acknowledges the basic continuity of human experience (the 'irreducible minimum of psychological traits and aspirations which are the common possession of all mankind')[5] plus a common desire for life and the means to support it (for social advantage and self-esteem, for freedom and self-realisation and so on), he finds the diversity in the real conditions under which we live compelling fundamentally divergent moral and political philosophies. The appeal to universal standards

erects a rude and finally superficial canopy over what are singularly
state-bound conceptions. Only the latter have practical force. Leaders
may speak the same moral language when they travel abroad, but when
they return they revert at once to regional dialects, and the ethical concepts they use among fellow statesmen from other countries are translated as such into the various and vernacular applications deemed
appropriate at home.

This is the logical extension of that notion of morality that depicts
the popular reference to right and wrong in terms of the human group.

> To the great mass of mankind, the dichotomy in western philosophy
> between the individual and mankind is meaningless: the individual
> is part of a tribe, clan, sect, family, village, and the like, and this
> serves as the effective middle term between him or her and the world
> at large. The essence of the group is its distinction from outsiders;
> morality consists primarily of right conduct towards the other
> members of the group.[6]

States consist of many such groups with their conflicting moral codes
but in the name of the state leaders can assume or assert a 'national'
morality to justify their actions in the global arena where they meet
with other such claims likewise articulated in national terms. Any area
of mutual consent constitutes 'international morality'; beyond this
there is, effectively, nothing more.

This sort of argument is a reasonable and an empirically efficient one.
Though states are very different in kind and coherence, their elites do
strive, nominally at least, to protect their separate sovereignty and their
domestic political domains. Indeed, from the pluralistic perspective 'we
have no warrant for thinking that loyalty to mankind, or to any system
of morality based upon common humanity, will prevail against the
morality of the state,' since the former 'either invites or commands
people to treat as equals those who are worse off than themselves . . . It
is an invitation to be worse off oneself.'[7] Privilege is very rarely surrendered without reluctance, and the state is more immediate and more authoritative than any rival collectivity defined in terms of religion, professional
interest, class or race. Too many elites in positions of local power owe
too much to their state-centric perspective to relinquish it readily.

Moral Universalism

And yet, as well as the systemic commitments to non-intervention and
the observance of mutual agreements and the conventions of contemporary

diplomacy the majority of state leaders have publicly endorsed, in one form or another, the Western doctrine of human rights. Though every moral system strains towards universal acknowledgement, the specific notion that individuals are entitled by virtue of their very humanity (suitably defined) to certain sorts of treatment, and are generally enjoined to provide the same to those denied them, is the first to have found anything like it. This is only one index of common concern, however. The workers and peasants who stand behind the world urban centres show little propensity to unite. We should not underestimate, on the other hand, the degree of transnational co-operation that is necessary on the part of those who rule them to sustain the capitalist world economy and to exploit the labour and the resources of a global periphery, which contributes in no small measure to the living standards of all who dwell in richer countries, plus those of peripheral state elites themselves. And we should not underestimate the extent to which the sovereign state is in fact a fundamentally compromised institution; that in the majority of cases it does not secure the interests of those it purports to protect and sustain and in all honest expectation cannot; that it has in many places successfully pre-empted such interests altogether in favour of those of a ruling elite or class, rendering their long-term realisation highly unlikely indeed.

The contemporary invitation to be 'worse off oneself' only applies to those who are already favoured by material security. To those with less who argue for more, or for the opportunity to realise a fairer share of the world's productive wealth, such ethical imperatives are a promise, not a threat. Such claims are made by state leaders in statist terms, but the moral constituency on whose behalf they advance them is a *transnational* one, and the genesis of that constituency, as well as its contemporary predicament, must be seen in the 'structuralist' terms which complement the 'pluralist' and in this sense partial view.

However much the fact of state divergence may frustrate the realisation of global norms, these do now exist, and they are derived (a) in terms of the *individual*, that is, in the form of *human rights*, and (b) in terms of *collectivities*, in the form of claims for *social justice*.

The two conceptions support each other, and it has been argued that the former may be directly inferred from the latter.[8] Claims for social justice draw added weight from those that are made by individuals seeking the satisfaction of personal rights, and the obligation to meet individual entitlements can be reinforced in turn by the collective sense that the entitlements in question are just.

In practice the latter are not readily realised. A world society that consists of a conglomeration of states and transnational entities overlain by a patchy but none the less identifiable global bourgeoisie, with a very mixed company of subordinate classes splayed out underneath, is not one that is likely to see the commonplace enforcement of universalistic norms. Local governments will respond to their more immediate dilemmas first, and as maintenance men in a global hierarchy highly prejudicial to the life-chances of a good many human beings, they tend, whatever they may say, to be on the side of the global privileged and not those who assert the moral claims of the daily dispossessed.[9]

The standards exist, however, and they have been given near universal enunciation. They have educative value and wherever the gap grows between good words and evil deeds people tend to note the disparity and ask, in whatever ways they can, the reasons for it, which they may then assess as valid or not.[10] In the case of overtly oppressive regimes it becomes that much less easy to accuse those who talk in terms of justice and rights of mouthing foreign propaganda, especially if the codes they employ to make their claims defend the very same values advanced by those in authority to justify their rule. Present circumstances need not always prevail, indeed, the ultimate efficacy of rights talk and social justice may only be manifest in the longer term: 'One generation's hypocrisy may be the next generation's fighting creed. Perceptions of people about themselves, what they want and what they are entitled to, are slowly changing.' Most people find it simpler to remain pessimistic than to accept the mantle of optimism with its activist resolve, but: 'History suggests that such widespread ideas and hopes are not easily stifled.'[11]

Moral Universalism: Human Rights

I would like to look a little closer at the dual conception of global norms introduced above. A 'human right' is a general moral claim.[12] It is the assertion of a just entitlement pertaining anywhere, anytime, to anyone coherent enough to be able to make it, to the enjoyment of certain goods or the satisfaction of particular interests deemed fundamental in some way. The decline of human rights is seen, at least by those who advance it, as justifying what may be a revisionist stance in political terms, or as good reason for opposing those who would deny them. Depending on the circumstances, they are an important source of support for political protest, and though as moral claims they are not always enforced by the positive sanctions of legislation and law, they are not to be sensibly despised. To establish a moral right that obtains in general helps individuals define what is morally wrong in the particular. It demonstrates to others that what ought to be done is either being done, or that it is not, as the case may be.

Several aspects of this definition are vague and philosophically vexed. For example, it is not intuitively obvious what 'human' means, and when a person may be construed a non-person or vice versa.[13] The status of 'personhood' has been gradually extended to include women, children, prisoners, even extra-terrestrials and trees, but the process has been far from automatic and the problems of definition can be acute. It is also difficult to say what is 'fundamental' about such claims, particularly when they conflict. The doctrine draws upon much the same moral impulse that led to the historic assertion of 'natural' rights, and before that of 'natural law', which is the code of right conduct laid up somewhere beyond the realm of the rules made by human-kind, accessible none the less to reason. The notion of 'natural law' derives in turn from what seems to be an irresistible human urge to locate absolute and certain concepts which can then be used to measure the more expedient, corrupt and partial dictates of political regimes, and when these are found wanting, to pronounce them unjust in all conscience, thus sanctioning the withdrawal of obedience and the willingness to respond to command. Even where these concepts are not manifest, in principle they are felt to be there somewhere.

It is easy to deride such an impulse as a presumptuous attempt to legislate for future generations, or to absolutise the relative – the temporally and culturally conditioned judgements that people make about what should be done. Thus:

> If natural law theory . . . looks beyond the particular judgment to
> an independently existing moral order, it is either barren, declaiming
> the existence of the unknowable, and therefore useless . . . or it leads
> to a rigid dogmatism which, so far from settling arguments, can only
> embitter them.[14]

It has proved less easy to despatch it altogether for it is a direct expression of our moral sense and shows no sign of terminal decline.

The dilemma is partly so acute because the notion of the 'natural' and the 'conventional' have been forced so far apart, and the idea of a 'natural law' as one that evolves beside human experience, universal still but party to human practice, has been long submerged.[15] It has not been lost altogether, however, and this basically Aristotelian approach does have modern parallels. Sydney Hook, for example, has attempted a modest justification of human rights in relativist terms as *proposals* to recognise as binding, on all and sundry who are relevantly situated to defend and/or enforce them a set of rules which within the historical and cultural context in which they are enunciated are more reasonable . . . They are derived not from the reason of things, or the reason in God, Nature or Man. They are justified by the consequence of rules of action. Nor can it be said that these consequences are such that they strictly *entail* any proposals or choices, but only that they render some more reasonable or less arbitrary than others.[16]

With its muted talk of consequences this might satisfy the utilitarians among us, but we miss, I think, the sense of superordinate accountability that gives the whole notion of global norms the power it can possess. We miss, in other words, a feeling for law as not only a 'measure of action' but a 'pronouncement on its value'. Thus: 'Law is an indication of what is good and evil. In turn, good and evil are the conditions of legal obligation.'[17] The law exists 'not only to make men obedient, but to help them to be virtuous',[18] or so a deep stream in Western thought predisposes us to believe.

Standards of good and evil come from human beings, however they are thought to be received. To this extent they reflect the moral preferences of their percipients. Too far down this road, however, and we reach the conclusion that there are fundamental conflicts between ethical systems that allow of no rational resolution at all. It has been argued that a moral stance of this sort was the critical implication of Niccolo Machiavelli's work,[19] and many would feel it to be a fine thing to have found. From it they draw the idea of liberal compromise, since absolute standards invite political extremism. Recognising the fundamental diversity of moral judgements, they say, can only encourage the sort of humility that sustains moderation and good sense. Others, however, have refused to limit moral debate in this way. They retreat from the notion that law and morality are contingent upon elites, not to be construed in terms of the common good of the world as a whole. And they have attempted to rescue something at least of the idea of universal standards, and its flair for humane reform.[20]

H.L.A. Hart, for example, has argued that all persons as persons, if they are able to make choices, possess by virtue of that fact alone 'at least one natural right, the equal right of all men to be free'.[21] And elsewhere he has posited a set of 'simple truisms' that allow us rationally to relate the 'facts of life' to legal and moral codes; allowing us, that is, to arrive at a basic list of what such codes must contain if, as we can safely assume, the majority of people at least most of the time want to stay alive and through society seek the means of doing do — a set of rules that do in fact prevail wherever groups have reached the point of discriminating between morality and law, and without which, being what they are, would have 'no reason for obeying voluntarily any rules at all'. Much is predicated upon the fact that 'without a minimum of cooperation given voluntarily by those who find that it is in their interest to submit to maintain the rules, coercion of others who would not voluntarily conform would be impossible.'[22]

Given our bodily vulnerability then, and the fact that we are, very approximate though this may be, equal entities; given our limited capacity for altruism, our limited resources, limited understanding and strength of will, Hart concludes that any society, to secure simple survival at the very least, will require constraints on killing, a system of mutual forbearance and compromise, respect for the possession of property (and not necessarily individual possession of property), organised sanctions against the unruly, and ways of creating confidence and co-operation (by enjoining honesty or truthfulness for example) so that commerce may proceed and contracts be kept. For a minimal list this has some rather comprehensive implications. Proclaiming the utility of 'mutual forbearance and compromise', for example, denotes liberal sentiments that would require an extensive political and legal commitment to make them work. *Some* list like this one would seem necessary, though, if the idea of basic standards is to have more than rhetorical value, and to the extent that a world society exists, these strictures will apply to that collectivity too.

Hart's approach still fails to affirm in a positive fashion, as advocates of natural law prefer, an explicit endorsement of 'good' over 'evil', and the feeling that this difference is evident regardless of cultural contingency and the workings of prejudice and whim. Perhaps any more ambitious statement could only survive by being correspondingly vague, hence open to any interpretation and well nigh meaningless as a policy prescription or a readily defensible reason for resistance or reform. And yet, rendering it down, as Hart does, to satisfy a secular and pragmatic age, the doctrine looks much like a rather anaemic anachronism. Older versions — the Romans reading from their practical experience of empire, the medieval divines from the word of God — had a robust if finally evasive sense of conviction that modern restatements lack. Modesty emasculates, but virtue is perhaps better defended that way.

The 'fundamental' character of human rights might be established more readily by demonstrating the existence of some transcultural consensus on individual entitlements and on what 'rightly' obtains in the relationship between the person and the group estate. The lessons of anthropological research over the last century have not been encouraging in this regard, and yet, when a decade ago the Division of Philosophy at UNESCO solicited statements from all over the world which reflected a local sense of human rights, a number of common themes did emerge, and the issues seemed, rather than just juridical ones, to be very much alive at all levels of human experience. The selection was highly eclectic and not all the ideas cropped up everywhere, but many subjects did recur which dealt with social solidarity and the sense of self, for example, the value of life and the duty to protect the lost, sick or weak, the right to die rather than submit, the idea of the legitimacy of power, the duty to rebel when power's legitimacy is lost, the limitations to be placed upon its arbitrary exercise, the idea of juridical impartiality, the civil freedom to travel and to work elsewhere, the freedom to think and publicly criticise, the toleration of social rights (to strike, work and so on), the need to secure freedom by securing economic well-being, the right to knowledge and learning, the right of a people to their identity, the universality of the human enterprise, and that universality itself as justifying rights. The compiler came to conclude that 'most human beings and most cultures contain something of the Kantian idea, that the human being should never be used only as a means, but because he can change, he has the ability of becoming,' and that this idea obtains even where, by violence or neglect, it is denied.[24] Human rights are difficult to uphold since there are always powerful interests arraigned against them. They are not, she decided, 'in this sense, natural . . . they are very much against nature . . . ', which is probably the best reason why, if human rights are to prevail, they have to be thought of in absolute terms.[25]

However haphazard and arbitrary one finds this sort of empirical survey, and however predisposed the compiler might have been to find common ground rather than highlight the discrepancies, common ground does exist and globally shared norms—often quite specific ones— seem to be part of the human endeavour as a whole. In this respect the process of Westernisation may finally prove to be one that systematises and renders explicit much of what is already there, rather than one that imposes all the mores of an alien culture *en bloc*.

What do the various codifications of human rights contain? Since the notion emerged under the auspices of growing European commercial elites who viewed the 'state' as an important impediment to their power to expand, its early expression, most notably by John Locke, fastened on rights to freedom and property, as well as those to life itself. Locke strove to justify the new social order that was rising in his day against the traditional authority of the English kings, and he did so in terms of personal prerogatives that no temporal power could morally prorogue. The more general sense of the individual as part of an ongoing, organic social whole with an appointed place therein and specific functions to perform was giving way to the atomistic endorsement of personal endeavour, individual conscience, individual property and personal faith. 'Capitalism' and 'Protestantism' were both the source and the expression of a sea-change in the individual's established relations with society and with social authority; and they had politically revolutionary implications.

The 'natural rights' proclaimed in the English Bill of Rights of 1689, the Constitution of Virginia of 1776, the American Declaration of Independence and the French Declaration of the Rights of Man and of the Citizen were the self-conscious expression of general claims of this sort and they were assumed to have universal validity. As statements of intent they were particular to each political purpose. Their collective example was compelling, however. The self-evident success of capitalist industrialisation and the spread of the European empires endorsed, even while in practice it denied, the ideology of natural rights that coincided with it, and the civil and political definition of what the individual could rightly claim against the state was taken up by subject peoples to become commonplace. It also led to such international measures as the abolition of slavery, rights for prisoners of war and for care of the wounded, and rights for cultural minorities.[26]

As the state assumed more of the responsibility for promoting private welfare by public means, the line that seventeenth- and eighteenth-century transatlantic radicals drew between the state and the citizen was progressively erased. Socialist states, in theory at least, abolished it altogether. The increase in the world's disposable wealth led to a growing awareness that human intervention could alleviate the plight of many of those who might otherwise expect to continue poor, malnourished, or politically abused indefinitely. The earlier doctrine had fastened on human freedom from state interference.[27] It became more and more concerned, in time, with cataloguing, sometimes to such lengths as to parody the original principle, a wide range of socio-economic rights as well.

The United Nations, the most comprehensive international body to meet to date, referred in its original charter to 'fundamental human rights', and in December 1948 the General Assembly endorsed an itemised account of them—'a common standard of achievement for all peoples and all nations'. They generally enjoined a 'spirit of brother-

hood' and combined civil and political claims for free speech and equality before the law with such social, economic and cultural ideals as the
right to marry, to work, to be educated, and to receive social security
and an adequate standard of living. This was the first Universal Declaration of Human Rights. It was not a treaty and therefore had no legal
force, but it did, however conditioned by clauses allowing state regimes
the ultimate say, establish a single set of global aspirations. These were
made even more explicit under the International Covenants on Human
Rights, one for Civil and Political Rights and another for Economic,
Social and Cultural ones. The Covenants were unanimously endorsed
by the Assembly in 1966, and they stand as a most singular achievement in the socio-legal history of mankind.

The extension of the doctrine to incorporate more than civil and
political principles has caused considerable anxiety. Maurice Cranston,
for example, has argued that social, cultural and economic rights are
not rights at all because for the majority of earth's people claims of this
kind are 'vain and idle' and cannot possibly be met by even the most
enlightened of poor state regimes.[28] In ranking values they are secondary ones anyway. Their affirmation only obscures what are the basic
issues at stake, clouding honest intent with pious Utopianism.

This position is not well held, however. On the first ground, that of
practicability, it would seem eminently reasonable to recommend that
governments do whatever they can with their resource capabilities, however modest these might be. And in terms of *paramount importance*,
while I would not resist the attempt to rank rights in some order of
significance, I cannot see that all those of a civil or political nature
should be placed automatically above the rest. Indeed, the realisation
of the one may depend directly upon the other; civil and political rights
may be quite irrelevant where they are not accompanied by conditions
of social and economic well-being. This connection was duly noted by
the UN Conference on Human Rights held in Tehran in 1968, where
the realisation of civil and political rights was seen to be contingent
upon the enjoyment of economic, social and cultural ones, and 'lasting
progress' in implementing human rights in general was declared a function
of economic and social development.

The real problem here is the opportunity it presents for autocratic
regimes to *reverse* the traditional liberal preference which puts civil and
political rights first; to place a commitment to the socio-economic construction of society before that of the protection of personal liberties.
In the name of social welfare a repressive government can abrogate what
those who live in Western democracies would consider basic freedoms

indeed; freedoms that the abrogating elite charge are paper undertakings wherever necessary socio-economic needs are not being met.[29] Securing such social goods as full employment and physical well-being is a long-term process, however, which usually means that the realisation of civil and political liberties can be indefinitely deferred. And when the political process is not open to popular censure, social, economic and cultural rights can be readily neglected without serious challenge too.

This debate turns upon an *individualistic* versus a *collectivist* conception of human rights, and constitutes the key difference between the ideology of the industrialised liberal democracies and that of a *mélange* of more or less paternalistic and authoritarian regimes.[30] The doctrine was originally derived to defend the individual against the state, a defence that has in fact been profoundly compromised by the inclusion of rights that require a collective administration. The doctrine itself is ambiguous, because in practice rights are held only in relation to a society. Thus the

> self-realisation which is the truest freedom can come only through living in a society where duties and rights are correlative aspects of an integral situation in which neither individual nor community can be understood in abstraction from one another . . . the concept of a right against society, of a right which is not intrinsically connected with the social structure which creates and protects it, is self-contradictory.[31]

It is possible of course to belong to various communities and these may espouse differing norms and ideals. We generally concede someone's rights if we share his or her communal values, the ones that he or she implicitly or explicitly endorses in making a claim. This is particularly significant when we come to consider rights as they apply to social structures in other parts of the world, structures that are centred, formally or informally, on the concept of reciprocal obligations.[32] Here the rights will be understood primarily in terms of their contribution to the good of the collective. Where individual obligations are enforced by the state, the totalitarian abuse of human ideals is not far behind; sanctioned by the customs of the community, however, and an enhanced sense of collective responsibility not only becomes part of the process of enforcement, but renders rights a shared experience and hence more humane.

This sense of collective identity can be generalised still further, since if what is claimed is a *human* right, then to be recognised we need to admit the concept of a general human community that stands above all the particular communities to which we belong; we need to admit the claimant as a member of the human community as a whole; and we need to endorse such values and ideals as that community may profess.

> The question, then, of whether human rights exist, or, better, whether any individual has a right as a human right, now shifts to (i) the defensibility of the notion of the human community and to (ii) the defensibility of any fairly concrete conception of the good life for mankind.[33]

Allowing this defence, to admit of rights as a community enterprise still does not sanction any one sort against others. If they are all potentially secured in a social context, then we have no help on this account deciding whether the social defence of the individual as a political animal should prevail over the social defence of him or her as an economic, cultural or social one.

This point continues to escape those who articulate competing global ideologies. The American perspective, for example, has been informed from the beginning by Lockean concepts of civil and political freedom. Its more contemporary restatement by President Carter and those of his administration continues to sanction this traditional emphasis. On 7 March 1977, Deputy Secretary Warren Christopher spoke of American recognition for a wide range of human rights. He noted primary concern for 'violations of the integrity of the person' and the protection of political and civil rights. The latter were accorded 'high priority', though it was seen as 'inevitable' that such concerns might conflict with a declared commitment to the goal of economic development at large. One month later in an address on 'Human Rights and Foreign Policy',[34] Secretary of State Cyrus Vance endorsed 'liberty' as the 'one great revolutionary cause', and in defining human rights cited three key categories. They were (1) the right to be free from government violation of the integrity of the person (torture; cruel, inhuman or degrading treatment or punishment; arbitrary arrest or imprisonment; denial of fair public trial; and invasion of the home); (2) the right (dependent upon the level of a state's economic development and the quality of commitment on the part of its elite) to food, shelter, health care and education; and (3) the right to civil and political freedom (of thought, press, movement within and without the state, and of participation in government). In May 1977 President Carter himself, elaborating human rights as the first of the 'five cardinal principles' on which he saw his foreign policy as based, cast the discussion entirely in terms of human freedom and the 'protection of the individual from the arbitrary power of the state'.[35]

From these brief but representative examples it is clear that the American understanding of the issue of rights, though cognisant of the need to promote social and economic well-being, is still primarily concerned with the liberal values that have historically informed its foreign political platform. And this experience is seen to be of pervasive global significance. 'Our policy', Carter asserted 'must shape an international system that will last longer than secret deals.'[36]

The Soviet Union reverses these priorities. In general terms the Marxist perspective rejects the notion of abstract individuals arriving at an understanding of their rights by ratiocination. The focus falls not so much on the citizen in his or her relationship to the state but on the place of the individual in society in an industrial age, and in particular, on his or her social context as this relates to the means of production. Human rights are understood, much as a pluralist sees them, by reference to group interests, but here such rights are the components of a class consciousness that is defined in turn by the evolution of the social substructure — the mode of material production. In capitalist states rights are distorted by the dominating influence of the bourgeoisie and the culture that it disseminates to delude and oppress the proletariat.[37] In socialist states, where working-class interests are declared paramount, economic, social and cultural rights are construed, in theory at least, as the basic principles that inform social policy, and political and civil rights are subordinate to them. Thus the Declaration of Rights of the Toiling and Exploited Peoples, adopted by the All-Russian Congress of Soviets in January 1918, makes its major commitment the suppression of all exploitation of man by man, the abolition forever of the division of society into classes, the abolition of the private possession of land and the means of production, and the placing of these in the hands of the workers. In 1949, Boris Tchechko described Article 118 of the 1936 Constitution which enunciated the right to work and the abolition of economic crises and unemployment under a socialist economy as 'the king-pin of the whole Soviet system', and the only way to ensure 'the true liberty of the individual'.[38] *Political* liberty was an anachronism, he said, since Soviet citizens were members of a classless society, and therefore 'without conflicting interests'. Since it referred to liberation from the capitalist state it could mean nothing under socialism, where the individual had 'no desire' to exercise such a right. In the Soviet Constitution of 1977, under the section entitled 'The State and the Individual', we find specific details about the basic rights, freedoms and duties of the Soviet citizen. One can fairly assume that the order in which these have been placed denotes some sense at least of the comparative importance attached to the various values themselves. They begin with the right to work, to rest and leisure, to health protection, social security, housing, education, the enjoyment of the achievements of culture, and the freedom to pursue scientific, technical and artistic creative endeavour. Having made these socialistic commitments, only then do we find a number of civil and political rights, suitably hedged about by the obligation to safeguard the interests of the society and state: the right to participate in the administration of state and public affairs, for example, to tender criticism without persecution, to free speech, press and assembly, to meet, demonstrate, worship and to hold inviolate the human person.

Given idealised versions of the Soviet and American stance, there is a good case each way. A conspicuous preference for civil and political rights may well obscure a bourgeois neglect of human charity, and a rather wilful evasion of the shocking reality of the contemporary living conditions of the global poor. It may, on the other hand, represent a quite rational respect for the long-term principles that experience has shown makes human welfare possible. Social security is in daily jeopardy if it is provided only at the behest of those who can waive the favour at will. The alternative attempt to realise economic, social and cultural needs first is all too often employed as a ruthless rationale for elite repression. Again, however, as indicated above, such a commitment may serve to rescue from conditions of appalling disadvantage many who would otherwise languish forever. Nothing succeeds like success, and the onus lies, I think, on either set of exponents to realise the globally accepted norms to which they lay a favoured claim, while minimising the human costs that accrue from the selective or generalised denial of the rest.

Such a burden is lightly borne where the global community is diffuse and where those who choose in practice to set it aside can do so with indifference. Which brings me back to the question of enforcement. There is a conspicuous lack of the concomitant means to impose rights where their verbal promotion is ineffective, or they are actively repressed. What means there are vary in their effectiveness depending on the issue to hand and its relative specificity, on the publicity it receives, on the level of the global consensus about it, and on the amenability of the regime to whom the suggestion is made to mend its ways. Publicity is a weapon of sorts and a number of non-governmental groups, from the venerable Anti-Slavery Society to Amnesty International, have used the device of

selective and open testimony to win change, or at least to force from
their target body a counter-justification. The sovereign realm is not an
uncontested one; even more so when we come to consider the extent
to which it is penetrated by other social structures. And mobilising
some sense of public opinion may make it possible in certain cases to
exploit global interdependencies to humane ends.

Enforcement raises the general issue of majority rule, for if we accept
majority rule as desirable in a local context, as Western democracies purport to do and as reformers would recommend for countries like South
Africa, for example, then it should apply to the human community as a
whole, to whom we attribute rights in the first place. It does not apply,
in fact, because the 'state' intervenes and rights are regulated by separate
elites. The majority principle prevails in the UN General Assembly, and
Assembly resolutions receive some public attention and possess some
global standing, but that is all. Nevertheless, enforcement of human
rights as they attach to individuals will only be legitimate in the end as
the expression of the human constituency as a whole, and that constituency must appeal to the majoritorian principle to decide contentious
issues if it is to employ the fairest means possible for doing so.[39]

Empathy seems to be a spasmodic emotion, and most people most
of the time are too preoccupied by more immediate interests to press
their governments to meet those of groups and individuals elsewhere.
The record is a depressing one when we look for sustained attempts on
an official basis to hold to account those who have violated human
rights; to make of these norms other than the most ephemeral foreign
policy issues. The Covenants deploy consultative sanctions only, and
the Optional Protocol of the civil and political one, which does actually
allow of the right of individual petition against state regimes, has not
been notably effective. Which hardly constitutes judicial control, with
the power to interpret, arbitrate and punish that one assumes a real
measure of implementation would require. The Final Act of the Declaration of Principles of the Conference on Security and Cooperation in
Europe that was proclaimed in Helsinki in 1975 saw the Soviet Union
and the United States, along with 33 other countries, endorse diverse
rights and freedoms for the individual. The results of this commitment
have been subject to review (a harassed process in the Soviet Union),
but the principles in it are sustained by nothing more stringent than
this, and in most cases they have not received further consideration at
all. Rights are political passengers and their recognition does not readily
lead to their implementation, even where the substantive issues to hand
meet with widespread approval.

Moral Universalism: Social Justice

The problem may be 'less that international declarations and conventions accomplish too little than that we expect too much',[40] expectations that will continue to be disappointed in a pluralistic world. The plea for social and economic rights over and above civil and political ones is in effect a plea for often quite revolutionary forms of *social justice*, and it is no accident that those frustrated in their revisionist resolve look beyond the package of human rights to analyse what is wrong with the world in structuralist terms. The recommendations that flow from such studies generally endorse some concept of global equity in the face of the highly unequal socio-economic conditions that actually prevail today. It is only by expanding the diagnosis of the problem, however, that one gains any realistic idea of its scope, and in this sense the structuralist perspective is indispensable.

The pluralist paradigm presents the world as an arena of state and corporate competition and conflict. There is no superior entity to which we can attach definitions of global good other than those that states and corporations create for their strategic and economic convenience. The means of applying effective power are seen to be dispersed, and holding state leaders to a particular moral argument or securing their compliance with any particular moral resolution is a tenuous and precarious enterprise at best.

The structuralist paradigm attempts to account for the social and political continuities that are contingent upon common modes of production and the contemporary persistence of economic imperialism. In establishing and sustaining global industrial enterprise core state political elites have progressively 'marginalised' the political influence and economic autonomy of the diverse peoples who live on the world's periphery in ways that seem 'unjust'.

Social *justice* pertains to society (in this case world society, both class-bound and statist) and its treatment of individuals and of subsidiary groups. Its underlying moral impetus flows from the choice to share the burden of socio-economic disadvantage, if burden there must be, rather than placing it all on others to alleviate the individual lot.[41] It is the name we give to 'certain classes of moral rules, which concern the essentials of human well-being more nearly, and are therefore of more absolute obligation, than any other rules for the guidance of life'.[42] All people should, such rules enjoin, be treated equally and under like circumstances alike, unless there is some good reason that makes for a better social balance by acting otherwise, by making allowance, that is, for non-arbitrary differences in terms of need, merit, desert, capacity, or prior contract. This is more than a procedural injunction since social justice always implies some notion of the good society and of right action, though it is not always identical with right and good as such. The perspective one adopts, at least notionally, is an extra-societal one. There is always the sense that anybody who stands outside the situation will tend to agree on the particular resemblances and differences deemed relevant to a just administration.

The concept of social justice constitutes, in fact, 'one segment of morality primarily concerned not with individual conduct but with ways in which *classes* of individuals are treated'.[43] Where the 'justice-constituency'[44] is viewed in terms of a world society of states and corporations, then social justice, as the authoritative admonition to distribute to the needy and compensate the dispossessed, prescribes a transfer of resources and productive capacities from rich countries to poor ones, thence presumably to those worse off within the latter, to ensure at least some minimum of subsistence for all. Should the justice-constituency be construed in terms of socio-cultural *classes*, however — an urbanised global elite sharing economic advantages that are denied to those living on peripheral city fringes and in the countryside — then we can place local regimes in their structuralist context, and we can appreciate that a redistribution or a restitution which sees the process in state terms *alone* will tend rather to reinforce a pattern that systematically impoverishes those it ostensibly seeks to sustain.

The prescription becomes more powerful the more ably we can demonstrate the historic passage of wealth from colonial possessions to developing imperial nations, and the continued relevance of this process in contemporary terms. The demonstration is a complex one, since it requires us to spell out the empirical mechanics of that transfer, and though there have been notable attempts, by 'dependencia' theorists for example,[45] to do so, it is not always clear what we should be measuring and how the qualitative judgements involved can be expressed in quantitative terms. We can look forever for capital flows, at terms of trade and tariff barriers, but somewhere we have to assess the 'unfairness' of the exchange,[46] a question that hangs in turn upon claims for a 'just' world economy.

Approached in formal terms, we do have one notable attempt to enunciate the notion of justice as fairness.[47] What differences in life-style and life-chances would global groups accept in relative ignorance, that is, *before* they knew who was to gain and who to lose under the circumstances that prevail in the real world? Though the original statement of this question has been a much debated one,[48] and indeed, has been curtly dismissed by one critic as 'a philosophical *apologia* for an egalitarian brand of liberal welfare-state capitalism',[49] the device suggested for approximating a just principle of distribution is sufficiently general, it would seem to me, to dispel the worst of the world's inequalities were we in any position to implement the conclusions even its partial application might provide.

Several attempts have been made to extend the notion of a just contract and the 'difference principle' John Rawls suggests to world affairs,[50] a theoretical endeavour mirrored by many of the sentiments expressed in the UN General Assembly's Declaration of the Establishment of a New International Economic Order in May 1974. 'Justice' is implicated, for example, 'wherever there is systematic economic intervention; for wherever there is regularized commerce there is an institution' in the sense of a 'public system of rules defining rights and duties'.[51] Since economic sovereignty has been compromised by the growth of global interdependence and trans-state dependencies, moral considerations cannot now be confined to those who make up each state apart.

If we imagine a meeting between the representatives of the world's *states* where they are ignorant of the conditions under which their own people live and the 'contingencies and biases of historical fate',[52] and where they are required to decide the basic rules under which conflict among them is to be contained, we can expect them to arrive, Rawls maintains, at such familiar tenets of international law as the right to national self-determination, the need for non-intervention, for the observance of treaties, for self-defence where it is justified and so on. We might also expect them to arrive at much more than this, at some shared commitment to world federation or world government for example, or some means of managing the stockpile of modern weapons and ensuring access to the natural resources so arbitrarily dispersed across the globe, or a socio-economic guarantee of well-being for those who turn out to be at a disadvantage when the 'veil of ignorance' is finally dispelled. As representatives of states, such a guarantee does not account, however, for the quality of justice that prevails within each one, and in the real world this would continue to exacerbate the plight of the poor and feed the interests of enclave elites.

If we imagine a counter-meeting between representatives of the world's main *classes*, again ignorant of where in the process of global discrimination they might emerge — as over-dogs or under-dogs or dogs in between — how would they be likely to structure affairs so as to secure the best possible package of group interests? They would probably elect to abolish classes altogether, and elites of all kinds. Short of this they would certainly elect to control any way in which the classes that benefit most directly from industrial society might skew other-world developments to their own advantage. Though patently Utopian, we see in this something of the promise of a sense of justice as much concerned with the process of *production* as it is with that of *distribution.* Inevitably, the victimised value would be 'liberty'. The sort of economic growth that would be necessary, and the sharing of the burdens involved, would not come about where production was allowed to proceed by *laissez-faire* means alone.

Any meeting like this would be mixed in fact, since those representing the state would be the same persons as those representing the global bourgeoisie, and if the procedural conditions of ignorance Rawls posits were strictly observed, the second, the structuralist solution, would be the most likely outcome anyway. In practice, however, the welfare needs of the *nationally* disadvantaged take precedence over those of the global poor construed in *class* terms, which is a predictable consequence of the realities of political pluralism. The concept of social justice employed above is particular to what have been called 'market' societies (in contrast to 'primitive' or 'hierarchical' ones).[53] Market societies, or at least those who control them, evaluate the social distribution of benefits in terms of ideal standards of desert and need.[54] The advent of a world market system and a world society has lent the conception global relevance. It is possible, however, to conceive of circumstances where it has none at all. I refer to the Marxist perspective, and though no one had a more acute awareness of the maldistribution of wealth and productive capacity than Marx did, it is an interesting fact that he never found this situation specifically 'unjust'.[55]

This is not to say that Marx felt nothing of moral outrage; he clearly did, and his sense of how contemporary socio-economic structures alienated and dehumanised the working man was acute. But his analysis and his critique of capitalism and its consequences were not made in terms of abstract principles of justice. Capital, he said, uses the labour of those who have only their capacity to work to sell. The difference between the contract price and the value of what is produced accrues to the capitalist as 'surplus value', to be re-invested or conspicuously consumed. Generating such a profit, and maximising it by buying labour as economically as possible, is the very nature of the beast. The notion of justice or injustice is quite irrelevant in such a context since in terms of the capitalist mode of production all this is perfectly 'fair' and anyway, a general notion of justice could only be derived from an abstract political or juridical concept of society and such a concept Marx explicitly rejected.[56]

Justice in this view, then, can never be construed as an independent value since our idea of right is contingent upon the prevailing substructure of material life. The notion of a more 'just' *distribution* is a mere palliative because

the central concern of Marxian theory, morally as well as intellectually, is with the mode of production, with man's activities as a producer, and with the conditions under which he carries on these activities. The theme of man as a creative being who expresses his nature in productive activities, foremost among which is economic activity or the production of material objects, is fundamental. Industry, for example, represents a huge complex of already materialized productive powers of the species, the human collective's tools of production. World history is . . . basically a history of production . . . [whereby] the species develops and realizes itself.[57]

To tinker only with the *distributive* terms of such a system would be worse than useless, indeed, it would be 'unjust'. The fundamental harm comes from the capitalist mode of production as a whole; the mode of distribution derives from the ethos itself, and constitutes only one of its operative components. To demand an end to capitalist exploitation because it is unjust is to urge an argument that conveys 'no rational conviction [−] to urge action with no practical basis toward a goal with no historical content'.[58]

This is a global question now, because, as Marx argued, the peculiar genius of Western civilisation lies in the way in which it has universalised itself:

the bourgeoisie has through its exploitation of the world market given a cosmopolitan character to production and consumption in every country . . . It compels all nations, on pain of extinction, to adopt the bourgeois mode of production . . . to become bourgeois themselves. In one word, it creates a world after its own image . . . Just as it has made the country dependent on the towns, so it has made barbarian and semi-barbarian countries dependent on the civilised ones, nations of peasants on nations of bourgeois.[59]

In Marxist terms, justice cannot be applied globally since capitalism has woven itself into the fabric of world society and the economic transfer it effects is intrinsic to the system itself. The sort of servitude that results can only be condemned on other grounds, since in terms of the logic of the exchange, labour is a commodity and is paid what it is locally worth and often more. Though the rate will vary widely from place to place it must be sufficient to provide what is necessary to survive within the local environment, which again will differ considerably. Any economic surplus will be the capitalist's own reward and his or her incentive to expand production further. Thus 'exploitation' is a feature of the exchange process as such, and it operates regardless of the real wages that are paid to the workers producing the goods.

All of which has not prevented diverse poor state regimes calling for what they call social justice and a greater degree of socio-economic advantage in the world, a claim that combines moral fervour with the more familiar desire to gain recognition as equal and independent entities under conditions that do not favour them. Given the shortage of resources and rewards, it is no surprise that many of the concessions that rich states do make are not passed on to the peripheral poor. And we begin to appreciate the force of the Marxist point against redistribution as such; that a different disposition of affairs, and a different sort of justice, will only proceed from the radical transformation of the whole global system of production itself. For Marx, such a change was implicit in this system. Transformation he considered the inevitable outcome of the contradictions embedded in capitalism. As someone who does not share his cumulative concept of history, I do not accept his deterministic conclusions. Subsequent experience has made us much less sanguine on this point, but only time will ultimately tell.

From the *pluralist* perspective the advent of a global concern for 'human rights' and 'social justice' is one ideological expression of the pursuit of power and influence in a world of states and nation-states, many of whom are struggling to define their collective identity in an environment antipathetic to them. It amounts to the reaffirmation, in another form, of the state system. It is through this system that those in command see the inequalities of their historical inheritance being redressed. The moral challenge on the part of poor state leaders is very much a 'traditional' one, made by juridically sovereign and largely independent entities in a competitive arena that helps those who help themselves.[60]

Certain new features are acknowledged. Although sovereignty is still seen to be a central concept in world affairs, the case for sovereign equality has been extended, in line with a general evolution in human expectations, to include socio-economic forms as well as legal and political ones: 'Equality is still synonymous with independence, but independence is itself given a new dimension in that it is seen to encompass and, indeed, to require the equal opportunity of states—above all the disadvantaged states—to develop their potential.'[61] Such potential can only be realised where preferential economic treatment favouring peripheral regimes has finally been provided. The consequences are pluralistic ones, since

> the emergence of the new egalitarianism not only reflects the state's universalization consequent upon the decline of empire. It also reflects the triumph of the state in depth; that is, the triumph of the state's persistent claims to men's loyalties. The equal opportunity that is demanded for states reflects the faith with which so many peoples have accepted the state, or the nation-state, as the principle institution for achieving a collective destiny so long denied them.[62]

From the *structuralist* perspective, however, this seriously misrepresents the complex character of global interrelations. State formation is not an autonomous process; it is a highly conditioned one. And in paying analytic deference to the fact of state difference we should not lose sight of the common concerns and shared interests of the diverse elites involved. Those in core states who proclaim human rights and social justice endorse the creed of individual deliverance (supplemented in the case of socialist countries by the notion that the welfare of each is secured by guaranteeing the good of all). This is an intrinsic part of the Western liberal tradition and a useful advertisement for its moral good. At the same time, however, they perpetuate a global system of production and of trade that defends their established interests, to the disadvantage, or so it is claimed, of a large proportion of Earth's people, in ways that deny the latter's rights and needs. And this not simply through the representatives of single states in competition with each other, but in an established and patterned fashion that retards the development of the disadvantaged and reinforces dependence.

In this view, those in positions of command in the periphery are quite critically placed. As the conduits of modern industrial culture and the products in many cases of the education systems of core states, the indigenous elites are quite familiar with the operative concepts, and they readily endorse them. Yet their own interests depend upon their subordinate peoples—the ones to whom such rights and distributions ostensibly accrue—generating the material and human resources that the world market requires, that they need to sell to sustain their cosmopolitan standards of living. They argue for reparations and equality of opportunity much as the pluralists depict them doing. This is done in more or less anguished class collusion, however, with those who own and control the global mode of production, and they act as a result in ways that effectively deny individual freedom and the egalitarian distribution of what wealth the people do manage to produce.

Effecting social justice in these terms entails transcending the global system as a whole. Not only is this not likely to come about short of ecological collapse, since too many people in positions of power have too many advantages to lose to let it happen, but we might ask whether social justice is our prime moral value anyway? If it requires so much, do we want it? The attempt to define the absolute needs necessary for human beings to survive does not always generate self-evident standards that universally obtain. And the radical advocacy of a new system asks us to sacrifice, to ambiguous advantage at best, whatever advances in freedom and welfare have been achieved. Hedley Bull has argued that, in general, 'justice in any of its forms is realizable only in a context of order,'[63] and many would agree that we should prefer 'order' as an elemental human concern where we have to choose between this and what is a contingent endeavour, the realisation of a just disposition of affairs. Which obscures, as I have mentioned already in a footnote, the extent to which the two concepts overlap, and the fact that short of the end of the world any 'order' at all will protect and advance the interests and values of some sections of the human enterprise over others. We should confront the moral consequences of that advance in terms of the right and the good, and the debate these moral concepts entail.

The argument is easier these days because of the prevalence of Western values, which provide a common frame of reference. The features of a 'modern' society are becoming only too familiar the world around. Where we do encounter this process it may seem to us only a thin overlay, and anyway, the majority of human beings are still rural residents immersed in their traditional environments. Nor can we claim convergence for the grand divide between rich and poor. And yet the European experience has proved a pervasive one and upon it has been built, by whatever means, a self-consciously modern global civilisation that has no historical parallel. This civilisation has made of the ethic of material advancement a normative machine of awesome influence and power. The rich promise of the industrial mode of production has carried with it a number of distinctive corollaries—patterns of bureaucracy, of constitutional government, styles of life, and ethical commitments too. By adapting in a selective fashion, non-European cultures have maintained a good deal of their intrinsic resolve. But the process of erosion is accelerating, not slowing down.

Most people have little objective knowledge of these forces in fact, forces that determine and shape their social world and much of their own social behaviour. There would be no collective existence, however, if people did not relate to their own interests and to the institutions and social organisations that they regard as realising their communal purposes. This relationship is established by means of myth, dogma and ritual belief as much as by intellectual inquiry, and here the symbolic representation of society generates a sense of the ineffable that sustains ordered life and serves to obviate the need for force.[64] Rights-talk and notions of social justice partake of this fundamental quality, and help lift social systems beyond the realm of the secular and the profane.

The core concept, and it has proved a thoroughly insidious one, is probably that of progress, of willed change in the direction of enhanced material welfare; change that is rapid, that can transform the physical life chances of whole sections of humanity in a single generation, and change in which all, potentially at least, can share. If the most recent Chinese revolution is any indication, the attitude may be transmitted where an industrialised economy is a supplemental factor rather than a central one. 'Every culture', Lewis Mumford once wrote, 'lives within its dream.'[65] If world culture can be said to have a dream surely it is this one. Or is it, as any Cassandra worth an ounce of credence might claim, the stuff of nightmare instead?[66]

Notes

1. H. Morgenthau, *Politics Among Nations* (Alfred A. Knopf, New York, 1966), 3rd edn, p. 259. This predicament inspired Morgenthau to a flight of quite graphic hyperbole:

> Thus, carrying their idols before them, the nationalistic masses of our time meet in the international arena, each group convinced that it executes the mandate of history, that it does for humanity what it seems to do for itself, and that it fulfills a sacred mission ordained by Providence, however defined. Little do they know that they meet under an empty sky from which the gods have departed.

2. G. Modelski, 'The World's Foreign Ministers: a Political Elite', *Journal of Conflict Resolution*, vol. 14, no. 1 (June 1970), p. 146. Modelski sent questionnaires to the 175 ministers who held office for the year 1965. Only 16.7 per cent responded — hardly a good sample, and his conclusions must be taken in this light.

3. Ibid., p. 148.

4. A point argued very strongly by H. Lauterpacht, *International Law and Human Rights* (Stevens and Sons, London, 1950).

5. Ibid., p. 262.

6. J.D.B. Miller, 'Morality, Interests and Rationalisation' in R. Pettman (ed.), *Moral Claims in World Affairs* (Croom Helm, London, 1979).

7. Ibid.

8. S. Benn, 'Rights' in P. Edwards (ed.), *The Encyclopaedia of Philosophy* (The Macmillan Co. and the Free Press, New York, 1967), vol. 7, p. 199.

9. Within all societies, but especially the more developed industrial societies, failure to implement valid rights is increasingly due, not to what men do, but to what they neglect . . . Liberal unwillingness is all too often what Marx claimed it was; a subtly self-serving mask of rectitude which in practice supports a bourgeois culture and an underlying structure of social power that are unresponsive to basic human needs (A. Kaufman, 'A Sketch of a Liberal Theory of Fundamental Human Rights', *The Monist*, vol. 52, no. 4 (October 1968), pp. 595-6).

10. There is an interesting statement of this theme in American President Carter's Notre Dame address of May 1977:

> I understand fully the limits of moral suasion. We have no illusion that changes will come easily or soon. But I also believe that it is a mistake to undervalue the power of words and of the ideas that words embody . . . In the life of the human spirit, words are action. The leaders of totalitarian nations understand this very well. The proof is that words are precisely the action for which dissidents in those countries are being persecuted (Department of State *Bulletin*, vol. 76, no. 1981 (13 June 1977), p. 623).

11. R. Bilder, 'Rethinking International Human Rights: Some Basic Questions', *Wisconsin Law Review*, no. 1 (1969), p. 217.

12. For the concept of general as opposed to that of special rights which arise from voluntary relationships or transactions, see H.L.A. Hart, 'Are there any Natural Rights?' *Philosophical Review*, vol. 64, no. 2 (April 1955), pp. 183-8.

13. C. Hill (ed.), *Rights and Wrongs* (Penguin, Harmondsworth, 1969), 'Some Philosophical Problems about Rights', pp. 8-11. Also S. Benn, 'Human Rights – For Whom and For What?', *World Congress on Philosophy of Law and Social Philosophy*, August 1977, Paper no. 53, pp. 11-13:

> It is a mistake, in my view, to make the distinction hinge on the difference between *human* beings and others: it is not their humanity, a simple biological characteristic having no necessary moral implications, but their personality that makes the crucial difference between right-bearers and other objects. The *natural personality* of nearly all human beings consists in their having a certain kind of self-awareness, a conception of themselves as initiators of actions that make a difference to the course of events.

Scarcely more than 100 years ago a court in Virginia, USA, could rule that 'so far as civil rights and relations were concerned, the slave was not a person but a thing.' C.F.R. Pucetti, *Persons: a Study of Moral Agents in the Universe* (Macmillan, London, 1968); C. Stone, *Should Trees have Standing? Toward Legal Rights for Natural Objects* (W. Kaufmann, Los Altos, 1974).

14. S. Benn and R. Peters, *Social Principles and the Democratic State* (George Allen and Unwin, London, 1959), p. 69.

15. E. Barker, 'Translator's Introduction' in O. Gierke, *Natural Law and the*

Theory of Society (Cambridge University Press, Cambridge, 1934), vol. 1, p. XXXV.

16. 'Reflections on Human Rights' in H. Kiefer and M. Munitz (eds.), *Ethics and Social Justice* (State University of New York Press, Albany, 1968).

17. A.P. d'Entréves, *Natural Law* (Hutchinson University Library, London, 1951), p. 80.

18. Ibid., p. 83.

19. J. Berlin, 'The Originality of Machiavelli', a paper delivered to the Political Studies Conference, Oxford, 27 March 1963, p. 1.

20. There will never be final agreement on such standards, but the attempt to define them will never cease either. This fact should not appall us. R.H. Tawney once pointed out that we can never be completely honest. We do not as a result, however, at least most of us do not, go out and rob little old ladies. The fact that we can never be completely clean does not prompt us to roll in manure.

Moral differences reflect in some part at least disagreements as to facts. To this extent, however conditioned they may be by time, place and cultural predilections, they are amenable to rational criticism and debate. It is through their factual components and premises that ethical concepts can be compared, and to understand a moral injunction is to understand how it might also be applied. Resolving matters of fact does not necessarily resolve matters of moral meaning of course. Ethics apply to social relations and social relations are not material things. We observe them as cultural events indirectly; we interpret other people's behaviour only in terms of the frameworks we invent that give them meaning for us. But we can observe their consequences, and we can try and establish what is necessary rather than contingent, which is important because what seems necessary is more difficult to criticise and lies closer to what our conception of the human condition might be. See also L. Strauss, *Natural Rights and History* (University of Chicago Press, Illinois, 1953), pp. 2-6.

21. Hart, 'Are there any Natural Rights?', p. 175.

22. H.L.A. Hart, *The Concept of Law* (Oxford University Press, Oxford, 1961), p. 189.

23. J. Hersch, 'Is the Declaration of Human Rights a Western Concept?' in Kiefer and Munitz, *Ethics and Social Justice*, p. 326.

24. Ibid., p. 330.

25. Ibid., p. 332.

26. Conor Cruise O'Brien has a droll comment to make on this last one, in its modern context. 'As a matter of experience I have found', he says,

> that people who are all in favour of human rights generally speaking are very likely to sit up and look suspicious where there is any question of *minority* rights. Human rights is a pleasing abstraction impregnated with our notion of our own benevolence. But *minority rights* evoke a sudden sharp picture of 'that lot' with their regrettable habits, extravagant claims, ridiculous complaints, and suspect intentions. Special rights for *them*? Not likely (G. Ashworth (ed.), *World Minorities*, vol. 1 (Quatermaine House, Middlesex, 1977), p. xix).

27. Economic and social rights, though not prominent in these antique declarations, were by no means unknown. See D. Raphael, 'The liberal Western tradition of human rights', *International Social Science Journal*, vol. 18, no. 1 (1960), pp. 24-5.

28. M. Cranston, *What are Human Rights?* (Bodley Head, London, 1973), p. 66. Cf. 'As there cannot be a duty to do what cannot be done, so there cannot be a right to what cannot be had' (E. Carritt, *Ethical and Political Thinking* (Oxford University Press, Oxford, 1947), p. 79).

29. The correlative obligation to political rights is the mainly passive one of

loyalty to the political order under which those rights are enjoyed. The corr'elative obligations to social and economic rights are active. If the new declarations of the rights of man are to include provisions for social services, for maintenance in childhood, in old age, in incapacity or in unemployment, it becomes clear that no society can guarantee the enjoyment of such rights unless it in turn has the right to call upon and direct the productive capacities of the individuals enjoying them (E.H. Carr, 'The Rights of Man' in the UNESCO Symposium, *Human Rights* (Allan Wingate, London, 1949), p. 22).

30. This roughly corresponds to the debate between *intuitionists* and *utilitarians* which colours a good deal of contemporary ethical philosophy. Intuitionists endorse the near sacred nature of individual moral judgements and convictions, which they call 'rational', though they may offer little that guides a reasoned choice between conflicting rights and helps establish their relative worth. Utilitarians stand in open support of the primacy of human happiness, a principle that they apply collectively to ethical and social disputes even if it means causing some persons' unhappiness to secure that of the rest.

31. J. Burns, 'The Rights of Man since the Reformation: an Historical Survey' in F. Vallant (ed.), *An Introduction to the Study of Human Rights* (Europa Publications, London, 1970), p. 28. Also Benn and Peters, *Social Principles and Democratic State*, pp. 96-7: 'there can be no right without a rule, to abstract man from society is to abstract him from the context of rules, and therefore to make a discussion of rights irrelevant.'

32. On this, see W. Clifford, 'Human Rights and Human Obligations', *World Congress of Law and Social Philosophy*, August 1977, Paper No. 66.

33. M. Golding, 'Toward a theory of human rights', *The Monist*, vol. 52 (1968), p. 549.

34. The Department of State, *Bulletin*, vol. 74, no. 1978 (23 May 1977), pp. 505-6. Interestingly enough, the US has not ratified the International Covenants ostensibly because of the ambiguous wording of those clauses that allow the limitation of human rights for national security reasons, clauses that apply to some but by no means all of the rights these documents have defined. The Soviet Union is in fact a signatory now, though it did not ratify the Optional Protocol of the covenant on civil and political rights that allows the Human Rights Committee to hear individual complaints from the citizens of signatory states.

35. Carter, Department of State, *Bulletin*, p. 623.

36. Ibid., p. 622.

37. See I. Kovács *et al.*, *Socialist Concept of Human Rights* (Akadémiai Kiadó, Budapest, 1966).

38. B. Tchechko, 'The Conception of the Rights of Man in the U.S.S.R. based on official documents' in UNESCO Symposium, *Human Rights*, pp. 161, 169.

39. For a detailed discussion of this issue, see T. Honororé, 'The Human Community and the Principle of Majority Rule', *World Congress on Philosophy of Law and Social Philosophy*, 1977.

40. Bilder, 'Rethinking International Human Rights', p. 207. Also E. Haas, *Human Rights and International Action* (Stanford University Press, California, 1970).

41. W. Frankena, 'The Concept of Social Justice' in R. Brandt (ed.), *Social Justice* (Prentice-Hall, New Jersey, 1962); A. Honoré, 'Social Justice' in R. Summers (ed.), *Essays in Legal Philosophy* (Basil Blackwell, Oxford, 1968); D. Miller, *Social Justice* (Clarendon Press, Oxford, 1976).

42. J.S. Mill, *Utilitarianism, Liberty, Representative Government* (J.M. Dent and Sons, London, 1972), p. 55:

the sentiment of justice appears to me to be, the animal desire to repel or retaliate a hurt or damage to oneself, or to those with whom one sympathises, widened so as to include all persons, by the human capacity of enlarged sympathy, and the human conception of intelligent self-interest. From the latter elements, the feeling derives its morality, from the former, its peculiar impressiveness, and energy of self-assertion (p. 49).

43. H.L.A. Hart, *The Concept of Law* (Oxford University Press, Oxford, 1961), p. 163.

44. The term is J. Stone's; 'Approaches to the Notion of International Justice' in R. Falk and C. Black (eds.), *The Future of the International Legal Order* (Princeton University Press, New Jersey, 1969), vol. 1.

45. There are useful summaries in N. Girvan, 'The Development of Dependency Economics in the Caribbean and Latin America: review and comparison', *Social and Economic Studies*, vol. 22, no. 1 (1973), pp. 1-33; S. Lall, 'Is "Dependence" a Useful Concept in Analysing Underdevelopment?', *World Development*, vol. 3, nos. 11 and 12 (1975), pp. 799-810. See also A. Emmanuel, *Unequal Exchange: a Study in the Imperialism of Trade* (MR Press, New York, 1972).

46. J. Caporaso, 'Methodological Issues in the Measurement of Inequality, Dependence and Exploitation' in S. Rosen and J. Kurth (eds.), *Testing Theories of Economic Imperialism* (Lexington Books, Mass., 1974), p. 91.

47. J. Rawls, *A Theory of Justice* (Belknap Press, Harvard, 1971); also its application by W. Runciman, *Relative Deprivation and Social Justice* (Routledge and Kegan Paul, London, 1966).

48. The literature on Rawls is now extensive. See B. Barry, *The Liberal Theory of Justice* (Oxford University Press, London, 1973); R.P. Wolff, *Understanding Rawls* (Princeton University Press, New Jersey, 1977); N. Daniels (ed.), *Reading Rawls* (Basil Blackwell, Oxford, 1975). Also the symposium in the *American Political Science Review*, vol. 69, no. 2 (June 1975); T. Scanlon, 'Rawls' Theory of Justice', *University of Pennsylvania Law Review*, vol. 121, no. 5 (May 1973), pp. 1020-69; R. Miller, 'Rawls and Marxism', *Philosophy and Public Affairs*, vol. 3, no. 2 (Winter 1974), pp. 167-91; and the obscure but suggestive J. Hinkson, 'Justice for the People: Implementing Rawls', *Arena*, no. 42 (1976), pp. 60-9.

49. Wolff, *Understanding Rawls*, p. 195.

50. For example, C. Beitz, 'Justice and International Relations', *Philosophy and Public Affairs*, vol. 4, no. 4 (Summer 1975), pp. 360-89; P. Danielson, 'Theories, Intuitions and the Problem of World-Wide Distributive Justice', *Philosophy of the Social Sciences*, vol. 3 (1973), pp. 331-40; Barry, *The Liberal Theory of Justice*.

51. Scanlon, 'Rawls' Theory of Justice', p. 1066.

52. Rawls, *A Theory of Justice*, p. 378.

53. Miller, *Social Justice*, Part III.

54. Ibid., p. 336.

55. R. Tucker, 'Marx and Distributive Justice' in C. Friedrich and J. Chapman (eds.), *Justice* (Atherton Press, New York, 1963); A. Wood, 'The Marxian Critique of Justice', *Philosophy and Public Affairs*, vol. 1, no. 3 (Spring 1972), pp. 244-82.

56. Wood, 'The Marxian Critique of Justice', pp. 257, 259-60.

57. Tucker, 'Marx and Distributive Justice', p. 319.

58. Wood, 'The Marxian Critique of Justice', p. 270. Thus:

The revolutionary who is captivated by the passion for justice misunderstands, in the Marxian view, both the existing production relations and his own revolutionary aspirations. He implies by his use of juridical conceptions, that his protest against the prevailing mode of production is a protest against evils which can and should be remedied by moral, legal or political processes, which in fact are only dependent moments of that mode of production itself (p. 271).

Likewise:

> The servitude of the wage labourer to capital is . . . an essential and indispensable part of the capitalist mode of production, which neither the passage of liberal legislation nor the sincere resolve by bourgeois society to respect the 'human right' of all its members can do anything to remove (p. 278).

59. *Manifesto of the Communist Party* (Progress Publishers, Moscow, 1952), pp. 46-8.

60. R. Tucker, *The Inequality of Nations* (Basic Books, New York, 1977).

61. Ibid., p. 67.

62. Ibid., p. 133.

> In rejecting the moral relevance of proximity, distance, or most critically a social grouping, the argument of a shared humanity rejects if not human nature then human history. It assumes the capacity of sympathetic attachment to those with whom the only tie is – or may be – a shared humanity, whereas a uniform experience indicates that the internationalization of the sense of obligation to sacrifice for the welfare of others depends if not upon proximity then upon discrete and identifiable social grouping. For better or worse, the nation-state has been the largest social grouping able to command such sacrifice (p. 151).

63. H. Bull, 'Order vs Justice in International Society', *Political Studies*, vol. 19, no. 3 (September 1971), p. 277.

64. Fortes and Evans-Pritchard, pp. 17-18.

65. L. Mumford, *Technics and Civilisation* (Routledge and Kegan Paul, London, 1934), p. 28.

66. Hence the large literature now on the dangers of industrialism, and the argument that the era of material progress is coming to an end as non-renewable resources, particularly energy ones, and the pressures of population growth and increased pollution make themselves felt. For a brief summary, see K. Kumar, 'Continuities and discontinuities in the development of industrial societies' in R. Scase (ed.), *Industrial Society: Class, Cleavage and Control* (George Allen and Unwin, London, 1977).

Part II: SOCIAL STRUCTURE

"*I hate to brag, but I __am__ the state.*"

4 THE NATION-STATE

The State

In the first section I attempted to establish the terms in which we may
sensibly talk of a 'world society' and the values and norms its individual
members profess. How is this world society structured? What concrete
forms have such significant social forces as industrialisation and modernisation served to shape? What is the context that they work to varying
material and mental effect within? Any answers to these questions will
be conditioned, I argued, by paradigmatic preconceptions — in particular,
whether our perspective is predominantly a *pluralist* or a *structuralist*
one.

Regardless of our choice of paradigm, however, somewhere we must
accommodate the fact of states, since they are real in that they have real
social effects which large numbers of people accept and in their social
practice serve to sustain — social effects which are integrative at the level
of local societies, and disintegrative for world society as a whole. The
characteristic institutions of the state are identifiable as such everywhere, and they develop an inertia and a momentum and diverse self-
perpetuating and self-justifying interests of their own. We can see them,
as pluralists do, as an example of instruments of social governance holding the political ring for group conflicts in the common interest, and
sometimes as the temporary captive of the most successful of these
groups. Elite theory views the capture as a permanent one. Or we can
treat them in terms of the machinery that one social class uses to
oppress another (which is closer to the structuralist point of view). But
the *idea* serves regardless to consolidate and regularise political commerce
within a recognised geographic range, in competition with others beyond
it. Whether the integrative process is a collusive or coercive one the
product, either realised or only intended, is some sort of a communal
entity with generalised jurisdiction over socio-economic, political and
strategic concerns, possessed of a more or less determinate territorial
boundary, plus personnel who legislate, administrate and adjudicate and
who can rely on a more or less popular sense of apathy or compliance
to win respect for their commands. This idea is now universal both in
its appeal and its conflictful application, and beside the class-building
capacity of modern modes of production is the most important social
agent in the contemporary world. So much is this so, in fact, that most

pluralists would attempt to define politics itself solely in terms of affairs of 'state' and inter-state concourse (though not all, as witness those who appeal to a 'systematic' perspective).

Every society known to us has some established means whereby its members can regulate their domestic relations and their contacts with other groups. Ethnological evidence suggests that the social hierarchies observed among apes and monkeys perform a similar function, so the practice seems to extend even beyond the human realm. It is tempting in fact to consider politics as one thoroughly pervasive form of social behaviour manifest whenever we bargain and compromise, order and obey, argue and agree. The political import of such behaviour may be remote: bargaining can be part of a purely commercial transaction, which common usage would not invest with any political connotations; ordering may occur in a military or bureaucratic context, again in terms which one does not equate with political behaviour; arguing may take place between rival professors who have nothing in mind but their competing hypotheses. None of the above play themselves out in a vacuum; hence they all sustain social relationships that are part of a particular political order. But this is a very diffuse connection, and we are wont to talk of political behaviour only when the *purpose* of what is said and done seems political, that is, when the bargaining, ordering and arguing serves to regulate social relationships in some way, feeding a sense of personal self-esteem or individual advantage, moderating conflicting interests, affecting or defending some personal or more public distribution of resources and goods. Purposes like these are pursued at all social levels — in families, small groups, clubs, tribes — anywhere in fact we find some-one manipulating somebody else to more than just functional ends (extracting a decayed tooth for example) or purely spiritual ones (con-verting them to a preferred faith). Deeds have political implications only where they are part of something discernibly political in intent. Political intent is a pervasive phenomenon, however, and cannot be confined to our understanding of those institutions that serve these purposes at the level of society as a whole.

This said, we may still acknowledge the inordinate influence 'state' institutions have over who is to receive social rewards and what the in-dividual must do in the name of social duty to avoid punitive sanctions. It is no accident that the attention of analysts should focus here. Organ-isations of this kind consist of individuals behaving towards each other in expected ways to calculated effect, but those who define these effects are in a strategic position to realise them, and to advance the interests they represent. And for good reason. As societies have grown in size there has been a discernible trend towards the centralisation and the formalisation of 'state' processes. Growth has been made possible by the very aggregation of governing procedures, and it is these institutional aggregates we designate in discussing the 'state'. There are other ways of serving the same political ends. Fortes and Evans-Pritchard, in a comparative review of African political systems, distinguish between centralised societies *with* governments and those *without* them, where the machinery for administration, adjudication and governance is dispersed.[1] The latter, they observe, rely on lineage systems of 'permanent unilateral descent'[2] to co-ordinate political tasks. The former, however, unite the largest numbers of people, lineage systems being appropriate (in terms of mobilising defence and regulating internal contention) to smaller societies only. Beyond this we do find communities where political and kin relations are totally integrated, but they are invariably the smallest ones, kin-based political structures being incapable of sustaining more than the most rudimentary governmental and defence capacities.

With the advent of industrialisation the 'state' has been expanded to accommodate and express new and highly insistent socio-economic realities. The intricate character of the world economy and of world society implicates a correspondingly complex polity in the process of maintenance and control. States have venerable antecedents, however, and it does not seem particularly useful to me to mark off their present-day manifestation as wholly different in kind from what has gone before. Wherever we find a political system on a reasonably large scale that is focused and not dispersed, that is governed by a 'government' within a framework that institutionalises power and not in some less formal (though not necessarily less effective) fashion we have what we can call a 'state'. Though we apply the concept retrospectively—this sort of political focus has been given different names at different times, names that denote real and significant differences in the sort of system that we find—the key feature, which I have talked about above as the bringing together at a social point of the capacity to compel individual compliance and to punish the disobedient within an established physical domain, is a characteristic aspect of what have otherwise been very varied institutions indeed. Whether this competence is used to exalt a dynastic majesty, or to proselytise a spiritual creed, or to defend and extend the interests of those who control the means of material production, or to solicit some more democratic sense of how it should be used whose delegates can then attempt to realise the majority preference in this regard, it is the capacity to predominate that defines the state. The focus can be very sharp or it can be quite diffuse. The governing process can be direct or indirect, centralised or comparatively decentralised. The territorial domain can be expanded by imperial means or smaller states may emerge out of the break-up of some more comprehensive entity. But the focus must be there, as a discernible and visible reference point for individual behaviour. And the social scale must be large enough, anomalies allowing, for such a formal way of conducting affairs to be necessary at all.

Origins

How did these centralised, formally administered systems arise – those we identify as states? Who or what made this one world of citizens, exiles and refugees? When a people wins a war, conquers another, and faces the task of controlling the vanquished we might expect to see focused administration of the 'state' kind. Oppenheimer speaks for an important analytic tradition when he asserts that:

> The State, completely in its genesis, essentially and almost completely during the first stages of its existence, is a social institution, forced by a victorious group of men on a defeated group, with the sole purpose of regulating the dominion of the victorious group over the vanquished, and securing itself against revolt from within and attacks from abroad . . . No primitive state known to history originated in any other manner.[3]

The human record is rife with this sort of behaviour, but it must on logical grounds fall short of universal derivation for how, then, do we explain the original State, the one that first imposed such dominion on others? Where did *it* come from? Surely not through its own defeat, for it must have been by definition the very first such organisation. What were the other forces at work that produced it? Once we identify these, however, there seems no reason not to suppose that they are not still at work elsewhere. What, for example, about the imperatives of subsistence? Can we go further and link state formation and determining modes of production? 'It is obvious', Fortes and Evans-Pritchard conclude, ' . . . that mere differences in modes of livelihood do not determine differences in political structure'[4] (though the way in which communal subsistence is secured, something that is heavily conditioned by environmental circumstance, will certainly affect 'dominant values' while 'strongly influencing' modes of social organisation, including forms of governance. It is influence at best, however, and not an ineluctable cause.) The argument that states derive from particular modes of production is not good enough then. Does it develop as a way of regulating domestic con-

flict? A political focus of a 'state' kind is indeed characteristic of societies divided within themselves, and the secular framework that centralised government and administration can provide has proved peculiarly
appropriate where a people diverge culturally and in terms of socio-
economic status. Again, however, this is not sufficient to explain why
states are formed, since they are found elsewhere among populations
already highly integrated. Is there perhaps a territorial imperative at
work? Focused political systems invariably have a specific geographic
reach, but once more, we can conclude that: 'Political relations are not
simply a reflexion of territorial relations. The political system, in its
own right, incorporates territorial relations and invests them with the
particular kind of political significance they have.'[5]

Historically, the Western tradition from which the contemporary
philosophy of statehood draws its primary understanding fastens first
upon the experience of the classical 'polis', particularly that of ancient
Greece. Greeks of the time saw their political system as a socially comprehensive one. How this system gained such power in the face of rival
identification in terms of kin and tribe is unclear, but predominate it
did, and continuing self-sufficient and independent, the city communities
of the Hellenic world allowed very full expression to those individuals
permitted to participate in them. The sense of community and its sustaining unity of values was closely guarded and maintained, breaking
down before external invaders only when the degrading effects of such
exclusivist control had become apparent, and disillusionment along with
such civic consequences as corruption and opportunism had become
commonplace. Released from central regulation, subsidiary associations
of many kinds proliferated and power became much more widely dispersed.

The rulers of the Roman Empire evolved a different system, which
allowed of a less thoroughgoing but physically much more extensive
political control. The heart of it lay in the Roman approach to law, and
their administration of distant domains owed as much in the end to a
considerable capacity for generating and adjudicating generalised codes
of conduct as to their armed might. The demise of this impressive civil
artifact left a political void in Europe which was not filled until the
modern age. The tribal groups that presided over the process of destruction re-established much more rudimentary systems in terms of their
military supremacy over immediate regions. These tended to fragment
further as local notables secured command of immediate resources in
their own interests rather than those of any collective estate.

The advent of feudal modes of economic and political practice helped sustain this pattern of highly localised authority. The distribution of power between lords and vassals precluded centralised coercive control, since despite the hierarchy of command, it placed important independent privileges at the disposal of whoever had been granted fiefs. Those contending for influence outside this system were the Christian church, the Holy Roman Emperor, diverse medieval and manorial authorities, and the proto-industrial guilds. The most important of these was the Church. The pretensions of those who would have made of the Papal focus a universal state, while successful in particular instances, were never realised, and they finally failed altogether in the face of temporal competition from ambitious kings and feudal elites. Winning a monopoly of the means of force was a protracted business.[6] Significant advances in military technology, however, as well as the growth of money economies and the advent of new sources of finance meant that those in a position to tax and levy could generate the capital necessary to sustain the sort of wars that could subdue and secure ever greater domains. These were then extended until they encountered other peoples with the resources sufficient to resist.

Generating renewed interest in classical philosophies of state omnipotence, the passing age arrived at its own celebration of this secular process in the doctrine of *raison d'état*, a doctrine still very much extant. The notion of state sovereignty, its implicit assumptions made explicit by the English philosopher Thomas Hobbes and the Italian theorist, Niccolo Machiavelli, gave coherent intellectual expression to what eventually became familiar fact. Supported by professional bureaucracies, West European governments co-ordinated within state frameworks a growing range of socio-economic functions. The conviction steadily grew that this was as it should be and further technical advances in printing, in communications generally, and in transport, made it possible to put this concept before very large numbers of people indeed. Competing ideas about individual freedom and competence became problematic in an industrial age so conducive to monopoly, and the totalitarian manipulation of entire populations is now imminent, where it is not already a daily event.

The key aspect of governance of the 'state' kind lies in its command of organised force. It is interesting, however, that the centralised systems Fortes and Evans-Pritchard discuss also possess a parallel class structure — distinct social inequalities of wealth, privilege and status which correspond to the distribution of authority and power. Dispersed systems do not display the same obvious differences and inequalities and one wonders, as Marxist theories would lead us to do, whether the former

coincidence is wholly inadvertent, and the lack of it in the latter is not
equally significant too. In a balanced system of dispersed social segments,
political initiative becomes a matter not of adjudication but of self-help.
The emergence of a powerful class, however, leads through self-interest
to the centralisation of the powers of social regulation and of communal
defence and their co-option by members of the dominant sector. Which
prompts one to ask where such inequalities come from, a problem I
shall pursue in the next chapter.

Holding this aside, it would seem reasonable to conclude that where
government in the form of the state does not exist, it will remain nascent
'unless some set of people who regard themselves as forming a distinct
group have an interest *of some kind* in establishing and maintaining
superiority over others among whom they are living'.[7] Elite self-interest
must include some notion of a *general* interest if authority is to remain
effective in the long term. However indirectly it is expressed, there must
be a modicum of public consent or of public indifference to the dictates
of the focal regime if social order is to prevail. The most effective device
here is for the ruling group to reproduce as a public sense its own particular concept of what is right and due. What it is that generates social
norms becomes a very important question indeed, since material interests
must be served by common sentiments if a society is to cohere. The
political order not only perpetuates the prevailing mode of production,
upon which day-to-day subsistence is based, it also secures respect for
rights, the performance of coincident duties, and the ethical and judicial
values that inform individual behaviour and belief. Ceremonial functions
reinforce such beliefs and persistent material security provides secular
proof that they work. In general, the penchant for spiritual significance
is as pervasive as the desire to see the satisfaction of more prosaic interests, and the successful political order will further either one in terms
of the other. Clearly focused regimes can carry the manipulation of
normative symbols to extremes. Attaching the value of an office to its
particular incumbent is a time-honoured means of celebrating the potency
of personal power. Sun-kings, with all the symbolic association the
concept can command, have been a well-nigh universal phenomenon, a
fact that is hardly accidental. In this sense, a people will get what it
believes, or more accurately, what it is taught to believe.

The 'state' is one means of organising the political life of a community,
but it is not the only way in which this has been done. That centralised
jurisdiction over a discrete domain has become the universal mode is
particular to our times. State boundaries abut each other and constant
pressure is placed upon adjoining peoples to reduce any socio-cultural

ambiguity about the adjoining geographic zone – to replace, that is, mixed and porous regions with ones that are consonant with lines on the map. This bears witness to the political preferences of those regimes that have made the running in the world for the last few hundred years. With their technically more sophisticated means of communication, commerce, administration and waging war, such regimes have succeeded in establishing this preference as the global norm. Most characteristic of large composite societies, the state is now as often as not to be found deliberately enjoined as a means of bringing expanded and more complex societies to life.

Like any political system, however, it must provide a modicum of real reward. Many would argue that under the difficult conditions that mass communities present, it does this better than any known alternative, though one might well hesitate to endorse a judgement that is made so often simply because 'states' are so very much a part of the present socio-political landscape. Historical precedents suggest a range of more or less familiar possibilities, but the 'state' has prevailed. Its approximate form is found in other times and places, but the contemporary ensemble of them – the plurality of such political systems, deliberately engendered and physically adjacent – is unique.

Forms

This point I would like to elaborate at greater length. The sort of political system I have depicted as typical of the 'state' occurs throughout human history. Though generally restricted in terms of those considered by its participants to be politically competent, the *city-state* has been one common version of this entity, and the example of the Greek 'polis' in particular has been, as indicated already, a particularly enduring one. Those who belonged to the polis (male and free) were active members of an absolute institution, and the exclusive character of their collective life, and the individual's capacity to participate in it, has remained a consistent reference point for contemporary state-builders.[8]

To focus coercive power fully it is necessary to eliminate any form of authority that might effectively intervene between the individual and his or her government. The influence of family and kin, priests and lawyers, military, commercial and manufacturing associations, security forces and voluntary groups of all sorts must be rendered subordinate to the sway of those exercising authoritative control. Under such conditions what is private becomes as far as possible a matter of public regard; society and state are one; and those manipulating the machineries of governance incorporate army, industry, family and Church into an extended political repertoire that exploits them all to integrative ends. Totalitarian control of this kind may be achieved by repressive means, by rigid discipline, fear and surveillance, or in some more subterranean fashion which conceals force behind a judicious blend of social welfare, media reassurance, moral education and regulated rewards. The degree of organisation necessary to implement either means is such as to defeat all but the most technically sophisticated state regimes. Most present-day administrations must resort to devices that require less to make and maintain, such as the persistent promotion of the idea of the state itself and its positive connotations for society at large. In the Greek 'polis' the link between society and state was the sense of community engendered by what in contemporary terms would be considered small-town life. On the larger scale, that of the modern territorial state, the sentiment most commonly inculcated as a surrogate for the immediacy of a sense of community is that of 'nationalism', which is an extended version of the same thing.

The doctrine of the state as a total entity was taken to its logical extreme by German theorists of the nineteenth century. The metaphysical ideal the state was presumed to approximate was, in Hegel's words, an expression of something 'divine',[9] concrete evidence of God at work in the world, the hidden but higher reality that those aware of the fact must logically promote. The rational surrender of the individual to the discipline of an integrated polity—the construct of a common will—was seen as a process of total liberation. Hegel himself, though he deliberately reified the state, was not the absolutist in this regard he is often made out to be. He considered cultural heterogeneity as irrelevant to the establishment of a public authority of this kind, and as wholly compatible with it. While proclaiming the dominance of the universal polity, he specifically denounced the notion of a society so regulated as to render personal initiative impossible. When he spoke of the state's 'organic unity' he was not depicting something solid and monolithic but rather a 'differentiated social structure in which relatively autonomous bodies counterbalance each other'.[10] He saw in the state an instrument of collective defence and social welfare that reserved to the individual none the less the freedom to pursue his or her own propensities and predispositions. Though the mass involvement and the intensity of interaction possible in a city-state is impossible over a certain population and size, and politics then becomes an indirect process involving representatives rather than immediate and personal participation, individual feeling for the polity is still possible. This feeling, Hegel said, would occur most readily if the 'state' could be seen as something transcending self-interest (which operated in another realm, that of 'civil society'); as an instrument, that is, of communal altruism and the political expression of individual human reason become conscious of its social self.

The celebration of the 'state' as an independent good is a predictable consequence of its contemporary prevalence and potency. There is a strong tradition that has continued to endorse the idea of the 'state', however disastrous actual examples of it have proved to be in global practice. Thus Bosanquet argued, in Hegelian fashion, that by the state 'we mean Society as a unit, recognised as rightly exercising control over its members through absolute physical power'.[11] Embodied in its law, its codes of common conscience and its purpose is the 'best life, as determined by the fundamental logic of the will'.[12] This will is a General Will, which is more than the aggregate of individual intent. Its sovereign exercise involves 'forcing men to be free'.[13]

I do not wish to rehearse here the debate about the idea of a Common Good and arguments on how and by whom it is defined. Suffice to say that in humane hands the concept has a constructive aspect that it quickly loses when it gets into reactionary and rather more dogmatic ones. The metaphysical concept of the state is plainly exultant, and in its very excess lie prime grounds for an effective critique. Where our index of individual felicity is the excellence of the state; where service to the state is exalted as that means whereby individuals realise their essential communal selves; we have an ideology of considerable potential good and of considerable potential harm.

To identify private purpose so completely with public life may well be a liberating and fulfilling experience, as committed exponents of the model of the 'polis' maintain. I would suggest that it is as likely to suffocate and enslave. Freedom means self-determination, but conformity to law and custom can secure a freedom that is more effective than anything possible under pre-civil conditions. Law and custom are enforced by governments, however, by individuals who are not always benevolent or self-less in their tasks, particularly over the long term. Thus:

> in the notion that the state has the authority of a common self standing above the individual, we have a principle which may but too easily develop into a complete denial of the organic conception, because, instead of recognizing that the value of the state lies in its service to the harmonious development of all its component members, it subordinates that development in each and therefore in all to the fictitious whole which contains them but is not them.[14]

The balance is a moving and a multidimensional one. Neither unmitigated individualism nor thoroughgoing collectivism can do justice to the human needs for both self-actualisation and group identification, since the one is not always and everywhere to be sought through the other. Undue deference to the claims of public authority can be effectively countered by reasserting the importance of a purely personal domain, just as the selfish pursuit of self-interest can be legitimately controlled to public good.

States come in diverse forms. The institutional capacity for social control can be focused in different ways, and just which of these ways obtains in practice can make considerable difference to the well-being and life chances of the subject citizenry. If we talk of the state in an abstract ideal sense, however, and if what is best for the society and for individuals is always and by definition what serves the state, then we have merely said the same thing in a different way. We need a separate notion of what the 'best life' entails, of what the 'logic of the will' is supposed to determine. Declarations about the 'best life' diverge fundamentally in fact, and unless one assumes that this divergence is somehow spurious, we have no one final definition of what is good for us, and any appeal to a single ideal alone is to opt in advance for the notion we favour most, investing it by fiat with universal validity as ultimately good. It is possible, of course, to construe civic submission as the best life. Thus the state can be seen as an end in itself, but only if we are prepared to sacrifice the concept of individual conscience and the importance of being able to formulate a personal critique of the means that those who exercise state power adopt in realising what is ostensibly the 'real' and 'general' will, but may be more or less remote from what people actually want. Though we respond to the dictates of authority out of habits of obedience, we are also apt to ask what such dictates imply in terms of our life projects and satisfactions. These are contingent upon the definitions that prevail in the society into which we are born and where we live, but they are also subject to individual scrutiny. To this extent the state cannot be justified simply because it exists and manages to secure some sort of ordered environment within which a citizen's purposes may proceed. We may rightly ask just what it is that the state does for us, and what the consequences of a specific government's policies happen to be for our separate as well as our collective selves. It can be a difficult equation resolving the benefits of obedience against those of dissent. But it is not one to be decreed by advancing some special concept of freedom, for example, or will. However worthy the 'polis' may have been, and however attractive ideal versions of it can be made to appear, the total democratic state is a mirage that we can only approach, and that I would not expect to see realised in political fact. Anticipating something less, we do well to think in terms of protecting individuals from the consequences of its failure to arrive.

As well as the *city-state* we have historical examples of *tribe-states* where a self-designated tribe possesses an internal political organisation sufficiently tight and complex to be construed in state terms.[15] We also find *empires* where the economic, political, social and cultural life of vanquished peoples has focused more or less intensely on that of the imperial regime. The hierarchy of dominance and dependence centres on the regulating power of the conquerors. We do not, however, identify the Roman Empire or the British Empire as a Roman or British state. Particularly where the imperialists attempt a form of indirect rule, subject populations may retain statist capacities or find these constructed for them where they did not formerly exist, as part of the pattern of core state control. Physical threat can call up a state from a conglomeration of groups in their collective attempt to co-ordinate defence. Once conquest has occurred, the process of managing the provinces is often solved by creating state-like mechanisms where they may not have been before. Any subsequent dissolution of empire will leave these part-formed creations behind as centralised control constructs, to grow more autonomous and concrete, or to fragment and fade away.

Most in evidence now, however, is the *nation-state*, and it is this form of the institution, or at least that model of it where the political focus falls upon a homogeneous populace, that has come to predominate.

> The fact that State and nation are not synonymous, and the States frequently incorporate several nationalities, indicates that authority of government is the ultimate force of national cohesion. The fact that State and nation are roughly synonymous proves that without the sentiment of nationality, with its common language and traditions, the authority of government is usually unable to maintain national unity.[16]

The coercive power of a centralised and territorially delimited authority is used to promote national identification for the state as well as having its own ideological position to promote and defend. Where social integration occurs under the auspices of state domination, and state power is used to inculcate the notion of nationalism, the process of integration is doubly enhanced.

Statist integration is achieved in practice by repression, for example police surveillance, military suppression of rebellions, the calculated use of propaganda and of control over the domestic flow of information and the systematic distortion of public opinion, attitudes and beliefs. This is the imposition of a more comprehensive socio-political form from *without*, or it can be achieved by some more positive and collusive process from *within*—by the ritual and symbolic expression of unity, for example, and the establishment of a 'security-community',[17] which is a social group that has eliminated war or the expectation of it within designated boundaries by rather more amalgamative means. The two can be run together in some grand strategy that is a blend of external and internal agencies. Historically, though, we tend to find either states that have grown from progressively more comprehensive 'attempts' to express a people's sense of themselves as a nation, or the reverse, where state formation occurs as a deliberate, conscious act which is then used to generate feelings of communal interdependence. Building a nation is one way of extending the state; of realising its potential for social integration by making more uniform the society over which it stands; of achieving some sort of consonance between the body of the citizenry, as it were, and their definitions of moral and legal right, a monopoly that is much easier to maintain in a society that is culturally singular and that is one 'nation' with a coherent and publicly sanctified code of beliefs.

Nationalism

The advent of the national state is, in fact, one of the pre-eminent political processes of modern times. In Western Europe it was the paradoxical achievement of a period of royal absolutism that has now passed. Monarchical supremacy in this region was achieved by consolidating or eliminating a wide range of competing social authorities—the word of the Pope and his diverse ecclesiastical representatives, feudal nobles, guild organisations and city-states. The idea of nationalism was crucial, for it was this idea that made the nation 'from an historical fact into a political ideology, into the one exclusive principle of legitimation of the State',[18] a principle then applied by kings and queens to assemble their separate realms. It was subsequently co-opted by an expanding bourgeoisie and enshrined in their diverse constitutions.[19] Loyalty, patriotism, these were the emotions used to link the nation and the state. Expanded to incorporate the sentimental endorsement of the whole citizenry, and the notion that a territorially delimited political domain not only may but should express the common ideals of a singular people became a most significant ideological, even quasi-religious force.

What is nationalism? Where does it come from? What purpose does it serve? Who constitutes a nation and in what does their national quality reside?

The debate about this is a rather sterile one now, but whatever definition we prefer, nationalism is loyalty, induced or coerced, to the nation, a group of people united by some 'pre-political' tie. This union 'might be that of religious belief, blood, or agreement on values and customs. Anything . . . and the more . . . the better.'[20] It ought to be 'natural' somehow, but it can be readily created by state perseverance where it does not already exist. A nation is a way of describing a group of individuals who actually or potentially share particular traits designated as 'national' ones. They aspire to a quality of collective integration that excludes those felt to be foreign, and they argue the superior value of self-government in the sense of rule not by aliens but by their confrères.[21]

Where they are represented in the modern world by those who wield the power of the state, nationals tend to identify directly with the policies their governments make, feeling themselves to be part of this political expression and part of a collectivity that is neither kin, Church nor association, but country. That they should do so is a psychological puzzle of its own. Realist theorists like Hans Morgenthau see the sense of identity prompted by the desire to wield power, a desire that is frustrated for most people by their own largely subject status within their more immediate community, which they then project abroad in vicarious support of the power of the state as a whole.[22] State elites will tend in their own interests to sanction this sort of behaviour, discouraging individual assertiveness while endorsing attempts to serve the name of the nation. Those most deprived of a sense of potency or more insecure about what power they do possess will be the most virulent in support of the national estate, though they may of course reject it outright. Thus:

> The growing insecurity of the individual in Western societies, especially in the lower strata, and the atomization of Western society in general have magnified enormously the frustration of individual power drives. This, in turn, has given rise to an increased desire for compensatory identification with the collective national aspirations for power.[23]

There is a cogent case to be made here. A sense of social insecurity and its complement, which is the sense of social opportunity, is endemic to industrial societies today. Declining codes of faith and custom, increased efficiency in control of work and of life-styles in general, economies that boom then bust, all these factors have contributed to the loss of a sense of personal competence, and the adoption of its surrogate in heightened support for the strength of the state. A surrogate of this kind does not readily abide dissent or social heterogeneity. It is not only relevant to the middle-class societies of the West, who having more, have more to lose, but also to the needs of poor states on the periphery, whose members, seeking autonomy and development, have a good deal more, they feel, to gain.

All this accords with Louis Snyder's definition of nationalism as 'a state of mind, an act of consciousness, a psychological fact . . . that socially approved symbol used by modern society in its search for security'.[24] Max Weber, in the context of a discussion of the economic foundations of imperialism, made a similar point in asserting that an 'emotional influence' like this is not on the whole one of 'economic' derivation. 'It is based upon sentiments of prestige, which often extend deep down to the petty bourgeois masses of political structures rich in the historical attainment of power positions . . .' The 'intellectually privileged' transmute the 'naked prestige of "power" . . . into other special forms of prestige and especially into the idea of the "nation"'.[25] So impressed was he by this process that Weber explicitly defined the nation (where he felt the concept could be given any credence at all) as that 'community of sentiment which would adequately manifest itself in a state of its own'.[26] He specifically denied that the idea could be given empirical referents that would distinguish those who might be included as nationals of one sort or another, and he saw it as meaning 'above all, that one may exact from certain groups of men a specific sentiment of solidarity in the face of other groups'.[27]

What, however, is this 'community of sentiment' that throws up states when sufficiently 'adequate' to the task? Where does it come from? Weber goes through some possible sources, dismissing them all. Mere membership of a given political system is not enough, he declares; nor is common language, common cultural values, or common ethnic origins. Indeed, so contingent is the quality of nationalism that it can be created quite quickly by specific initiatives directed to that end, and just as quickly renounced by those who determine to do so. A common 'political destiny' will, he concedes, produce common sentiments, by which he seems to mean a people's memory of their political history. Furthermore, a state organisation that already exists is able, particularly

in terms of foreign threat, to consolidate its citizens along nationalistic
lines, which reinforces a definition like Morgenthau's that is power-
based. The mark of a nation is the emergence of a state. The state can
pre-date the nation, however, and can be used to create it, in which
case it can hardly be evidence for what is in effect its creature (unless
we want to talk of a 'latent' nationality which the appropriate state
then makes 'manifest'). And as Weber admits himself, not all states are
nations, since belonging to a given polity is not, in common parlance,
evidence itself of national solidarity. So we are left with the notion of
'common political destiny', which may help explain certain historical
circumstances where social coalescence has occurred, but is hardly
adequate to our understanding of why nationality occurs here and not
there, unless we wish to say that all the negative cases lack the quality
of 'commonality' the definition requires. We are justified, then, in
looking beyond such a crude conception of the psychological imperatives at work to consider what other forces make for national sentiments and their political expression.

'Nationalism provides an escape from triviality.'[28] It helps define a
state of conflict; it ennobles and dignifies distress; it provides hope and
purpose to human endeavour. Nationalism grants those 'distortions of
reality' which 'allow men to cope with situations which they might
otherwise find unbearable'.[29] Is this the reason for its popularity? But
then, why 'nationalism'? why not some religious creed or an ideology
like capitalism or socialism? These latter have their adherents, of course,
but in the contemporary world they must complement the notion of
nations.

Perhaps the task is more specific than this. In a world fraught with
radical social change, is nationalism a strategy for coping with change,
with industrialisation and modernisation and the drive to economic
development? Greater social mobility for the individual leads to more
uniform modes of culture, to shared language and shared values; for
what in a traditional environment is given, in a contemporary one has
to be contrived. What gets built here is appropriate to larger-scale and
more dynamic societies, which cannot tolerate excessive regional
eccentricity if they are to function efficiently or even function at all.
The sort of metropolitan society sustained by the developed industrial
infrastructure that has become the near-global ideal is only possible, it
is felt, where much of the traditional diversity of identity is surrendered
and a common attachment to one language and one hierarchy of educational achievement is put in its place. I shall return to this point in a moment.

In direct opposition to the Weberian view, Benjamin Akzin specifically defines the nation as an ethnic phenomenon. Ethnicity he describes in terms of a shifting mosaic of personal characteristics that are relatively prevalent in a particular human group, the group itself being of sufficient size to constitute a political force. Objective indices like language, culture, common descent and religion are cited; to which Akzin adds subjective forces such as the inculcation of coalescence by political will.[30] Ethnic identity competes with ideologies that exalt the autonomy of the individual or allegiance to some comprehensive transnational creed. Consolidating a sense of communal loyalty has had to contend with the inertia of beliefs that still prevail on a local level, as well as traditions of worship or obedience that endorse social distinctions other than ethnic ones. It is a general observation, however, that given long enough, 'integration seems to constitute the most plausible outcome of the cohabitation of several ethnic groups living in close proximity, especially when they live under common rule and where the territorial delimitation between their respective areas is incomplete.'[31]

Here Akzin points up the 'pressure of social contacts' as the catalytic agent, a rather vague notion that he sees intensified by such factors as social mobility and mass education and communications. More important, perhaps, are state-made initiatives. All societies are now more or less multi-ethnic, and where integration is a specific state policy the nature of that policy will vary depending upon the social balance between the various minorities. Where one group is dominant and has co-opted the power of the state it will tend to use that state to support and extend its own national interests. Where the mix is more confused, the state is often given a neutral value that all can endorse, which distracts from the potentially divisive consequences of ethnic dissension. The general tendency is so significant though, that Clifford Geertz calls it an 'integrative revolution'. By this he means the search by peoples, in new states in particular, for a discrete identity, and the wider recognition of their presence in the world as a notable one. As societies, such peoples are often disparate and incongruous. A civil order that transcends the most prevalent 'primordial sentiments' is not to be constructed overnight: 'born yesterday in many cases from the meager remains of an exhausted colonial regime . . . superimposed upon . . . [a] finespun and lovingly conserved texture of pride and suspicion', the nascent state attempts to transmute this stubborn material into a coherent tapestry of contemporary design.[32] It is no mean task, and the one common approach to it seems to be to collect together the more close-knit traditional groups into a nation, defined at first by civil order. Aggregation does not mean displacement, however, and we find rather the reconciliation of one cultural context to another and the promotion of a collective and more comprehensive sense of the individual and his or her social context.

Karl Deutsch has spelled out the development of nationalism in some detail,[33] and it springs in every case, he says, from the emotional need for security, from the feeling that one can trust those with whom one shares common habits of communication. Again and again, in fact, analysts return like this to the psychological dimension of the concept. Hans Kohn, another academic who has specialised in the subject, flatly asserts that 'first and foremost' nationalism is a 'state of mind, an act of consciousness'.[34] People possess an ego-consciousness and a collective or group consciousness which will be attached to many different social entities. They tend to fasten, however, upon one group as the object of ultimate loyalty, and this results in the decision to form a nation. There are antecedent historical processes that make the mass expression of the emotion possible. 'Nationalism is inconceivable,' Kohn maintains,

> without the ideas of popular sovereignty preceding – without a complete revision of the position of ruler and ruled, of classes and castes. The aspect of the universe and of society had to be secularized with the help of a new natural science and of natural law . . . the traditionalism of economic life had to be broken by the rise of the third estate, which was to turn the attention away from the royal courts and their civilisation to the life, language, and arts of the people.[35]

Nevertheless the well-spring is the idea itself 'which fills men's brain and hearts with new thoughts and new sentiments, and drives him [*sic*] to translate his consciousness into deeds of organised action';[36] a potent brew, and decanting it into the container of the sovereign state is apt to produce synergistic effects. A fundamental distinction exists, Kohn argues, between a nationalism that precedes or accompanies the formation of the nation-state (the product of a domestic move towards a liberal constitutional government defined in terms of the value of the individual as well as the unity of humankind and with its prime base in a burgeoning middle class) and a nationalism derived from earlier cultural contracts and imbued with rather more emotional and universalist notions that find their political expression in an authoritarian state (aristocratic or mass-based), which is generally opposed to liberal, rational ways. The fundamental instinct is the same, however – the desire to belong, and to share some concept of a larger self.

What I find unhappy here is the rather circular nature of the argument: nations are nations (variously defined) that are called forth, as it were, to celebrate the state. What does the calling? Ideas are mental artifacts and have no life of their own. They can be granted emotional allegiance without any obvious rational or material interest being involved. Nationalism and the concept of the nation have this capacity for comparatively independent support and the writings of Machiavelli, Hobbes, Locke and Rousseau remain relevant because they give articulate expression to the moral sense of what identifies the people with the state. However, what was a Western European phenomenon might have stayed that way but for the expansion of the capitalist system and the radical change in productive, specifically industrial power that accompanied it.

The real engine of the process of global dissemination, of the notion of nationalism, has been this twin socio-economic force. The European empires carried more than conquest to the colonies. And they generated there a motley provincial bourgeois class, its recruits drawn from the clerical, legal, medical and educational professions as much as industrial or commercial ones, who with the more or less witting connivance of landowners and mostly peasant majorities came to demand self-determination and economic development for their subject domains. Their demands were usually made in the analytic language of the alien overlords themselves, conceptual frameworks as often as not derived from the educational institutions of the metropolitan capitals by those who had made it out into the world through the channels the imperial connection did provide. The key conditioning process was that of political modernisation, in the context of an international capitalist and industrialising economy, and in looking back to common factors of history and culture with which to construct a nation those who took local command were also looking forward to a future where all of these factors would be modified by the conscious and unconscious effects of cultural assimilation into the wider world. This has proved a difficult and often very destructive process.[37] Since the qualities of national continuity do not themselves derive from the workings of the global economy and the political hierarchy assembled within it, they are not always compatible with them either.

Nationalism: The Marxist Case

The most coherent statement of the case above is in modified Marxist terms; modified since the Marxist insistence on the primacy of class analysis does not adequately account for the realm of ideas, even where we allow for all the subtleties with which ideological controls can be inculcated and sustained (a conclusion, incidentally, that would be condemned in Marxist terms as a thoroughly bourgeois one). The emergence of capitalist states from their feudal antecedents was not an accidental process, and the subsequent advent in Western Europe and beyond of broader based and more uniform social entities owes a great deal to the impact of modernising policies and industrialisation. We can push the explanatory power of such a connection a good way, it seems to me, without becoming reductionist.[38] Marx and Engels themselves did not resolve the ambiguities implicit in their own doctrine here and subsequent Marxist theorists have not found the task any easier;[39] but their general statement remains a central one.

Rosa Luxemburg, for example, particularly in her polemics against Polish nationalism, stands out as an opponent of the right of national self-determination and a supporter of the concept of a revolutionary proletarian alliance that the separatist force of social patriotism could only undermine. In her frame of reference the latter was a bourgeois concept anyway, since to her the nation and national independence was secondary, and the fact of classes and their disparate interests came first. Small potential states like Poland were not, she argued, economically viable, and in what was an age of imperialism and of great state rivalry over global domains it seems hardly surprising that she should have seen the notion of national interest as somewhat irrelevant to the real play of political and economic power. Her position was not wholly consistent though, for elsewhere in her writings she did allow of the phenomenon of national independence as an expression of deeply felt cultural sentiments. And one can argue that she consistently denied the importance of an autonomous realm of political aspirations, which is a criticism generally true of most, though not all, Marxist analysis. In the end events went against her anyway. Political aspirations were to have revolutionary effects in Eastern Europe, Central and East Asia, and Africa, particularly once nationalist movements had managed to generate the support of the peasantry. These effects were often comparatively independent ones, and extremely potent too.

Lenin rejected Luxemburg's stance and attempted a strategic reconciliation of the forces making for nation and class. His argument was, in essence, for self-determination first and proletarian internationalism second. The former created the conditions for the latter, and the fact that this precise progression did not actually take place does not invalidate the analysis as a practical response to the political realities of the time. Thus (and note the order of instruction):

The Marxists' national programme . . . advocates, firstly, the equality of nations and languages and the impermissibility of all *privileges* in

this respect . . . and the right of nations to self-determination . . . ;
secondly, the principle of internationalism and uncompromising
struggle against contamination of the proletariat with bourgeois
nationalism.[40]

Using this formula Marxists could account for the evident developmental
impact of capitalism as it spread across the world, generating national
movements in its wake, and yet not seduced by its bourgeois consequences. Capitalism functioned most effectively, Lenin asserted, where
markets were linguistically unified and free, and this had produced the
most profound propensity for forming nation-states. Since they were
economically advantageous, state self-determination had been the
'typical and normal' outcome of an era in which Europe, secure within
its own transnational frame, had extended its reach around the world.
This understood, Marxists could then go on to take advantage of capitalism's more mature influence, which was the demolition of the national
differences it had earlier created in favour of an international unification
of capital, politics and science. This latter process Lenin approved as
productive of the 'greatest historical progress, the breakdown of hide-
bound national conservatism . . . especially in backward countries'[41]
(among whom he explicitly numbered his own).

Having given nationalism its due, it remained to draw the line. Hence
'awakening the masses from feudal lethargy' was all very well, and one
could support national liberation as such, but anything beyond this
limit involved actively promoting the concept, which meant siding with
the bourgeoisie. As he pointed out himself, this threshhold could be
difficult to discern, but in practice Lenin felt it was there none the less,
and a critical point to watch.

Consolidating nationalism within a certain 'justly' delimited sphere,
'constitutionalising' nationalism, and securing the separation of all
nations from one another by means of a spatial state institution —
such is the ideological foundation and content of cultural-national
autonomy. This idea is thoroughly bourgeois and thoroughly false.[42]

The class interest of the proletariat lay beyond the limit. It existed in
every force that might reduce distinctions and assimilate nations one to
another that was not coercive or the product of privilege, hence Lenin's
support for the 'fullest freedom of capitalist intercourse' and his eager
anticipation of its mature consequences and the opportunities that
these would present for proletarian solidarity against the bourgeoisie —

'the antagonism between internationally united capital and the international working-class movement' that would then, in Lenin's parlance, come to the fore.[43]

Lenin's strategy was left deliberately flexible and if the bourgeois preference for nationalism could be used to secure equal rights for the working class, then it could be used to serve the greater cause and the creation of more opportune conditions for class struggle. Conditional collaboration was in order. The obvious problem, of course, was the perennial propensity for means to contaminate ends. The means-end dichotomy is not a dichotomy at all, it is a process. And while the proletariat or those acting on its behalf might well work to ensure the overthrow of the bourgeoisie, should they do so by endorsing nationalism, however inevitable and obvious the presence of nation-states might be and however 'negative' the endorsement remained, the danger was always there that the proletariat would not recognise Lenin's Limit and would become bourgeois-style nationalists too. The alliance of the workers of all nations could never then come to pass. In establishing a right to self-determination, in other words, Lenin sailed too close to the wind. Proletarian unity seems more remote now than it has ever been, and a global proletariat divided by diverse and mutually exclusive national allegiances, however inimicable to its 'real' interests that division might be, shows no sign of amalgamating on an international basis to confront the bourgeoisie, whose own particular notion of nationalism has come to encompass all competing conceptions of social class, race, religion or ideology.

National identity continues to divide the bourgeoisie as well, though here the Marxist case is more cogent, as I shall indicate in the next chapter. Each of the new political regimes around the world has hampered to some extent, at least, the broad play of capitalism's cosmopolitan compass. The development of the global economy has been very uneven, and along with the dramatic rise in the number of nations pressing on to the world stage from the wings, and the growing sense that nations should be responsible in a collectivist fashion for the social welfare of their citizens, there have been diverse developments in the nationalisation of economic affairs.[44] Inside the global economy there are now many national economies more or less preoccupied with securing their own part of the world's productive wealth.

Has this trend been decisive? Do we see now the final effect of the fact that 'human society consists essentially of several hundred different and discrete "nations", each of which has (or ought to have) its own postage-stamps and national soul'?[45] The question can readily mislead, because it moves away from the structure of global society as a whole and the macro-process of socio-economic change that has followed the Industrial Revolution, towards what seems an undue emphasis upon shared cultural traits and the human need to 'identify'. The fact that certain people share similar values or behaviour patterns does not tell us why the importance placed upon what is shared should receive such support. We need to reconcile subjective elements with those material imperatives that inform so much of the contemporary world. We need to look closer at the process of change, and its irregular and heterogeneous results.

The spread of industrial culture across the globe has not, as one might expect, been equable or easy, but those in command of the power of industrial production have on the whole been able to build a capitalist world economy with it, placing their own countries at the core. The building process was in many respects a disconcerting one, and to secure at least something of the industrial largesse, leaders on the periphery of this system had to bring into the process (where they did not actually invent them) whole peoples in whose name hierarchic control could be rearranged to satisfy more local, if no less selfish and elitist interests. 'Nationalism' was the only potent resource to hand which might mobilise large numbers of people. The movement of capitalist enterprise around the globe came to be met by ramshackle coalitions defined in terms of a grab-bag of whatever 'national' attributes could be identified for the purpose of a political response. In this sense, as Tom Nairn argues, 'nationalism' is a product of the periphery, received back again by core states only as it becomes a tangible ideological presence in the world. '"Uneven development"', he comments, 'is a politely academic way of saying "war" . . . that "development war" (as one might call it) which has been fought out consistently since the irruption of the great bourgeois revolutions.'[46] It is hardly surprising then that the most extreme and the most aggressive sort of nationalism should have been generated by core states like Germany who thought they were falling over on to the losing side; who could remember what it meant not to be developed, and yet had a sufficiently contemporary infrastructure for resolute mobilisers to create Fascist states and to strike out in force against their systemic degradation. Again, the potent animator was a sense of nationalism, here carried to pathological extremes. A posture of defence was transcribed into one of aggression, since the sentiments involved are quite capable of being turned to either account. 'Thus does nationalism stand over the passage to modernity . . . As human kind is forced through . . . it must look desperately back into the past, to gather strength wherever it can be found . . .'[47] The fervour of mass nationalism provides that strength. It is one pervasive response—both sick and sane—to rapid socio-economic change.

The State in Post-Colonial Society

All of which cuts across any effects that global class consciousness might be able to claim. The 'developmental' and 'mature' aspects of world capitalism, as Lenin depicted them, have not occurred in that sequence. The construction of nation-states has not given way to a truly potent cosmopolitanism. The Marxist assumption of a global proletariat confronting a global bourgeoisie has proven false. The two aspects of capitalist expansion do exist, but they have taken place at the same time and to complex effect. In core states, in terms of the part they play in the world economy, almost the whole population may be construed as bourgeois. In the periphery the strategic force is usually that of Westernised intellectuals, military or civil, who must manufacture a local version of the ideology of nationalism, at the same time sustaining an indigenous group of 'developers' who promise to make modernisation happen in terms of industrial and material progress. Those who would hope to control more closely, where they do not completely reject, the inroads of the global economy, remain in the minority. Popular demands for 'development' and its goods and services continue to grow and this works directly to the advantage of the modernisers and against those who would secure other values. It is far from clear that a majority of people in the periphery specifically demand industrialisation in fact, but they do generally look for its products and its promise of social mobility and advancement, if not for themselves then for their children, and the only mode of production known to be able to fulfil requests like these *en masse* is the industrial one.

The class picture is highly diverse. It would be too crude by half, as I hope is clear by now, to depict a 'simple contradiction between a world-proletariat and a world bourgeoisie working its way through all levels of social practice'; rather, we find the 'simultaneous combination of several modes of production with their own working together of economic, political and ideological levels as well as their working together as modes of production with each other'.[48] The social and political consequences are confused. There are differences between bourgeois owners of labour power, loan and industrial capital, and land. And as I have indicated, in terms of the global division of labour and of styles of life and the mechanics of exchange, the rich states may be construed as bourgeois in a way belied by their domestic class patterns, since as states, as representatives

of their citizens, they are capital-owning industrial entities. The bourgeoisie on the periphery is also very mixed, and the part it plays in controlling the government in particular, and the whole state apparatus of
administrative and bureaucratic organisations, military and police forces
and judicial bodies in general, can vary widely too. Hamza Alavi discriminates in the South Asian context between three separate propertied
classes—the indigenous, 'metropolitan neo-colonialist', and land-owning
ones, each with its own social base and class interest. Under the conditions that usually prevail following a colony's formal receipt of independence we find another group, however, that of a 'bureaucratic-military'
oligarchy, which is the administrating legacy of the former colonial
power and which tends to re-emerge to mediate between the different
fractions of the bourgeoisie while co-opting in the process the machinery
of the state. (Since imperial regimes dominated all social groups, the
machinery they built to do so became relatively 'over-developed' as an
òrgan of political control, a fact more conspicuous once independence
was achieved.[49])

In this sense the state in post-colonial societies is a relatively autonomous one and not the agency of a single class,[50] though it must accommodate competing bourgeois interests and secure what is the shared concern
of all—the social order as such and the institution of private property. It
also has direct access to whatever economic surplus exists, which is used
to instigate 'development'. The pattern is further complicated where
there are political parties sharing state power. Often closely associated
with the construction of the nationalist movement that established the
right to self-determination, the incumbent politicians must adapt to,
where they have not actually been displaced by, the bureaucracy and the
military. This usually involves an intricate strategy of endorsement and
command. The relationships of the three propertied classes to each other
are also intricate—the landowners servicing the links between the state at
the centre and the rural areas where they are most powerful and where
the possibility of peasant insurrection can be acute; the indigenous
bourgeoisie working jointly with the metropolitan neo-colonial one to
import goods and more advanced technologies and export primary
products (though the collaborative nexus is not always as automatic as
this commercial formula makes it appear); and so on.

East African analyses suggest a less balanced pattern than this, where
landed classes and the indigenous bourgeoisie are nowhere near such a
self-evident social force.[51] Furthermore, the importance the state
assumes in economic planning and production would suggest that those
who man it may well possess not only mediating and control functions,

but class interests of their own. In this sense the state bureaucracy, either run by the military or by civilian personnel or both, *is* the indigenous bourgeoisie – a 'political class' of high-salary officials and administrators, senior political advisers and party officials, senior military and policy officers, plus the more numerous and diffuse 'petty bourgeois' elements of both new and more traditional origins.[52] Here the state apparatus looks less and less like the one Alavi describes. Where what is done in terms of development is altruistically conceived, the ruling group commits a sort of 'class suicide'. More cynically engendered, 'development' becomes the pursuit of self-interest by other means. In either case the picture is quite different from that of Alavi's India, Bangladesh or Pakistan.

Colin Leys has questioned the whole notion of the 'top-heavy' state, arguing that such post-colonial establishments tend to have been relatively small in relation to their own populations and economies and those of advanced capitalist countries, and to have experienced expansion only after independence. The preoccupation with their structural significance obscures more important questions about the *composition* of the bureaucracy (and the military for that matter) and the distinctions to be made between the personnel within it, as well as its class character and its connections with the larger petty bourgeoisie of rich peasants, traders and small manufacturers. One should remain mindful, as well, that 'in post-colonial societies in Africa there can be little doubt that the *dominant* class is still the foreign bourgeoisie,' and the key question is the extent to which the local state serves or denies these external interests.[53] There are examples where even this must be qualified simply because the state is 'dependent but not dependable . . . too weak and too internally compromised to stabilize society and economy'.[54]

State and Class

The question of the autonomy of the 'state' has always presented problems for those who would talk in terms of class analysis. These are closely related to the perennial debate about the autonomy that political initiatives possess in the light of economic, or more generally, material constraints. Marx and Engels themselves distinguished in Hegelian fashion between 'civil society' and 'the state', a distinction that roughly correspond to the difference between a private sphere and a public one. By 'civil societ' they meant 'the whole material intercourse of individuals within a definite stage of the development of productive forces'. The concept was felt to embrace 'the whole commercial and industrial life of a given stage and, insofar, transcends the State and the nation, though, on the other hand again, it must assert itself in its foreign relations as nationality, and inwardly must organise itself as State'.[55] Civil society was the basis of the state, though the latter stood as a separate entity 'beside and outside' it; 'nothing more than the form of organisation which the bourgeois necessarily adopt both for internal and external purposes, for the mutual guarantee of their property and interests'.[56]

Since state organisations are political institutions that concentrate and organise social force, any class that seeks the upper hand has first to 'conquer for itself political power in order to represent its interest in turn as the general interest, which in the first moment it is forced to do'.[57] Thus, Marx considered the state the key instrument of political change (while asserting at the same time that a proletarian revolution would result in its demise).[58] A truly autonomous state of Alavi's sort, mediating from outside the arena of conflict, could exist only where there were no classes as such, or where no one class was predominant.

The origin of the state lies, in this view, in the division of labour that Engels in particular considered the root of the division of society into classes.[59] Class conflict necessitates social control; a public power that can assume a progressively more detached and supreme position above society, taxing and coercing it. This power moves into the possession, where it is not the immediate product, of the ruling class. It is the 'machine' whereby the ruling class exploits and oppresses subordinate groups. Given its clearest expression in the famous formula of the Communist Manifesto ('The executor of the modern state is but a committee for managing the common affairs of the whole bourgeoisie'), the point was exploited by theorists like Lenin in confirming Marxism as a strategy for revolutionary change and post-capitalist rule.[60] (The state-after-the-revolution Lenin depicted in terms of an expanded postal service,[61] where state officials would be subordinate in their tasks of accounting and control to the state power of armed workers; where the bourgeoisie had been overthrown and bureaucratic functions, rather than standing above the people; had become the province of all.)

Marx himself did acknowledge political occasions when a state might not be the agency of the ruling class pure and simple, and possessed independent power of its own. In his analysis of the Asiatic mode of production he seemed to subscribe to the notion of a state divorced from class rule altogether. Likewise in discussing the French Second Republic he had to account for Napoleon Bonaparte's capacity to manoeuvre the social forces of France in a voluntaristic way and to construct an authoritarian bureaucratic-military regime based on something like a broad class balance with the endorsement—more implicit than positive, perhaps, but support none the less—of both the peasants and those with property. In the course of this study Marx indicated that a ruling class was most vulnerable where the fact of its rule was most evident, which leaves the option of suggesting bourgeois governance at one remove, and ways of conducting affairs that leave the ruling class less directly exposed to the resentments of the repressed. He also recognised that 'states', while sharing basic common features, were different from country to country and that they could be used quite convincingly to effect change. This, in turn, allows of a more independent political realm that is more than the vulgar reflection of particular economic substructures. It makes any doctrine that depicts state forms playing out the imperatives implicit in society's material underpinnings much more difficult to apply with predictive worth.

In a contemporary statement of this general theme Ralph Miliband asserts as 'obviously true' the fact that the capitalist class, as a class, does not 'govern'; that it confronts the state and the state elite as a 'separate entity'.[62] Class power and state power are actually distinct, however much the one may employ the other to its own ends. This represents what has been termed the 'instrumentalist' strand of Marxist thought on the capitalist state,[63] an approach that attempts to establish with some empirical precision the links that bind the ruling class and the state together. As a way of understanding the subject it tends to revert to *pluralism*, placing the ruling class as only one group, albeit dominant, within the social arena, and it loses some of the force of the rather more unalloyed Marxist view. Since policy cannot always be explained as the outcome of ruling class machinations, a competing tradition has grown up, rather more 'structuralist' in its focus, which attempts either domestically, or increasingly now in a global context, to map the capitalist system as a whole with all its internal problems and its policy-pertinent constraints.[64] From this perspective it is our comprehension of the underlying social structures that is important, structures that persist regardless of who precisely wields state power. The state in the structuralist sense functions to reproduce day by day the capitalist world economy and its national variants, while standing sufficiently apart from the capitalist class to be able to reconcile or contain the conflicts that occur within it. However impelling this may be in theory it is often difficult to see why such a scheme should work as it says it does in practice. It can also come close to economic reductionism, where it is not indeed a brand of structural functionalism in Marxist guise. Which need not be a bad thing, but the conservative bias of any structural functional approach, fastening as it does on the conditions necessary for the persistence of the particular system under review rather than its potential for change, ought to alert us to the ideological preference this sort of social analysis can imply. We might note a third strand too, termed the Hegelian-Marxist tradition, which considers more the part the *idea* of the state plays in contemporary political consciousness and ideology. Antonio Gramsci, for example, who developed the notion of 'civil hegemony' to describe the way human understanding must be changed and a truly class-specific conception of moral, cultural and political values be inculcated at large if that class is to prevail, saw the successful regime as exerting mental and moral authority far beyond, and preferably before, the mere assumption of power.[65] In this sense the state is 'the entire complex of practical and theoretical activities with which the ruling class not only justifies and maintains its dominance, but manages to win the active consent of those over whom it rules'.[66] It will raise the mass to whatever cultural or moral level might be necessary to service the needs of production and the interests, in capitalist states, of bourgeois control. Gramsci draws attention to a definition of the state that illuminates a growing historical trend, that is, the heightened capacity through the media, the schools, political parties and religion to reproduce a hegemonic sense of state legitimacy (and hence the legitimacy of the class the state represents and its preferred modes of material production). This sort of analysis moves away somewhat from the idea of substructural determination that pervades Marxist thought in general, a determination that has grown more important in contemporary times where states have come to play a greater and greater part in the whole process of production. It is no less suggestive because of that, though. While centralised organs of social coercion like the state have a growing influence over much of what a society can produce, they also feed on its expanded influence in all those fields that generate modern ideologies. 'Above' or 'beside' society, they come to share much of the means whereby society defines and perpetuates itself and its myths and its common values.

The three approaches outlined above pertain to advanced capitalist states.[67] What of the state in 'communist' countries, so called? Under conditions of Communist rule the 'state' directly dominates both economic and political arenas and we face 'state capitalist' formations representing a ruling class of Communist party politicians and bureaucrats. Lenin's idea of armed workers reconstructing society themselves has never been eventuated, though the Chinese, under Maoist inspiration, made a more sustained attempt than the Bolsheviks did in this regard. Communist states possess centralised powers of coercion exceeding even those of capitalist states, power likewise beyond and above the ordinary citizen and employed in hegemonic ways to educate and persuade as well as to coerce. In advanced capitalist states, however, the ruling class stands beside the state, penetrating it at every point but a component still of a civil society at large. In the Communist case, the bureaucratic apparatus of political and economic power is the overt and explicit arm of the ruling class, a connection made in the name of workers and peasants but none the less comparatively detached from them. Hence state and civil society are the same. State power is class power; not, however, the dictatorship of the proletariat envisaged by Marx and Lenin, but rather that of party officials and their military, administrative and judicial appointees.

This sort of theory makes of state formation and state maintenance (and the actions of governments within states) a dependent process. In an age following upon such a profound change in the primary mode of production as the advent of industry this does not seem to me to be an unreasonable argument. Nevertheless, as the process of differentiating classes has proceeded apace, the political consequences have been more complex than the Marxist model might suppose. As far as advanced capitalist states are concerned, for example:

> What Marx could not yet see, is that neither of the two industrial classes would acquire the *sole* faculty of ruling the nation. In the *welfare* state the organised employers and the organised working class became the ruling class*es* of the state in antagonistic cooperation with one another.[68]

The common result has been a process of horizontal integration — horizontal in the sense of a global social field within which we find centrally administered groups that we can distinguish one from another along territorial lines. Though fraught by domestic divisions it would mean the denial of a vast body of historical and contemporary evidence to maintain that those who govern do not nowadays seek and to some extent succeed in aggregating and disciplining their subject peoples as certifiable citizens of nation-states. The process of integration by fiat predominates here over that of social differentiation by some other socio-economic force, which must proceed then within the confines of the territorial overcoat. From this container governments construct coalitions with other states. They defend their borders, and attempt to bolster the unity and coherence of their domestic domains. Horizontal integration of this kind segments world society into many different groups, and such is the kernel of the pluralist conception of world affairs.

It is a compelling and a familiar one, but we must place it in the context of an understanding of the world put together from top to bottom as it were, in ways that belie the exclusive acceptance of a state-bound view.

Notes

1. M. Fortes and E.E. Evans-Pritchard (eds.), *African Political Systems* (Oxford University Press, London, 1948). Also L. Mair, *Primitive Government* (Penguin, Harmondsworth, 1962), Part One, 'Government without the State'; J.P. Nettl, 'The State as a Conceptual Variable', *World Politics*, vol. 20, no. 4 (July 1968), pp. 559-92.

2. Fortes and Evans-Pritchard, *African Political Systems*, p. 6.

3. F. Oppenheimer, *The State: its History and Development Viewed Sociologically* (Vanguard Press, New York, 1926), p. 15.

4. Fortes and Evans-Pritchard, *African Political Systems*, p. 8.

5. Ibid., p. 11.

6. For an account of this process in Marxist terms, see P. Anderson, *Passages from Antiquity to Feudalism* (New Left Books, London, 1974); *Lineages of the Absolutist State* (New Left Books, London, 1974). Anderson argues:

> Absolutism was essentially just this: *a redeployed and recharged apparatus of feudal domination*, designed to clamp the peasant masses back into their traditional social position . . . The Absolutist State was never an arbiter between the aristocracy and the bourgeoisie, still less an instrument of the nascent bourgeoisie against the aristocracy: it was the new political carapace of a threatened nobility

driven, in its turn, 'by the spread of commodity production and exchange' (p. 18). The pressure of the mercantile and manufacturing classes was a secondary determinant, for the need to accommodate their interests was an immediate one. States were 'machines built overwhelmingly for the battlefield' (p. 32), and they drew their strength from their tax and office systems, their diplomacy and their trade.

7. Mair, *Primitive Government*, p. 125.

8. For a brief but enlightening account, see H. Kitto, *The Greeks* (Penguin, Harmondsworth, 1951), pp. 64-79.

9. *The Philosophy of History* (Dover, New York, 1956), p. 41.

10. S. Avineri, *Hegel's Theory of the Modern State* (Cambridge University Press, Cambridge, 1972), p. 168.

11. B. Bosanquet, *The Philosophical Theory of the State* (Macmillan, London, 1923), p. 172.

12. Ibid., p. 173.

13. Ibid., p. 217.

14. L.T. Hobhouse, *The Metaphysical Theory of the State* (George Allen and Unwin, London, 1935), p. 97. See also H.J. Laski, *The State in Theory and Practice* (George Allen and Unwin, London, 1935), particularly Ch. 1, 'The Philosophic Conception of the State'.

15. L. Krader, *Formation of the State* (Prentice-Hall, New Jersey, 1968), p. 4. Krader also nominates *consanguineal-states* too, which he describes as those with defined territorial limits whose subjects are related to one another by kinship ties. The Fortes and Evans-Pritchard classification discounts this latter type. There is

also some mention of *empire-states*, though I would designate these as rather states-having-empires.

16. R. Niehbuhr, 'State Morality' in W. Browne (ed.), *Leviathin in Crisis* (Viking, New York, 1956), p. 184.

17. A.P. d'Entreves, *The Notion of the State* (Oxford University Press, Oxford, 1967), p. 176.

18. L. Snyder, *The Meaning of Nationalism* (Rutgers University Press, New Jersey, 1954), p. 37.

19. F.H. Hinsley, *Nationalism and the International System* (Hodder and Stoughton, London, 1973).

20. K. Minogue, *Nationalism* (B.T. Batsford, London, 1967), p. 11.

21. . . . it has been a mark of nurture, if not of nature, for human beings since the dawn of history to possess some consciousness of nationality, some feeling that the linguistic, historical, and cultural peculiarities of a group make its members akin among themselves and alien from all other groups. But not until very modern times have whole peoples been systematically indoctrinated with the tenets that every human being owes his first and last duty to his nationality, that nationality is the ideal unit of political organisation as well as the actual embodiment of cultural distinction, and that in the final analysis all other human loyalties must be subordinate to loyalty, to the national state, that is, to national patriotism. These tenets, again, are the excuse of modern nationalism (C.J. Hayes, *Essays on Nationalism* (Macmillan, New York, 1926)).
(See also L. Doob, *Patriotism and Nationalism: their Psychological Foundations* (Yale University Press, New Haven, 1964).)

22. H. Morgenthau, *Politics Among Nations* (Alfred A. Knopf, New York, 1966), p. 103.

23. Ibid., p. 104.

24. Snyder, *The Meaning of Nationalism*, p. 197.

25. H. Gerth and C.W. Mills, *From Max Weber: Essays in Sociology* (Kegan Paul, Trench, Trubner, London, 1947), pp. 171-2.

26. Ibid., p. 176.

27. Ibid., p. 172.

28. Minogue, *Nationalism*, p. 32.

29. Ibid., p. 148.

30. B. Akzin, *State and Nation* (Hutchinson University Library, London, 1964).

31. Ibid., p. 83.

32. C. Geertz (ed.), *Old Societies and New States* (Free Press of Glencoe, Illinois, 1963), p. 119.

33. For a summary of his view, see *Nationalism and its Alternatives* (Alfred A. Knopf, New York, 1969).

34. H. Kohn, *The Idea of Nationalism* (Macmillan, New York, 1945), p. 10.

35. Ibid., p. 3.

36. Ibid., p. 19.

37. For a cogent attack on the nationalising impulse see E. Kedourie, *Nationalism* (Hutchinson University Library, London, 1966). This in turn has been closely criticised by A.D. Smith, *Theories of Nationalism* (Harper and Row, London, 1971).

38. Many theorists explicitly deny this, e.g. Smith, *Theories of Nationalism*, pp. 73-85. For a typical statement of the type I mean, see M. Mann, 'States, Ancient and Modern', *European Journal of Sociology*, vol. 18, no. 2 (1977), p. 262:

the relationship between State and Society in large-scale societies changed dramatically with the advent of industrial capitalism. Prior to that development, the State and the state bureaucracy played a substantially autonomous role *vis-à-vis* the class structure of civil society. After that its autonomy has been negligible: indeed, for most analytic purposes the State can be reduced to class structure.

39. See H. Davis, *Nationalism and Socialism: Marxist and Labor Theories of Nationalism to 1917* (Monthly Review Press, New York, 1967); M. Löwy, 'Marxists and the National Question', *New Left Review*, no. 96 (March-April 1976), pp. 81-100.

40. 'Critical Remarks on the National Question', *Collected Works* (Progress Publishers, Moscow, 1964), vol. 20, p. 27. Compare Stalin's *Marxism and the National Colonial Question* (Lawrence and Wishart, London, 1936).

41. Lenin, 'Critical Remarks on the National Question', p. 30.

42. Ibid., p. 35.

43. 'The Rights of Nations to Self-Determination', *Collected Works*, vol. 20, p. 401.

44. E.H. Carr, *Nationalism and After* (Macmillan, London, 1945), pp. 17-26.

45. T. Nairn, 'The Modern Janus', *New Left Review*, no. 94 (November-December 1975), p. 6.

46. Ibid., p. 15.

47. Ibid., p. 18.

48. M. Dunn, 'Marxism and the National Question', *Arena*, no. 4 (1975), p. 32.

49. H. Alavi, 'The State in Post-Colonial Societies: Pakistan and Bangladesh', *New Left Review*, no. 74 (1972), pp. 59-81.

50. Ibid., p. 62.

51. J. Saul, 'The State in Post-Colonial Societies: Tanzania', *Socialist Register* (1974), p. 352.

52. R. Murray, 'Second Thoughts on Ghana', *New Left Review*, no. 42 (1967); also C. Leys, 'The "Overdeveloped" Post Colonial State: a Re-evaluation', *Review of African Political Economy*, no. 5 (January-April 1976), pp. 45-6.

53. Leys, 'The "Overdeveloped" Post Colonial State', p. 48.

54. J. Saul, 'The Unsteady State: Uganda, Obote and Generalism', *Review of African Political Economy*, no. 5 (January-April 1976), pp. 12-38.

55. K. Marx and F. Engels, *The German Ideology* (Lawrence and Wishart, London, 1977), p. 57.

56. Ibid., p. 80.

57. Ibid., p. 53.

58. G. Lichtheim, *Marxism* (Routledge and Kegan Paul, London, 1964), p. 375.

59. F. Engels, *The Origin of the Family: Private Property and the State* (Charles H. Kerr, Chicago, 1902).

60. Lenin, 'The State and Revolution: the Marxist Theory of the State and the Tasks of the Proletariat in the Revolution', *Collected Works* (Progress Publishers, Moscow, 1964), vol. 25.

61. Ibid., p. 427.

62. R. Miliband, *The State in Capitalist Society* (Quartet Books, London, 1973), p. 51.

63. D. Gold *et al.*, 'Recent Developments in Marxist Theories of the Capitalist State', *Monthly Review*, vol. 27, no. 5 (October 1975), pp. 29-43.

64. See, for example, N. Poulantzas, *Political Power and Social Classes* (New Left Books, London, 1973), and his debate with Miliband, the original statement of which can be found in R. Blackburn (ed.), *Ideology in Social Sciences* (Fontana, London, 1972). Also E. Laclau, 'The Specificity of the Political: the Poulantzas-Miliband Debate', *Economy and Society*, vol. 4, no. 1 (February 1975), pp. 87-110.

Poulantzas specifically rejects the 'structuralist' label and the dichotomy as such in 'The Capitalist State: a Reply to Miliband and Laclau', *New Left Review*, no. 95 (January-February 1976), pp. 63-83.

65. A. Gramsci, *Selections from the Prison Notebooks* (Lawrence and Wishart, London, 1971); J. Joll, *Gramsci* (Fontana, London, 1971).

66. Gramsci, *Selections*, p. 244. Cf. on this point Laski's observation:

> Men cease to regard slavery as 'natural' as it becomes difficult, by its means, adequately to exploit those forces. The rights of women are transformed from a philosopher's eccentricity into claims socially recognised by the law when the relations of the productive process require that recognition. Education becomes a state-matter instead of one of purely private concern as soon as industry requires a corps of workers who can read and write (*The State in Theory and Practice*, pp. 114-15).

67. For further analyses along these lines see Gold *et al.*, 'Recent Developments in Marxist Theories of the Capitalist State', *Monthly Review*, vol. 27, no. 6 (November 1975), pp. 36-51. See also C.B. Macpherson, 'Do We Need a Theory of the State?', *European Journal of Sociology*, vol. 18, no. 2 (1977), pp. 223-44; B. Jessop, 'Recent Theories of the Capitalist State', *Cambridge Journal of Economics*, vol. 1, no. 4 (December 1977), pp. 352-73. Jessop distinguishes six classical themes: the state as a *parasitic* institution, as an *epiphenomenal* reflection of property relations and class struggle, as the *factor of cohesion* in a given society, as an *instrument of class rule*, as a *system of institutions* (where no general assumptions are made about its class character) and as a *system of political domination* (with specific effects on the class struggle). Additional themes are developed in J. Holloway and S. Picciotto (eds.), *State and Capital: a Marxist debate* (Edward Arnold, London, 1978), particularly their introductory essay 'Towards a Materialist Theory of the State' and that of C. von Braunmühl 'On the Analysis of the Bourgeois Nation State within the World Market Context'; and the pluralistic reply by C. Crouch (ed.), *State and Economy in Contemporary Capitalism* (Croom Helm, London, 1979).

68. G. van Benthem van den Bergh, 'The Interconnection between Processes of State Formation and Class Formation: Problems of Conceptualisation', Institute of Social Studies, The Hague, *Occasional Papers*, no. 52 (August 1972), p. 12.

5 CLASS

We can consider, as I have done above, state formation as a comparatively autonomous process, finding its modern form first in Western Europe, and then precipitating similar structures from social solutions around the world. We can also describe these entities and their derivatives as a single system, and discuss the transformation of that system as industrialisation and modernisation proceed apace.[1] The extraordinary pervasiveness of the transformation will still elude us, however, unless we confront it for what in considerable part it is, as constituting a radical change in the dominant mode of production with concomitant effects upon the social relations of all those involved, both locally and on a global scale. The advent of industry has made a profound difference to the material bases of modern life and there have been far-reaching effects. One of the most far-reaching, it seems to me, has been the advent of the collectivities most commonly categorised in terms of social 'class', in terms, that is, of class formation and various kinds of class action. Furthermore, this particular effect proceeds at both the level of the state as well as that of the world system and the world society it contains.

The basic questions are simple to ask, but they are extremely difficult adequately to answer: what is the relationship between industrialisation and modernisation and the pattern of human stratification? More particularly, what is the relationship between the formation of global classes and those of the separate states; and how do we assess both of these and their political consequences in the light of the development of a capitalist world economy?

Class

Human communities, almost without exception, are stratified, that is, we find them arranged in differentiated subgroups which their members evaluate, or we can evaluate analytically, as higher and lower with respect to some ordering principle like age, authority, or political or economic clout.[2] Characteristic of the modern milieu, however is stratification in terms of 'class', which I derive here as an ordering principle from the productive arrangements of industrial society at large.

It is possible to speak of contemporary 'class' orders in much more general terms as a functional consequence of the division of labour any society will make to survive.[3] By offering differential rewards such societies induce individuals to serve in those necessary capacities that might otherwise go unattended, the latter a state of affairs that would soon jeopardise the persistence of the whole. Societies thus evolve sorting devices in terms of valued incentives to ensure an adequate supply of personnel for the positions that must be filled if they are to be maintained. These rewards parallel the differential value placed upon the various roles that have to be performed, which issues in turn in a social hierarchy of them. In this view, social 'strata' constitute a vital aspect of any reasonably complex community, and social inequality is the means whereby society locates its members within the matrix of necessary communal roles.

Gerhard Lenski,[4] in one notable study, attempts to move beyond this functional approach to accommodate a more precise concept of classes and class conflict. He posits societal survival in terms of our need to share what we produce in maintaining those whose labour in turn sustains ourselves. Any surplus will be co-opted, he says, due to resource scarcity and human self-interest, by those in 'power'.[5] In this sense a class is any aggregate of individuals that we can locate at the same or similar distance from the focus of communal command, and since power is derived from several sources — political activity, wealth, occupation or ethnic identity, for example — we find in any particular society a number of ranking systems or hierarchies that persist side by side. Any individual may stand at one and the same time higher or lower in a political 'class' system, a property 'class' system, or an occupational, educational, age or sex 'class' system, each of which embodies its own discrete principle of distribution.[6] Each can on occasion conflict, and 'class' struggle pits these principles against each other in ways that reflect their varying importance and complexity, their span and shape, the amount of mobility within and hostility between them, and the degree to which they have been institutionalised. Depicting patterns of social stratification in this way, in terms of a multi-faceted distributive system, gives us a coherent general picture, it is argued, of several hierarchies arranged to diverse though still related effect.

W.G. Runciman has elaborated the distribution of power, which he denotes as differential access to and use of political privilege, in a not dissimilar way. He outlines six model systems — a class one (based on property ownership), an elite one (force and/or guile), a race type (ethnicity), a pluralist type (technical expertise), plus those either socialist (bureaucratic status) or revolutionary in style (role among leadership cadres) — each of which has its own discrete features with respect to its degree of concentration and cohesion, the turnover and recruitment of its elite, its justifying ideology and its 'achilles heel'.[7]

Note the way in which 'society' is reified here as a needful, problem-solving entity, and the strain towards an integrative theory of social stratification where specialised functions arise from an agreed sense of what is useful and good. Hierarchy is also seen to serve a beneficial purpose rather than a malignant or dysfunctional one. Criticisms of such an approach can be and have been made along both these lines (plus others). The approach does, however, attempt to account for that often inchoate sense that people in a particular place seem to possess of the relative worth of separate social roles, albeit in an abstracted and rather organismic way, and it does confront the concept, more or less widely shared, that the communal order is somehow harmonious and just. Significant problems remain. The value placed upon differential rewards is a social one. Individuals learn it and develop it *in situ*. It is highly pertinent then to know just who defines the useful and the good and to what ends. Furthermore, a sense of the justice and harmony of a particular set of social arrangements can also fail. We need a notion of stratification that accounts for more than mere social competition for scarce resources and power, that accounts for the disintegrative potential — no less creative in the long run perhaps — that social hierarchies seem to possess beside their integrative one.[8]

We need, in other words, a more immediate appreciation of the impact of industrialisation and modernisation. As our emphasis drifts towards job descriptions, towards ranked orders of occupational importance and prestige, we lose our sense of coalitions of control built directly upon the material order and the industrial means of production. We lose sight of any evidence of a ruling collectivity or class behind the plural display of diffracted groups. To re-establish the second perspective, the traditional understanding of stratification as a 'system of structured inequality',[9] we need to reconsider the work of Karl Marx, who in his scholarly attempts to account for the class-forming capacities of contemporary capitalism prompted a much broader understanding of the way the material life of humankind generates characteristic social groupings.

Marx depicted societies as progressively polarised — an expression of deep conflicts and contradictions that could only be resolved once they had been transcended by new ways of producing and relating — and he gave the concept of class *conflict* special prominence beside that of class *formation*. His own concept of class, however, rather curiously given the importance it possessed in his scheme of things, has to be culled from the corpus of his work as a whole, or from the work of more or less faithful followers like Bukharin or Lenin.[10] He did not invent it as a socio-

logical category to describe socio-economic aggregates, nor was he alone
in fastening upon class formations or the conflict between class formations as significant social events. He made this disclaimer himself. What
he did do, however, was to draw a straight line between the way material
wealth is produced and the sort of social divisions societies display. These
social divisions inevitably lead, he argued, to conflict; to the ultimate
demise of the system they divide and the ultimate demise of classes
themselves.

To Marx, a class was a group that shared identifiable economic concerns. One either owned the means of production or one did not, and
any society could be seen to fall into these two components.[11] This was
an objective distinction that stood on its own terms. Classes were also,
however, he argued, groups subjectively aware of themselves as such,
consciously sharing particular outlooks and special interests and cognisant of their comparative and relative class locale; this awareness reaching its fullest expression in political action against another class (the 'an
sich/für sich' dichotomy).[12] Class interests could always be determined
by reference to productive processes and the relations of authority they
predisposed. These obtained regardless of any differences between individual class members. And at its simplest the pursuit of a class interest
was 'the effort of classes to increase their share in the distribution of
the total mass of products'[13] (though Marx also emphasised the psychologically alienating effects for the proletariat in particular of working
under the demeaning conditions of the industry of his day). Such interests
could only be effectively expressed when members of the human
aggregate who carried out the same sort of productive tasks had been
concentrated in cities, had learned to communicate readily with each
other, and had become aware of themselves as a class and of the deprivation explicit in their collective plight.

In all this Marx was concerned primarily to explain not social stratification as such, but social change in terms of evolving social structures,
hence his propensity to reduce the class complexities of the real world
to a dialectic confrontation between two of them, a model that had
more to do with the heuristic statement of ideal types than the strict
representation of any particular society.[14] Politically Marx was concerned with the contradictory forces at work in the advanced capitalist
societies he found about him. The bourgeoisie, a progressive force in a
feudal context, became a reactionary one, he said, when it fell to realising
the potential of its own mode of manufacture and exchange. An excess
of productive endeavour engendered cyclical crises. The bourgeoisie then
strove to limit productive capacity, or to exploit it by expanding markets

and modes of *de*struction, but they could only postpone the date of their ultimate demise. Capitalism was fundamentally irrational due to the basic contradiction between the way it produced goods and how it was organised socially to do so — through private ownership of the means of production and the competitive pursuit of profit where labour and a market were comparatively 'free'.

The Marxist approach has met, as one might expect, with sustained criticism.[15] First, we find the political point that the notion of historical necessity it sustains, especially in the hands of those wielding absolute power, all too readily allows personal revelation to become public oppression. Apprehension on this point is amply served by reference to the Stalinist regime and any other such attempt dogmatically to realise what are ostensibly social scientific predictions. Secondly, the predictions themselves have been declared untenable. The material capacity of modern industry has proved so prodigious, it is claimed, that the workers in the developed societies have been spared the mental and physical impoverishment Marx saw as their inevitable lot. The bourgeoisie has become more open rather than closed, and the dramatic process of dichotomisation — on the state level at least — that prompted the Messianic aspect of the Marxist vision, has failed to take place. (I shall consider the global prospect in a moment.) Thus the groups between the proletariat and the bourgeoisie have not suffered the polarising effects of maturing capitalism, though this may be as much because of a change in their composition as anything else. Marx saw in advanced capitalist societies a *middle* class of self-employed capitalists. This group has in fact significantly declined, as Marx thought it would, only to be replaced by a stratum of bureaucrats, officials and diverse white-collar types.[16]

It is a further general criticism that the scope for political intervention is now much greater than that apparent in Marx's day:

In situations where the political authorities can overtly and effectively change the class structure; where the privileges that are most essential for social status, including that of a higher share in the national income, are conferred by a decision of the political authorities, where a large part or even the majority of the population is included in a stratification of the type to be found in a bureaucratic hierarchy — the nineteenth-century concept of class becomes more or less an anachronism, and class conflicts give way to other forms of social antagonism.[17]

Ralf Dahrendorf has argued, in like vein, that the 'post-capitalist' societies of the advanced world today have successfully managed to dissociate 'industry' from its social context. The social relations of industry and the conflicts arising from them have been encapsulated and institutionalised within the larger political rubric, and deprived thus of their primary effects on society as a whole; the patterns of industrial and political conflict, while still closely related, are no longer superimposed one upon the other; the antagonists of industrial society — capital and labour — can no longer be considered at one glance in terms of a proletariat coming to confront a bourgeoisie.[18]

Attempts have been made on the other hand to extend rather than refute Marxist analysis. Given a definition of class in terms of the ownership of property, for example, we can re-introduce the functionalist account of the comparative precedence various occupations command in the social market. The hierarchy of occupations is the 'backbone of the class structure, and indeed of the entire reward system of modern Western society',[19] a vertebrate member that could eventually come to articulate the world. We might also note attempts to complement class analysis with such concepts as race,[20] ethnicity, and most important of all, 'status'. Thus Max Weber, in his well known treatment of the latter theme,[21] attempted to supplement the Marxist approach by giving separate credence as components of communal power to 'parties', and more especially to ranked systems of social prestige. 'Class', he argued, was an expression of the economic order of a society, which is a materialist conception in the Marxist sense of 'property' versus 'lack of property'. Unlike Marx, though, he stressed relative social control over the distribution and use of economic goods and services rather than production *per se*, and class situation as ultimately a market one. 'Status' he derived from the social order, the distribution of 'honor' made manifest by particular life-styles and the way in which goods are consumed, a system of stratification that may petrify in time into castes. 'Classes' he did not consider as communalistic aggregates, but 'status' groups, however amorphous, were conscious in and of themselves. They did not need, as in the case of class, to seek definition in terms of their action against other groups.

Class distinctions and status distinctions remained, in Weber's view, separable in analysis and in fact,[22] but they were also linked and they moved across each other in patterned ways. Thus:

When the bases of the acquisition and distribution of goods are relatively stable, stratification by status is favoured. Every technological repercussion and economic transformation threatens stratification by status [however] and pushes the class situation into the foreground. Epochs and countries in which the naked class situation is of predominant significance are regularly the periods of technological and economic transformations.[23]

Given the fact that in our present epoch we are witnessing the most extensive technological and economic transformation in the history of the human enterprise, a transformation now of global extent, we might expect by this assessment to find class formation and conflicts of class interest very much to the fore.

Global Stratification: the Pluralist Paradigm

To the 'pluralist', in the paradigmatic sense in which I have used the term, we best view the world as one where more or less sovereign states compete to realise their various interests with whatever resources their leaders can command. Here class analysis does not impinge. States can be ranked, like the people within them, as social units possessing particular general attributes of an economic, political or social sort.[24] We can compare, for example, the size of their populations, both urban and rural, or their military expenditure and armed capacity, or their past prestige, or the number of diplomatic missions they host in their capital, or the extent of popular literacy, or industrial or agricultural productivity as measured by components of GNP or income *per capita*, and so on.

Gustavo Lagos, for example, in a typical essay of this sort, treats states as interacting entities within a total social system and ranks them with reference to their economic stature, power and prestige. When we map out the rankings required, however, we are confronted with an apparent discontinuity, a radical inequality between rich states and poor ones. This fact is at variance with the ideology of a pluralist world, which is rather more egalitarian and grants the same status, formally at least, to all constituent sovereign states. This sense of discrepancy Lagos calls 'atimia',[25] and most poor states, he asserts, are engaged in reducing it, in securing enhanced real status through economic development. The newer ones must do this at a considerable disadvantage since they enter a system that is already highly stratified, and they must make their way in the face of dominant and often highly domineering countries that condition what progress they might make at every point.

This system may manifest different tendencies. Thus Johan Galtung, in what he terms a 'structural' theory of imperialism (though his analysis proceeds from pluralist premises), identifies an exploitative pattern of vertical interaction in the world where differences in productive processing levels permit dominant states to collude, while peripheral ones must proceed in domestic disarray.[26] Alternatively, top-dog states may feud among themselves, seeking allies and reasons for ideological support from strata lower down. There are, in fact, a number of analogous situations that obtain like this in domestic societies, which may be applied internationally to heuristic effect.[27]

Global Inequality

The schematics of the pluralist picture are comparatively clear. In gross terms, as industrialisation has developed and spread, a growing proportion of the human race has received higher incomes.[28] If we take the poorest forty states, however, we find the one-quarter of mankind that dwells within generating less than 5 per cent of the GNP of the quarter that lives in developed sectors of the Western and Soviet-bloc worlds.[29] The latter regions account for more than three-quarters of the world's state-reckoned income.[30] In an era of unprecedented expansion in the human capacity to manufacture and distribute material goods, we find poverty on a massive scale. The residual category of 'less developed' states is a disadvantaged one too (an ambiguous exception being the OPEC countries), though not to quite this heinous extent.

Patterns of global industrialisation have tended to exacerbate rather than alleviate this situation, since the industrial sectors of poor states tend to be peripheral components of rich ones, tied to rich state technologies and economic interests.[31] Looking closer we discover, however, that the plight of the population of poor states is not all of a piece. In the typical case of a subsistence agrarian economy, growth in one modernised fraction of it has very uneven results. The income of 5 per cent of the people, those who constitute the dominant economic elite, rises dramatically. That of the poorest 60 per cent declines, as does that of the middle 20 per cent, though less so. For the worst off — the majority of poor state citizens — the relative *and* absolute disadvantages of economic growth take a generation at least to begin to reverse, unless there is specific governmental intervention to effect some sort of socio-economic rescue through policies which promote income distribution rather than expansion alone. Economic modernisation shifts income distribution towards the upper end of the sociological scale (most commonly 'ruling coalitions of expatriate businessmen and indigenous property owners') and there is 'no automatic, or even likely, trickling down of the benefits of economic growth to the poorest segments of the population in low-income countries'.[32] Their position thus deteriorates *absolutely*.

Why should this be so? What are the socio-economic mechanisms that operate to such deleterious effect? The systematic analysis of stratified rankings for states as a whole, on whatever dimension we care to nominate, does not allow of the discussion of the sort of domestic dimensions just described. Nor does it explain such rankings in terms of the most pertinent socio-economic forces that persist today. We can cite differential historical opportunity, derived perhaps from the largely fortuitous endowment or lack of it of intellectual and material riches and the comparative advantage such differences bestow, but we are provided with little else of explanatory as opposed to descriptive value by such a point of view. We need a different perspective that makes more sense than this of the processes at work.

Only if we shift our analytic focus from the states and groupings of the pluralist paradigm and the world system to a view of world society as a whole can we begin to appreciate the extent to which 'political boundaries are not always coterminous with the boundaries of production systems'.[33] If in our analysis we distinguish between 'regions or areas *within* a system of production (even though these areas are politically bounded) and the boundaries of the system of production itself'; if we define the perimeter of a production system by the scope of its division of labour; then we can see the industrial system of production as an extensive one, encompassing in turn the multiplicity of states, which is a perspective that has important analytical consequences. We begin to see, albeit dimly, the productive workings of this world economy affecting both the comparative ranking of states in *pluralist* parlance, *and* the stratification patterns within them and between them in a *structuralist* sense as well.

How are these effects produced? Fundamentally, by virtue of the fact that the world economy operates as a system of production as a whole, in such a way as to generate and sustain patterns of stratification that allow different states, and different classes within states, preferential control over the productive process. This makes for 'dependency' and disadvantaged states, which exhibit a different class structure from dominant or intermediate ones. Privileged liaison elites, their interests most commonly centred upon the export of raw materials and the regulation of trade, turn to core states, and tend to detach themselves in important ways from the peripheral sectors of their own populations. In the metropoles on the other hand, where manufacturing capacities have resulted in far more egalitarian class conditions, the same degree of domestic inequality does not occur.

Global Stratification: the Structuralist Paradigm — 'Imperialism'

I am reaching here, of course, for an explanation of global inequality
and subsequently global stratification patterns, both international and
domestic, in terms of past and contemporary 'imperialism' — my own
response to the simultaneous appearance in history of 'great and dramatic forces' and the inevitable feeling that they are causally related
somehow.[34] States are not only unequal (which is a fact of life) but
their inequalities are reproduced by a specific process of subjugation in
patterns that bear very close scrutiny.

'Imperialism' is a complex concept that can be evoked in several
different ways.[35] It has been used very broadly to describe any act by
one people that tries to impose its collective will on another, and in
this sense it refers to every attempt, explicit or implicit, economic,
political or military, to establish or retain formal control over subordinate societies.[36] Such control can be very subtle and it is an important
part of the subject to determine just how close to informal influence the
imperial process can come and still remain effective. Since the Industrial
Revolution, however, many analysts have fastened upon *economic* factors, taking their cue from the productive forces at work in the world
and their varied socio-political effects. World society emerges in this
view not as a consequence of 'power' relations or decision-making
routines or the rest of the paraphernalia of a traditional approach, but
as a function of or reaction to the world economy. And the early
explanations of imperialism in terms of the pursuit of plunder, prestige,
or cultural or religious predominance are reshaped in ways that emphasise material factors and concomitant social forms.

History is rewritten to oblige the new view. With the advent of the
great European empires from the sixteenth century on, with the growth
of a world market system, capitalist in construction, and more particularly with the hasty grab for land by the European powers at the end
of the nineteenth century, a significant development is seen to have
taken place.

> The merchants, adventurers, financiers, and sovereigns . . . set out on
> an international quest for gold, spices, and new lands, but the really
> important discoveries were made at home. Superficially, the expansion
> of foreign trade and the growth of merchant and finance capital
> resulted, along with other factors, in the disintegration of the traditional
> non-market domestic economy and the setting free of labor from its pre-
> capitalist forms of production. This newly-created wage-labor force,

when harnessed by industrial capital first into manufacturing, then into modern industry, unleashed an explosion in productivity that provided society with an entirely new material basis for its existence and ushered in the modern world.[37]

The process was complex and difficult; merchant capital vying with industrial capital, for example, the former promoting new modes of production in the periphery while serving as often as not to sustain pre-capitalist political and economic systems, to secure its place and to constrain the proletarianising preferences of the latter.[38]

The part played by 'the state' was a critical one throughout, for countries that failed to reconstruct their own societies and effect a primitive accumulation of capital fell victim on the whole to those that did not fail to do so. The whole system's propensity to expand and then contract, and the social effect of populations siphoning into manufacturing centres and towns and mobilising politically in their own interests generated much more elaborate political mechanisms and reinforced the development of focused regimes. Pushed by their own momentum, or pulled by a host of opportunities, by cheap raw materials and cheap and docile labour supplies, new markets and opportunities to invest to advantage, industrialised capitalist states grafted their vigorous capacities on to the root stock of a large part of the rest of the world (a root stock as often as not already warped by metropolitan practices) and in their highly dynamic way prompted the social structures both between and within states that have come to divide rich and poor. In this sense the 'underdeveloped' components in the system are every bit as contemporary as the 'modern' and 'developed' ones.[39] The genesis of the 'widening gap' has been an extended one, and its convolutions are the consequences of past practices that now reach wide and deep.

Many keen minds have confronted this phenomenon and tried to unpack its well-springs and motive power.[40] Hobson, Hilferding, Luxemburg, Lenin, Bauer, Bukharin, Kautsky and Schumpeter are all names that come immediately to mind, all having placed their own particular emphasis on the fundamental factors involved — the imperatives of finance capital versus those of industrial capital, for example, or the relative effects of underconsumption and overproduction. On the whole, those of a Marxist persuasion have cleaved closest to the line that modern imperialism is an expression of modern capitalism, particularly in its present 'monopolistic' phase, and that as long as capitalism remains a dominant world force, imperialism will too. The general principle was expressed by Bukharin thus:

For a consistent Marxist, the entire development of capitalism is nothing but a process of a continuous reproduction of the contradictions of capitalism on an ever wider scale. The future of world economy, as far as it is a capitalist economy, will not overcome its inherent lack of adaptation on an ever wider scale.[41]

In this form the connection does not exclude the notion of imperialism as a deliberate political or military ploy, pervasive in the past or emerging once again in the future. However, in equating the two so closely, Marxists have generally looked to the latter persisting with the former, finally to pass in revolutionary fashion. The demise of the capitalist system would in this sense be both necessary *and* sufficient to end imperialism— a proposition that has occasioned much debate and is, indeed, highly debatable.

Even within the Marxist camp, the range of opinion is a broad one. Luxemburg saw imperialism as a consequence of an acute propensity for capitalist economies to over-produce (or underconsume) and the felt need as a result to secure markets for export goods that did not exist at home. Capitalist states must increase the extent of their geographic range, she said, in competition with others if need be, to capture what they cannot achieve by more intensive means within their own boundaries. Once it had exhausted these resources, capitalism would collapse; though socialist revolution ought to pre-empt that event.

Lenin likewise defined imperialism exclusively in terms of capitalist expansion—capitalism here in its highest stage, having passed into the hands of monopolists and financiers. This particular definition he built upon Hilferding's, who in his book of the same name singled out 'finance capital' (a term Marx had formulated) and the key role of the banks as the hyphen between the two. Unlike industrialists who tend to seek free trade, Hilferding argued, financiers prefer capital concentrated, centralised and domestically secure behind tariff walls. Their exclusivist interests extend to colonies too, where surplus capital can be invested under the protection of the state.

Bukharin, who paraphrased the same thesis, saw in this as Marx had before him the fundamental cause of a radical global division:

It follows that world capitalism, the world system of production, assumes in our times the following aspect: a few consolidated, organised economic bodies ('the great civilised powers') on the one hand, and a periphery of underdeveloped countries with a semi-agrarian or agrarian system on the other.[42]

Kautsky also saw finance capital (closely linked to industrial capital) and the urge to export it as seminal, but he was less convinced than Lenin that the system as a whole was incapable of reforming itself, and in fact he suggested the possibility of transnational collusion between imperialist powers in their efforts to manage exploitation on a global scale. Bauer went further and saw colonies as a relative necessity at best, emphasising what he saw as capitalism's revisionist capacity to sustain itself on more intensive terms.

At this point on the analytic continuum we move to liberal scholars like Hobson who, in common with those sharing a Marxist perspective, saw modern imperialism as a direct consequence of the excess of capital and productive power that accumulates in advanced industrial economies, and the urge that arises, through competition for profit, to dispense with the surplus. Unlike the Marxists (except Bauer), however, he found nothing intrinsic about the imperial solution as such. By redistributing the power to consume, by raising workers' wages and legislating to eliminate the capacity of the bourgeoisie to over-save, the business cycle of boom and bust could be broken and the pressure for imperialistic expansion relieved: 'It is not industrial progress', he said, 'that demands the opening up of new markets and areas of investment, but maldistribution of consuming power which prevents the absorption of commodities and capital within the country.'[43]

Josef Schumpeter went to the other extreme and divorced imperialism from capitalism altogether, defining the former as the 'rational and objectless disposition on the part of a state to unlimited forcible expansion',[44] and specifically excluding any concept of class interest in favour of an anachronistic 'instinct' psychologically to dominate and cause wars. Clear in the historical case of the 'people's imperialism' of a warrior state, for example, or the personal whim of self-aggrandising sovereigns, such an instinct was originally derived, he argued, from the social struggle to survive. It had persisted, largely redundant, into a later age, though it was still obviously capable of serving the interests of particular groups: 'It is an ativism in the social structure, in individual, psychological habits of emotional reaction.'[45] Given that the original grounds on which it had grown no longer existed, Schumpeter said, imperialism is doomed to disappear. In an increasingly democratic, individual and rational age, traditional instincts had no place; and a 'purely capitalist world . . . can offer no fertile soil to imperialist impulses'.[46] Capitalism being 'by nature anti-imperialistic', capitalists could only be at most the allies of those making for imperial policies, those, that is, who have inherited the autocratic state and would further its essentially pre-capitalist designs. All of which is quite at variance with the Marxist view, where capitalist ruling classes are seen to be directly responsible for reactionary policies: where superstructural repression and growing grievances are the logical result.

The sort of arguments used above are open to criticism on both methodological and empirical grounds;[47] they have been variously categorised as either fallacious or beside the point.[48] The heart of the debate is the question whether imperialism is a matter of necessity or choice; an act of policy or an ineluctable stage through which capitalism is obliged in some deterministic way to pass before its ultimate collapse. The impulse of non-Marxists has been to do two things — to separate political and economic affairs and to hold them separate for analytic purposes, allowing overlap only under particular circumstances or for particular events. And in a related fashion, they deny the matter of inevitability; the quality of 'this-therefore-that' where economy and policy do connect. In particular they see capitalism for all its dog-eat-dog characteristics as a basically co-operative enterprise, and the division of labour as evidence of an intrinsic harmony at work.[49] It is *political* competition that leads to conflict, they say, that then exploits whatever means, including economic ones, it can turn to account. It is in this way that politics and economics, capitalism and imperialism become confused. Modern empires have done '[no] more than call upon the most effective economic system that has yet existed to lend them support'.[50] And sustaining this general impulse is the sense that capitalism is not a specific concept but a generic one, germane to many historical systems; hence the *industrial* capitalism Marx analysed in its nineteenth-century English context and depicted as typical of capitalism at large is not the transitory phenomenon he considered it to be, but much more pervasive and likely to persist.

To sophisticated Marxists the dichotomisation of economy and polity is a vulgar reduction of the much more subtle instrument of historical materialism, and they rightly resist critiques that adopt this device. Likewise the sort of multidimensional analysis that accords some sort of combined significance to them both, plus whatever is felt to be relevant from factors of a social or philosophic kind. I am also not sure that it provides much solace to argue that capitalists do not *have* to behave in exploitative ways, that they simply *prefer* to do so, like 'water seeking its own level . . . [looking] out the paths of least resistance to profit — the most lucrative markets and investment opportunities, the least costly sources of raw materials'.[51] The line of least resistance (and maximum return) drawn across the last four hundred years by sharp capitalist practice may still lead to the inequalities apparent today. If despite the evidence of gross asymmetry the poor are not condemned to perpetual exploitation by such a global economy; if there is nothing inherent about the system that says they must remain so deprived; why have they done so when possibilities exist for alleviating such circumstances? What emasculates their countervailing power?

'The Internationalisation of Capital'

Though the present-day world is in many ways a different one from that discussed above, the terms of this debate still persist. With the formal dissolution of direct European dominance 'empire' has receded as a public enterprise. The resources/trade/investment equation is variously seen to permit an informal 'neo-colonialism' or 'neo-imperialism', however, that has taken up where more immediate control has been relinquished or lost. The internationalisation of capital has continued, with opinion still divided on the implications of this for the inequalities that separate the rich and the poor, and particularly for its effects on the internationalisation of patterns of employment (labour), and the capacity of the system as a whole for reform.

The great engines of expansion are no longer just governments; we have to account now for transnational corporations and the competition between them, and for their capital requirements as a group, a phenomenon which has created an integrated global market of quite a new kind.[52] This process implicates socialist states as well as capitalist ones.[53] At the same time the dynamic modernising sectors of poor states have been significantly internationalised by the corporations through their control of commercial technology, which they have used with considerable success to restructure external and internal markets to profitable ends, and palpable socio-political effects too. Poor countries constitute a considerable reservoir of surplus labour, with large and conveniently aggregated urban populations consuming comparatively little in the way of services and food, schooled to industrial purposes at least, and eager to work and earn. Transnational corporations are turning to this supply more and more. One ever-present tendency is for state-centric competition between the big firms to be sublimated by their need for oligopolistic understandings on global terms. At the same time we have seen the growth of a capital market within the world economy as such, a development that continues to enhance the common concern of otherwise disparate states in maintaining the corporate system.

The great pull of this system toward international class consciousness on the part of capital can be illustrated by the ambivalence of the successful industrial capitalist in underdeveloped countries. In the short run he may find it better to remain independent of international capital and continue his successful challenge, but his long-run interest often lies elsewhere;[54]

as the local representative of some transnational enterprise with all its technical capacities and commercial reach, plus the privileges that accrue from foreign status in the domestic arena itself.

The convergence that occurs within corporate structures becomes more visible towards the top: 'At the bottom . . . labour is divided into many nationalities. As one proceeds up the pyramid, nationality becomes more homogeneous and increasingly more European,' an international division of labour that keeps 'the head separate from the hand, and each hand separate from each other'.[55] Which makes for hierarchy, not equality; for cohesive cores, however competitive, and diffused peripheries. We might go so far as to posit a transnational class consisting of those who manage transnational conglomerates;[56] to the extent that they serve to perpetuate rich state hegemony they serve to perpetuate neo-imperialism.[57] We should not lose sight at the same time of the extent to which transnational corporations remain state-based. The quality of their multinational endeavour often resides more in the scope of their operations, and in their capacity to cross state boundaries to maximise the profits of their subsidiaries as a group, than in the class patterns just adduced.

The foreign personnel who staff overseas subsidiaries constitute none the less an important and comparatively denationalised sector of the local bourgeoisie. As the 'managerial' fraction of that class they can play an important part in promoting transnational cohesion. 'It may be enlightening in this regard to think of the worldwide corporate and managerial bourgeoisie as a class in formation and the transnational corporation as the key instrument in this developmental process.'[58] Corporate internationalism appears in these terms as a growing social entity with shared class concerns;[59] the corporate bourgeoisie of the industrial capitalist economies joining with 'managerial' groups of businessmen, professionals, politicians and bureaucrats in the non-industrialised states to promote conglomerate profits and national growth defined as 'development' for defensive purposes at home, and as 'progress' abroad.

Apart from those merely puzzled, many see this as all to the good, and transnational enterprise with its class-forming capacities as the next step in the global process of political evolution. The nation-state, they argue, has proved too narrow and constricted an institution to accommodate modern modes of production and the large-scale manufacturing and marketing units that a revolution in transport and communications has made possible. A truly rational world order should not have to wait upon its separate state sectors and the need, whether by co-option, seduction, subversion, threat or force, to obtain their permission to proceed. Others are more guarded in their acclaim, though unlike the Marxists and neo-Marxists they are fairly readily convinced of the utility and desirability of such conglomerates, as well as the inevitability of their global presence. On balance, they would say, transnationals have had beneficial effects for all concerned, and they perceive no threat in the fact that within a very few years much of the world trade will pass through the hands of only 300 companies, of which 200 are housed in one country, the United States. The political and social costs are outweighed, they feel, by the enormous potential of such groups for generating material progress. Thus Samuel Huntingdon sees a place for both the state and the corporation, and indeed, where states begin to disintegrate, he argues, transnational entities, including those of a corporate kind, may serve to hold them together because of the links they can use to support the dangling pieces.[60] One might wonder how benign or benevolent this supportive purpose would be, but the case can be made even stronger than he puts it. State and corporation are actually complementary, convinced protagonists argue, and standing outside the state system, fundamentally disinterested in sovereignty, the trans-state corporations and other such entities are the only ones likely in the end to be able to transcend it.

Regardless of our polemical preferences in the above debate the internationalisation of capital has clearly helped shape, where it does not directly provide, the contemporary programme of industrialisation in the Third World. And we cannot understand the social formations this latter and increasingly significant process generates without acknowledging the influence of the corporations, and the patterns they predispose within the structure of North-South relations as a whole.

'Social Formations in the Centre'

None of this should be allowed to obscure the differences apparent between centres of transnational capital themselves, as well as the conflicts implicit and explicit between the rich capitalist states and between them and core socialist countries (differences which it would do well not to exaggerate in turn).[61] It is common to argue that the difference it makes, in terms of social structure at least, of having a totalitarian political regime as opposed to one that merely supplements a market is decisive. In the former stratification patterns are one instrument of policy itself; in the latter planned political intervention is combined with the effect of economic forces in a much more confused way.

The point is easily overdone, however. The class structures of the rich market societies bear many similarities to each other and to those of 'developed socialist' states, a fact that bears witness to the common denominator of their industrial base. The property-owners who exist in the one do not in the other; the distinctions between manual and non-manual workers are far less acute in socialist states, while a discrete intelligentsia is more in evidence there. But public control of production by members of the Communist Party, through the bureaucracy, has made for 'bourgeois' preponderance just as effectively as in the more privatised systems of the West. It remains to be seen how closed the socialist version becomes if and when the opportunities for mobility by special promotion grow more restricted and begin to turn more upon the influence of the family and patron-client relations than upon such recruitment mechanisms as political loyalty ('redness') or education ('expertise').[62] In terms of privilege and reward, in terms of their own definition of social class as a relation to the process of production, the 'new class' of 'bureaucratic collectivists'[63] is very much in evidence in the Soviet state and its satellites, and more and more in China as well, however amenable this group has been to members moving into it from beneath, and however subordinate to party control.[64] In Marxist terms, too, class consciousness may develop more readily in 'socialist' states simply because the source of occupational promotion and material return, that is, the party and the bureaucratic state, is more evident as such than under capitalism, where it requires a rather abstract understanding of the structure of the system before its class-bound character comes clear.

Industrial societies require particular skills if they are to prevail. We can see in both East and West that a ranking of occupations relates directly to the relative importance placed upon specific occupations, since valued industrial skills tend to receive more both materially and in terms of social regard than disvalued ones. Thus, 'those in professional and managerial positions are allocated a more favourable share of resources than are manual labourers primarily because they command the type of skills whose scarcity-value furnishes them with the power to stake larger claims,'[65] a position that in their own self-interest they may actively attempt to preserve. This is modified somewhat by other social influences, and in the East it is subject to party-political power, but the correspondence holds. Whether we divide those who own and control productive resources like factories and land from those who do not, or extend this division to the formal and informal political dominance that Marxists would argue accompanies it, we have still to account for hierarchies of this functional kind which industrialisation makes possible and helps to sustain wherever it abides.

'Dependencia'

Corresponding patterns of domestic dominance and dependence are paralleled by, where they do not directly derive from, similar structures in the wider world. Following the lead given by the neo-Marxist/neo-Leninist literature on imperialism referred to above, these patterns have been given very specific scrutiny by the 'dependencia' analysts, whose insights, originally derived to explain the persistence of 'underdevelopment' in Latin America, have now been generalised to describe and explain socio-economic inequalities in other regions as well.[66]

Their central emphasis falls upon the pre-emptive effects that the international environment has for national late-comers, and the more or less typical dimensions of that influence. There is less of a sense of a response in this view to some internally engendered 'crisis of capitalism', like the 'falling rate of profit' or 'underconsumption' for example, which animates on the whole the analysis of 'imperialism'. There is more of the notion — often contradicting the 'neo-imperial' approach — of a tendency (it need not be a law) for capital to accumulate in centres of rapid advancement and power, exacerbating poverty at the complementary social pole by whole systemic means.[67]

As those who talk of neo-colonialism are wont to emphasise, a 'dependent' state knows an 'unacceptable' degree of political influence. 'Unacceptability' can be understood in various ways, in terms, for example, of the symmetry of the relationship it refers to, how systematic this seems to be, the various functions it serves (beneficial between core states perhaps, but exploitative between rich and poor), and how 'alien' the received political forms and practices feel. 'Dependent' states are seen to be debilitated by economic disadvantages too, manifest in terms of a lack of trained personnel, or elite consumption patterns derived from those of the metropoles, of an undiversified productive capacity controlled in large part by foreign capital anyway and usually concentrated in particularly important sectors like mining and agriculture. These debilitating influences limit in turn the potential for a nationally beneficial programme of industrial growth. The whole syndrome reflects one of acute handicap that persists, where it is not the practical result of, a historic and continuing relationship of 'unequal exchange'.

A generation ago Paul Baran argued, in Marxist terms, that the general effect of European imperialism in colonial countries had been to preserve the domain of merchant capitalism at the expense of the development of the industrial sort.[68] A.G. Frank went further to depict linked channels of exploitation, stretching from the hinterland of poor Latin American states through their provincial towns to their state capitals, and thence to the great commercial and manufacturing centres of the world.[69] These channels have effectively run off much of the economic surplus that might otherwise have been available to support self-reliant development, he argued, and have led instead to the *overall* underdevelopment of the satellite states. Where development *has* occurred it is only a reflection of the expansion of another dominant and in this sense independent political economy, a pattern of growth that forwards the commercial interests of the over-dog rather than those more general social needs of the dog underneath.[70] A 'comprador' class facilitates the flow of primary exports and the promotion of specific and subordinate industries in its own material interests, in collusion with, where they have not already been co-opted by, the bureaucratic machineries of state.

A similar picture is sketched by Samir Amin and others for Africa too. Amin distinguishes two basic patterns of capital accumulation and of economic and social development, one that takes place at the global centres 'characterised by the dominance of economic activity to satisfy mass consumer needs and the consequent demand for production goods', and the other that occurs in the dependent peripheries 'dominated by production of luxury goods and exports and the consequent lack of importance of internal mass markets'. In the latter case this accompanies

> inequality, technological dependence, political weakness among the oppressed—in sum, marginalisation. Restructuring of these economies requires a break with the international economy, and self-centred development which establishes the dominance of production for mass needs, though there are particular difficulties for individual countries attempting such a break and ultimately a solution can be found only if such changes take place internationally.[71]

The process of colonialisation, as elsewhere, destroyed much of the pre-existing infrastructure and the intracontinental links that joined region to region.

One can see how the re-shaping of Africa into an externally oriented, dependent economy was carved into the very geography of the continent by coastal concentration and development and by the simultaneous impoverishment of the interior. The resulting massive migration has in its turn further accentuated regional disparities. Furthermore, political balkanisation, rooted in the process of unequal dependent peripheral development, has created the conditions for smaller 'sub-imperialist units' within a system which on the whole, is dependent.[72]

A like process has prevailed, it is variously claimed, in South-East Asia too.

Johan Galtung[73] posits this mechanism as the result of differences in levels of processing—poor states exporting primary products that are returned to them by the rich plus a log of attendant costs, the latter having benefited also from the effects that processing produces because of its demand for social skills and other technical supports. This argument becomes weaker as poor states grow more industrialised, and there are important exceptions to it as a universal explanation of dominance and dependence.[74] The effects of industrialisation are particularly difficult to discern. On the one hand we find those impressed by the extent of the diffusion of capital and technology into poor states and its socio-economic consequences in calling forth indigenous middle classes. State sovereignty, furthermore, has given political regimes a greater capacity to exploit rich state differences to local advantage; a plausible degree of autonomy can be and has been used to enhance national economies at the expense of imperialistic intervention of all kinds. On the other hand, measured growth rates do not necessarily denote development, since assessed *per capita* rather than state by state the progress made is very unimpressive. Furthermore, poor state industry is, to an important degree, an 'assembly plant' enterprise, and a very different affair from that taking place in the metropoles. It usually proceeds to the detriment of poor state agriculture too, unlike in the rich states where 'industrialisation' has been applied to primary production as well as to the secondary sort. All of which tends to result in a different pattern of class formation with its own inhibiting effects.

A handful of poor states, it is true, are doing notably better now and better by no mean proportion of their citizens; the majority are doing badly, however, and that majority contains a large proportion of the population of the world.

This sort of poverty, the result in considerable part of foreign capitalisation that ignores national needs, can have independent structural consequences of its own. Aghiri Emmanuel, for example, has attempted to demonstrate how being poor generates a discrete logic that only deepens one's plight.[75]

> The advanced countries are nowadays too rich not to be able to absorb themselves, without difficulty, all the new capital that is formed in them, and the underdeveloped countries are too poor to offer attractive investment prospects to this same capital . . . All this, in turn, keeps them poor, or makes them even poorer.[76]

Capital is placed by those who have it where it works to most profitable effect. Labour, however, is not so portable (though its migration continues on a notable scale). Global wage-rate differentials and the tendency for rates of pay in poor states to remain depressed permit a trading exchange that is unequal. A disguised volume of value accrues to rich states, therefore, by simple fact of the disparity in their high-wage situation relative to that elsewhere. Since on the whole capital shuns markets where wage levels are low, the capacity to cater for consumer demand never comes to be established, and the causal stream that leads to heavy industry fails to flow. Capitalism as such swims the other way.[77] By this calculation its pernicious effects are inadvertent, since it blithely perpetuates poverty and stalls the rate at which more developed enterprise can be established by default rather than any more insidious intent.

'Dependencia' analysts tend to see the global structure as much more malevolent than this, as positively imposing subordinate status on the underdeveloped in a systematic fashion that underdevelops them. And not, as traditionalists tend to argue, as a matter of mere 'convenience'. 'Development and underdevelopment, in this view, are simultaneous processes: the two faces of the historical evolution of the capitalist system.'[78] And: 'To speak of a "Third World" or a "dual society" in our day produces and is utter confusion.'[79]

As an intellectual framework it has drawn a mixed critique.[80] Rather than dichotomise dominance-dependence one might argue the analytic advantages of a scale for each dimension. Dominant nations have different interests, and they vary in their vulnerability to the boycott of strategic resources. Dependent ones are equally scattered over the range of relevant qualities, which obviates any necessity to push what are empirically complex entities into one sole set or the other. Political sovereignty, furthermore, has made it more difficult for what we do identify as dependent states to be manipulated in position. They use what leeway a world of competing states and transnational enterprise provides to realise more of their autonomy by neo-mercantilist means, or by making alliance with others to unionise their demands. They can be co-opted by more radical elites at home, too, who are far less happy with their liaison role in servicing structural links, and are less than co-operative in global terms as a result.

Again I will not attempt to establish in detail my own conclusions on these questions. The problem may well lie with the spread of the capitalist mode of production and the way peripheral misdevelopment ('dependent capitalist development')[81] is culled of its surplus by the metropoles. On the other hand, we have the global system of consumption and exchange that inhibits real development where it does not actually de-develop (by misallocating their resources) those who have substantially less to begin with. Perhaps the answer lies in some combination of the two depending upon the particular place and time. It does well to remember however, that even if 'all capitalists may be imperialists . . . it does not then follow that all imperialists are capitalists',[82] and likewise, while the world capitalist economy directly induces 'dependence', not all 'dependence' is exploitative in effect. In a world where the capitalist mode of production and its prime conveyance, the industrial means of manufacture, are so pervasive, this might very well seem to be the case though.

'Social Formations in the Periphery'

I am more directly concerned with the social formations these processes have produced, not so much in the core states referred to above, but where mass poverty persists—on the global perimeter. Economic changes that denote dependence directly implicate social structures. As the economic fate of the periphery can only be understood by referring to that of core states, so its social structures must be understood within the overall context of the social structure of the globe. The phenomenon is a varied one as befits the differing roles different sectors of the periphery in Asia, Africa and America have played at different times in the development of the world economy. Most of the groups involved have possessed concrete interests that they have tried to defend by attempts to co-opt the political heights of their respective societies, which implicates the political process in turn. Those who constitute the 'internationalised' sectors in poor states—the bourgeoisie and the proletariat ('labour aristocracies')[83]—look to the external source of their prosperity and support as well as to the state, while such disadvantaged groups as the peasants and sub-proletariat turn, if they turn at all, to the latter alone. Hence:

as the process of internationalisation of dependent nations progresses, it becomes difficult to perceive the political process in terms of a struggle between the Nation and the anti-Nation . . . the anti-Nation will be inside the 'Nation' so to speak, among the local people in different social strata.[84]

One becomes aware of the existence of symbiotic socio-economic 'colonies' actually *within* the state, all the more evident where pre-capitalist conditions still prevail, sustained and intensified, as they have been, by the impact of core states and an expanding world market.[85]

These social changes have occurred as a direct consequence of all historical aspects of the movement by the West into the wider world. Precolonial trade prompted new sources of social power, or reinforced old ones. Direct and indirect imperial control instigated primary and secondary effects that persist in post-colonial times. Peasant societies no longer produce for localised needs only; they cater also now for those of the 'market'. 'Workers' have appeared in the contemporary sense of those without land and labouring for a wage. Mines and service industries, commercial enterprises, the administration itself, the professions and the security forces; all have created opportunities for individuals to advance their personal life-chances in material terms and in those of social prestige, which is not to forget that tucked into the interstices of the burgeoning social structures of the 'new' states we find all sorts of other groups sharing both traditional and modern class features. Indeed it is the pre-capitalist formations that have often proved the most pervasive. Capitalism with its propensity to dichotomise society along bourgeois/proletariat lines, while it may be the major influence, is not the only one. In Latin America, for example, it may be seen to have reinforced the feudal relationships of an earlier era in systemic expansion rather than to have replaced them — and to reactionary political effect.[86] In several African states wage labourers move between the 'modern' sector and the 'traditional' one where they work for themselves, cash-cropping or serving subsistence needs, in a semi-proletarianised fashion that complements as well as conflicts with the requirements of industry and primary resource extraction.[87]

In general, class supremacy in poor states derives from political power, a result of the 'virtual absence of a proprietorial relationship and the presence of a low resource base'.[88] Those who rule attempt to consolidate their position by connecting financial, political, professional and security elements into a self-sustaining network that in sufficiently concrete instances constitutes a 'political class'.[89] To one side stand those elements directly involved in comprador activities, though the line of separation is very indistinct. And we may also discern, where they have expressed some sort of self-conscious social action, 'working classes' (the whole shot through with ethnic differences where ethnic stratification intrudes on that of a class kind). The patterns are highly heterogeneous, for several historical episodes have had diverse consequences that persist together in overlapping ways. The most radical changes, furthermore, are often only just beginning. Behind any more general proposition we might make lies a wide range of established and emergent social entities. Poor countries are still largely agricultural, but agricultural endeavour has not been untouched by the expansion of the West, which has involved even the most remote regions in the world capitalist economy. Peasants and tenant cultivators work smallholdings in feudal or communal circumstances quite different from those of rich states, but there are wide variations also from state to state across the Third World. Likewise for the other strata, the agricultural and industrial proletariats, the 'semi'-proletariat groups, the industrial, trading, financial and rural bourgeoisies, and the pre-capitalist feudal and commercial groups.

It is still possible to speak of common features, however. Despite their manifold differences all peripheral formations—excluding socialist ones—share four major characteristics:

(1) the predominance of agrarian capitalism in the national sector; (2) the creation of a local, mainly merchant, bourgeoisie in the wake of dominant foreign capital; (3) a tendency toward a peculiar bureaucratic development, specific to the contemporary periphery; and (4) the incomplete specific character of the phenomenon of proletarianisation.[90]

Each aspect deserves description at greater length,[91] and I shall be looking again at some of their implications in the next chapter, but the general effect has been growing inequality in the social distribution of income and growing unemployment within an integrated world system that supports, as I have already indicated, a bourgeois world society. Whether this really leads to a significant amount of global polarisation is debatable. While an international bourgeois class may grow more conscious of itself and its shared interests in preserving and extending the world capitalist economy, this has not prevented conflict and rivalries, even outright war, between politically discrete segments of it, and is unlikely ever to do so. And however apparent a world proletariat may be in terms of the functioning of the global system, the development of an explicit consciousness of its place and role, particularly where it is heavily fragmented by national and other loyalties and constraints, would seem to require a degree of socio-economic awareness that specific life situations all too readily obscure.[92]

Nevertheless, the concept of classes on the periphery does make a useful contribution to our understanding of social change. The tendency under capitalism towards social polarity can be seen writ large in the growing income gap between rich and poor states, a gap that was first reproduced in its contemporary form within poor ones by imperialism, a process increasingly sustained now by industrialisation.[93] The division of labour, of task specialisation (different people doing different things), is subordinated to the prime fact of *appropriation*; the way that classes crystallise within local societies, and within the world system as a whole, is a component part of this appropriating process. When they find common cause they become a political force. The bourgeoisie, where aware of its common interests (and ever cognisant of its manifest differences) can be considered a class both of itself and for itself — at a state level and that of the world society they in fact define. Subordinate social aggregates can be located in shared arenas with reference to the pattern of global production, and are variously self-conscious in their local domains. They remain largely unaware of their common global concerns, however, constituting classes there in a nominal sense only, and remaining politically inert.

A Synthesis

It is a challenging task to arrange the complex picture of class formation at the state level, and that of the world as a whole, around the common historical expression of particular modes and means of material production. The structuralist approach attempts to place human beings in the social context that accompanies industrialisation as it evolved in Europe and has impinged on pre-industrial societies. In doing so its protagonists (and particularly the Marxists among them) emphasise the extent to which capitalism is incompatible with their preferred values. This attitude tends to lead to indifference towards what many people would see as feasible for now, and in the foreseeable future. The alternatives prescribed for development *without* dependence tend to austerity or at the very least selective affluence, and a sort of 'welfare imperialism' with its tangible (if ill-distributed) socio-economic benefits, and the politics of conflict resolution and repression if need be.

How effective we find such alternatives will depend upon our more general understanding of the world system and world society; an understanding that enables us to locate in the specific instance the constraints and opportunities implicit in the global economy and the global strategic balance. The hypotheses derived from the notions of imperialism and dependency go a good way towards this picture, but I find the link they posit between the world market and world production and the multiple interactions of the constituent polities too close. I would resist, in other words, the argument that 'in the last analysis' it is the former that decides the latter. 'In the last analysis' is used, like the Judgement Day that never quite arrives, to affirm a faith rather than a history or a science. The chosen return from their mountain, their prophecies falsified, the world sinful but still very much extant, to wait another day and wonder why the end is not more near; why the 'lonely hour' of the final instance has not come.

The materialist philosophy of history depicts human behaviour as ultimately determined by modes of production. We can resist the inevitability of this influence and still admit, however, the extent to which human initiative is conditioned by the way life's necessities and luxuries are produced, particularly in an age as industrious as our own. Marx argued that we do in fact make our own history, though not as we might please. Locating the realm of the voluntary within that of necessity is a central analytic task, and we should resist capitulating to either imperative in advance. Even if we admit the 'last analysis' as somehow decreed—no mean leap of the critical imagination—a good deal of 'non-material' derivation can happen short of that.

We can, it seems to me, assimilate the levels of analysis involved here—those of the state and the whole system—if we develop the 'dependencia' approach further in something of the way Immanuel Wallerstein has done. A holist perspective will see the world system as one outcome of the Eurocentric world economy that emerged originally four centuries ago, that

> has since grown through cycles of expansion and contraction in its geographical scope . . . in its productive capacity (capital formation), in its integration as a whole (world-scale interdependence) and in its penetration and organisation of social relations ('commodification' and class formation)[94]

to encompass the globe. As a 'world' system the European 'world economy' was not originally contiguous with the geopolitical whole, though it came to be so eventually. It was just more extensive than the city-states

and nation-states of the day. It was an economic entity (involving
cultural and political supports), but unlike an empire, it was not a political one. Former world economies in this sense (China, Persia, Rome)
invariably became empires thus defined. The novelty of the contemporary system is that it has not; the techniques of modern capitalism and science have served to sustain its expansion without recourse
to centralised political arrangements. And as the mode of production
of the world economy, capitalism directly influences the social relations
within its domain, now to global effect.

There are three basic dimensions to this sort of approach: an economic one that traces the development of the global division of labour;
a political one that describes the formation of states; and a social
(cultural) one concerned with human communities defined by other
means. Generally:

> The modern world-economy might be said to have been tenuously
> integrated when it emerged in the sixteenth century. But we might
> say the same of the several political jurisdictions, or monarchies,
> which the emergence of the world-economy brought into increasingly
> sustained relations with one another. The progressive formation of
> these polities as stronger and weaker states in relations to one another
> in the emerging European (later, international) state-system went
> hand in hand with the cyclically evolving division of labor between
> the increasingly 'core' areas of the world-system and the increasingly
> 'peripheral' areas. And the world-economy became basically structured
> as an increasingly interrelated system of strong 'core' and weak 'per-
> ipheral' states, in which inter-state relations—and hence patterns of
> state formation and, in that setting, the formations of nationally-
> organised 'societies'—are continually shaped and in turn continually
> shape the deepening and expanding world-scale division and integration
> of production. These basic trends are fundamentally antipathetic, and
> what the states try to unify, the world-economy tears asunder.[95]

(I would interpolate here the propensity states clearly have to *dis*integrate
the world system, and the contrary capacity for the world economy,
through colluding classes, to integrate it again.)

Identifying what is core, what is peripheral, and what is the external
arena beyond the system as a whole, depends upon the patterns apparent
in global transactional traffic. Busy regions are designated as central, the
less involved constitute the hinterland to the core, and those hitherto
touched in only selective ways make up the external arena. In addition

we find *semi*-peripheral states that serve core functions with respect to the peripheral arena, and peripheral ones with respect to the core. Their function is a necessary, not an incidental one, too. They help to defuse the conflict potential of a system that grows progressively more bi-polar, and they allow capitalists to escape 'wage-productivity' freezes in leading sectors, thereby preventing what might be serious economic and ultimately political consequences at large.[96] The general effect has been to sustain and extend the division of labour that defines the three sectors of the system itself, sectors that have persisted despite the significant revisions that have occurred over time in productive processes, and the geographic pattern of the states involved. Capital accumulates on a system-wide basis and in the form of national capitalisms competing as home markets within a world one, both commercialising land and proletarianising labour. And by definition it would seem impossible for all states 'to develop simultaneously. The . . . widening gap is not an anomaly but a continuing basic mechanism of the operation of the world economy.'[97] Some make it, but unless productive forces can be expanded to meet the needs of all earth's people, reciprocal effects and the propensity for capitalism to compete to seek a profit mean others tend to fail. The emergence of a Communist component does not alter the picture, since its state members participate in the capitalist world market, albeit in a more marginal way, just like non-Communist countries do.[98]

In this sort of picture 'stratification' denotes the differential distribution of productive tasks within the world system as a whole,[99] the core always specialising in 'comparatively highly-mechanised, high-profit, high-wage, highly skilled labor activities', the periphery the obverse, and the semi-periphery some combination of the two. Particular states will always in practice display the features of differing sectors, not just one, but we can still attempt to classify them as such. Furthermore: 'the state's political structures will tend to be determined by the needs of the predominant zones.'[100]

Statehood itself disturbs the open play of the system. State leaders can manipulate the costs of production locally or employ any one of a number of devices that intervene in the market to their immediate advantage. Their capacity to do so will vary with the decision-making efficacy of the state machines however, which tend to be stronger in the core and weaker on the periphery. And they remain 'consequent' to a significant degree upon the growth and change of the world-system as a whole.[101] Thus:

to understand the internal class contradictions and political struggles of a particular state, we must first situate it in the world-economy. We can then understand the ways in which various political and cultural thrusts may be efforts to alter or preserve a position within this world economy which is to the advantage or disadvantage of particular groups located within a particular state.[102]

New light is also thrown on the persistence of nationalism, too, as an expression of the transnational conflicts that arise within the world system as a whole.[103]

A synthetic framework like the one outlined above requires a clear sense of the disjunction between economy and polity, between economic decision-making and the political realm. Historically, capitalism did much to provide just such a disjuncture; indeed, it would seem one central aspect of its original argument that 'economic factors operate within an arena larger than that which any political entity can totally control.'[104] This may have been an aberration since the concept of a discrete economy subject to its own market mechanics, realistic where that market is comparatively 'free', has given way almost universally now, at the state level at least, to the idea of planned political control of economic affairs. State formation itself and the advent of civilly unified geographic regions played a key part in the growth of national capitalism, encouraging economic competition within an ordered domestic environment and allowing competition to proceed without the need for private armies. Industrialisation, having heightened class interdependence, has caused polity and economy to converge once more.[105]

With capitalism generalised over the world system the disjunction can be viewed as still prevalent *at that level* however. Globally, we encounter a hierarchy of occupational tasks that reflect global market forces, and with no world government to reconcile economy and polity overall the distance between them is still in evidence there. This of course continues to inspire materialist analyses, and to good reason. It also tempers any understanding of the world that attempts to analyse it solely in terms of 'state' power and strategic interaction. It cannot, however, replace such analyses since state formation, conditioned though it might be by the world economy, remains a process possessed of a logic of its own, and indeed, even as committed a structuralist as Samir Amin has declared a shift in the dominant role in the world capitalist system to 'politics' (undefined).[106]

Beside these whole-system sectors 'stratification' also denotes patterns of class formation and class conflict *within* states. The assertion of class consciousness still tends to occur in a national context rather than a global one, though as already indicated this pertains more to the proletariat than to the bourgeoisie. Social conflict tends to polarise societies. The modern world society, as described here, is unitary rather than binary, with the bourgeoisie progressively more conscious of itself as universal and as standing in opposition to a plethora of other groups and strata, a global social class. Supranational awareness of this sort was not unknown in earlier eras, but it has remained a difficult sense to consolidate since heterogeneity and regional inequality have often been integral to the way the whole system works. State machines have grown more concrete too, and as growing bureaucratic skills have allowed more efficient taxing and managerial tasks, those who command them have developed culturally, linguistically and spiritually sanctioned concerns of their own.

From class analysis we learn of the differentiating effect of industrialisation, and particularly that of the capitalist world economy, which has played the most conspicuous part in building social structures biased towards property-owning and profit-seeking groups and away from the rest. These structures are globally dispersed, and the separate states reflect the bias more or less faithfully, depending on the way in which those possessed of capital have approached the political management of their productive capacities and its social effects, as well as the pre-capitalist context in which they have had to proceed. An exclusive concern for the nation as the conduit for social reform and the raising of living standards must miss the currents that move through and around this institution, however. Inequality is a feature of a transnational pattern of class difference that cannot be understood in terms of separate states competing for influence and power alone. To declaim that class differences in poor countries are strictly secondary to the conflict taking place between poor states and rich ones as such is to over-simplify the effects of the forces at work in the world. If anything, it is the other way around.

Nevertheless state-making, urged on and variously constrained by such material influences, cannot be wholly comprehended in their light alone. Historically nation-states and capitalism evolved together, though the link is not inevitable or irresistible either way. Patterns of class formation cannot wholly explain those of the state, nor 'state' explain 'class'. Though the development of capitalism did encourage and condition that of states, the latter cannot be seen as always and only a consequence of capitalism and class struggle since they sometimes preceded it, have certainly been evolved outside it, and the development of the capitalist mode of production itself involved more than a class analysis allows.[107]

If we reify the structural aspects of a comprehensive capitalist economy and a plural world polity, treating them as consequential rather than causal components of some huge systemic machine, then we have no problem explaining a wide range of social events all over the globe. This comes close, however, to a deterministic view of individuals as vehicles only for abstract relations which obey a logic independent of human will. It tends to exaggerate the influence of the 'system' on lesser units of analysis and to downplay their heterogeneity and the differences between them. Concepts and not people become the motive force of historical change. If we allow for human agency, regardless of how unwitting or constrained the individual choices may be, then we can envisage state formation as proceeding on its own terms. Social power flows not only from control over production, distribution, 'service' and exchange — though in an era under the influence of a means of production as potent as 'industry' it might well seem so — but also from control of the means of destruction, social discipline, diplomacy, education and communal co-ordination as well. In many instances the same sets of individuals will master both; in others not. Hence the inter-state alliances and conflicts that express the functional requirements of the global division of labour; hence the whole spectrum of policy-making that proceeds oblivious to the long-term secular trends in the capitalist world economy. Which is not, in turn, to say that patterned trends cannot be constructed from the long historical view, and cogent ones at that.

The cruel problems persist: of threat of nuclear annihilation, and of global inequality and the plight of the poor. The violence of war is too familiar to need restatement. But we must account for the violence of not-war, for political repression and for structural violence

> when people are killed prematurely as a consequence of a particular societal order. Peace research has been able to demonstrate that already today the number of victims of such violence in international society has reached the number of victims predicted by military strategists for the case of a potential nuclear war between . . . East and West.[108]

The immediacy of the one cannot obscure the enormity of the other. Armageddon and mass poverty are preventable diseases, I believe, but the complex interplay at a global level of class integration and state differentiation, and at a more local level where states integrate and classes divide, may thwart their cure. Is this the best that the human enterprise can do? Where 'development' denotes a state of grace, as has come to do in the modern world, I suspect not. 'Salvation' has been 'naturalised' now for many of its members, and 'man's lot' is 'no longer synonymous with "man's fate"'.[109] The prodigious capacity of industry has generated new modes of production. Their promise is self-evident. They prompt in turn re-perceived possibilities for socio-economic rewards, and once the realm of human expectations has been revised, contingency willing, reality conforms.

Notes

1. E. L. Morse, *Modernization and the Transformation of International Relations* (Free Press, New York, 1976). Also C. Tilly (ed.), *The Formation of National States in Western Europe* (Princeton University Press, New Jersey, 1975); but cf. B. Hindess and P. Hirst, *The Pre-Capitalist Mode of Production* (Routledge and Kegan Paul, London, 1975).

2. For a brief discussion of the differences between egalitarian, rank, stratification and state society see M. Fried, 'On the Evolution of Social Stratification and the State' in S. Diamond (ed.), *Culture in History* (Columbia University Press, New York, 1960). 'The decisive significance of stratification', Fried asserts,

> is . . . that it sees two kinds of access to strategic resources. One of these is privileged and unimpeded; the other is impaired . . . The existence of such a distinction enables the growth of exploitation, of a more complex type associated with involved divisions of labor and intricate class systems. The development of stratification also encourages the emergence of communities composed of kin parts and non-kin parts which, as wholes, operate on the basis of non-kin mechanisms (p. 72).

3. See the now much noted statement of this position by Kingsley Davis and Wilbert Moore, 'Some Principles of Stratification and Selections from the Ensuing Debate' in L. Lewis, *Social Stratification* (Harper and Row, New York, 1974). Also, T. Parsons, 'Equality and Inequality in Modern Society, or Social Stratification Revisited' in E. Laumann (ed.), *Social Stratification* (Bobbs-Merrill, New York, 1970); R. Mousnier, *Social Hierarchies: 1450 to the Present* (Croom Helm, London, 1973).

4. G. Lenski, *Power and Privilege* (McGraw-Hill, New York, 1966).

5. Ibid., pp. 44-5.

6. Ibid., pp. 74-87.

7. W.G. Runciman, 'Towards a Theory of Social Stratification' in F. Parkin (ed.), *The Social Analysis of Class Structure* (Tavistock, London, 1974), pp. 62-3.

8. There is a radical/conservative dichotomy implicit in this between those (radicals) who see society more as an arena of discussion and conflict arising from social inequalities that are maintained by policies of coercion; where classes of social groups vie for predominance and co-opt the instruments of state to further their interests; and others (conservatives) who view it as a system in itself with its own requirements, founded fundamentally upon consensus, to whom classes are names more than palpable social structures. See, for example, Lenski, *Power and Privilege*, pp. 22-3. These two competing intellectual traditions have been characterised elsewhere, in the light of the rise of modern industry, thus:

Conservatives idealised the image of society in which every individual was born into a class where rights and duties were also his. Instead the industrial order imposed on each the burden of his freedom, with obligations enforceable only by legal sanctions, not by the morality of sacred tradition. . . . Hence, the classes of industrial society were simply aggregates of men similarly situated in the society. They were held together only by their economic interests.

Radicals responded to the experience of industrialisation in an opposite though not in a wholly dissimilar way. They, too, saw in this experience a crisis in human history. But they did not view it with despair . . . [they] were impressed by the conflict between the classes of owners and workers, a conflict which seemed to grow in intensity with each increase in the use of machines and the productivity of labour.

The fundamental problem of industrial society is construed, then, on the one hand as the 'weakening of ties between the individual and the group, which [has] generated a felt need for a process of reintegration', and on the other as 'oppression, the cruel and unusual deprivation of opportunities for individual development' and the concomitant urge to create social conditions conducive to human dignity and self-realisation. This differential construction still prevails. With global industrialisation, however, it now applies on a global scale. R. Bendix and S. Lipset (eds.), *Class, Status and Power* (Routledge and Kegan Paul, London, 1954), pp. 9-10.

9. F. Parkin, *Class Inequality and Political Order* (Paladin, London, 1972), p. 17.

10. N. Bukharin, *Historical Materialism: a System of Sociology* (International Publishers, New York, 1925); V.I. Lenin, 'A Great Beginning' in *The Essentials of Lenin* (Lawrence and Wishart, London, 1947). See also Ralf Dahrendorf's attempt to complete the famous unfinished chapter of Das Kapital III in *Class and Class Conflict in Industrial Society* (Routledge and Kegan Paul, London, 1959), and the assemblage by R. Bendix and S. Lipset, 'Karl Marx' Theory of Social Classes' in their collection, *Class, Status and Power.*

11. 'It is their different function in the production process', Bukharin reiterated, 'that constitutes the basis for the division of man into different classes', a conception that draws directly upon the materialist conception of history whereby the basis of life is seen to lie in the material process of production and the structure of society being its structure of labour, its relations of work (*Historical Materialism*, p. 144). 'In his character of revolutionary, economist and sociologist, Marx inherited all three basic types of conceiving the class structure which are encountered in the history of European thought. These are the dichotomic scheme, the scheme of gradation and the functional scheme' (S. Ossowski, *Class Structure in the Social Consciousness* (Routledge and Kegan Paul, London, 1963)). Marx emphasised class divisions in dichotomous terms, as exploitation (the appropriation of surplus value), and oppressors against the oppressed. He also attempted to account for historical competition between classes in more complex and more general terms. And to good reason, for as Ossowski argues:

> If all political or religious struggles are to be interpreted as class struggles, if we are to correlate the various literary and artistic trends with underlying class relations, if we are to look for a reflexion of class interests and class prejudices in moral norms, then we must make use of a greater number of classes than the two basic ones in the *Communist Manifesto* (p. 88).

12. His conception of social classes should not be regarded as describing the economic characteristics of particular aggregates of individuals. It is rather that the situation of individuals with regard to property provides a basis for statements about the probability of certain types of social, especially political, action (T. Bottomore, *Sociology* (George Allen and Unwin, London, 1973), p. 200).

One might also note here W. Wertheim's warning that: 'Social structure can be no more permanent than the social consciousness deriving from a more or less explicit system of values that is at the base of a given structural principle' (*Evolution and Revolution* (Penguin, Harmondsworth, 1974), pp. 94-5).

13. Bukharin, *Historical Materialism*, p. 285.

14. Dahrendorf, *Class and Class Conflict*, p. 19.

15. For a brief summary, see T. Bottomore, *Classes in Modern Society* (George Allen and Unwin, London, 1965). Also the comprehensive work by L. Kolakowski, *Main Currents of Marxism: its rise, growth, and dissolution*, 3 vols. (Oxford University Press, 1978).

16. Ossowski, *Class Structure*, p. 183.

17. Ibid., p. 184.

18. Dahrendorf, *Class and Class Conflict*, p. 268.

19. Parkin, *Class Inequality and Political Order*, p. 18.

20. E.g. L. Kuper, 'Race, Class and Power: Some Comments on Revolutionary Change', *Comparative Studies in Society and History*, vol. 14 (1972), pp. 400-21.

21. See H. Gerth and C.W. Mills (eds.), *From Max Weber: Essays in Sociology* (Kegan Paul, Trench and Trubner, London, 1947), Ch. VII, 'Class, Status, Party'. Also O. Cox, 'Max Weber on Social Stratification: a Critique', *American Sociological Review*, vol. 15, no. 2 (April 1950), pp. 223-7.

22. Parkin, *Class Inequality and Political Order*, pp. 28-44.

23. Gerth and Mills, *From Max Weber*, pp. 193-4.

24. See the work on 'rank-disequilibrium theory' by J. Galtung, 'A Structural Theory of Aggression', *Journal of Peace Research*, vol. 1 (1964), pp. 95-119; 'East-West Interaction Patterns', *Journal of Peace Research*, vol. 3 (1966), p. 146. Also G. Lagos, *International Stratification and Underdeveloped Countries* (University of North Carolina Press, Chapel Hill, 1963).

25. Lagos, *International Stratification*, p. 10.

26. J. Galtung, 'A Structural Theory of Imperialism', *Journal of Peace Research*, vol. 8 (1971), pp. 81-117.

27. E. Luard, *Types of International Society* (Free Press, New York, 1976), Ch. 9, 'Stratification'.

28. S. Patel, 'Collective Self-Reliance of Developing Countries', *Journal of Modern African Studies*, vol. 13 (1975), p. 572, Table 1.

29. H. Singer and J. Ansari, *Rich and Poor Countries* (George Allen and Unwin, London, 1977), pp. 16-17.

30. Ibid., p. 34.

31. I. Adelman and C.T. Morris, *Economic Growth and Social Equity in Developing Countries* (Stanford University Press, California, 1973), p. 196.

32. Ibid., pp. 178-83, 189. Also the *1974 Report on the World Social Situation* (United Nations, New York, 1975), pp. 13-14; K. Griffin, *International Inequality and National Poverty* (Macmillan, London, 1978).

33. R. Robinson, 'The World-Economy and the Distribution of Income within States: a Cross-national Study', *American Sociological Review*, vol. 41 (August 1976), pp. 638-59.

34. E. Winslow, 'Marxian, Liberal, and Sociological Theories of Imperialism', *The Journal of Political Economy*, vol. 39, no. 6 (December 1931), p. 755.

35. R. Koebner and H. Schmidt, *Imperialism: the Story and Significance of a Political World, 1840-1960* (Cambridge University Press, Cambridge, 1964).

36. B. Cohen, *The Question of Imperialism: the Political Economy of Dominance and Dependence* (Basic Books, New York, 1973), p. 16.

37. S. Hymer, 'International Politics and International Economics: a Radical Approach', *Monthly Review*, vol. 29, no. 1 (March 1978), pp. 17-18.

38. G. Kay, *Development and Underdevelopment: a Marxist Analysis* (Mac-

millan, London, 1975), particularly Chs. 5 and 6; also the review of this by H. Bernstein, 'Underdevelopment and the Law of Value: a Critique of Kay', *Review of African Political Economy*, no. 6 (May-August 1976), pp. 51-64.

39. P. Sweezy, 'Modern Capitalism', *Monthly Review*, vol. 2, no. 2 (June 1971), p. 3.

40. For a relaxed overview see V.G. Kiernan, 'The Marxist Theory of Imperialism and its Historical Formation' in Kiernan, *Marxism and Imperialism* (Edward Arnold, London, 1974). Also T. Kemp, *Theories of Imperialism* (Dennis Dobson, London, 1967).

41. Bukharin, *Historical Materialism*, p. 143.

42. N. Bukharin, *Imperialism and World Economy* (Howard Furtig, New York, 1966), p. 74.

43. J. Hobson, *Imperialism: a Study* (University of Michigan Press, Ann Arbor, 1965), p. 85.

44. J. Schumpeter, 'The Sociology of Imperialism' in Schumpeter, *Imperialism and Social Classes* (Basil Blackwell, Oxford, 1951).

45. Ibid., p. 85.

46. Ibid., pp. 90, 91-6. See also O.H. Taylor, 'Schumpeter and Marx: Imperialism and Social Classes in the Schumpeterian System', *Quarterly Journal of Economics*, vol. 65 (1951), pp. 525-55.

47. See, for example, the lucid critique by Cohen, *The Question of Imperialism*, pp. 49-72.

48. Winslow, 'Marxian, Liberal, and Sociological Theories of Imperialism', pp. 757-8. Also E. Winslow, *The Pattern of Imperialism* (Columbia University Press, New York, 1948).

49. Winslow, 'Marxian, Liberal, and Sociological Theories of Imperialism', p. 756.

50. Loc.cit.

51. Cohen, *The Question of Imperialism*, p. 121.

52. S. Hymer, 'The Internationalization of Capital', *Journal of Economic Issues*, vol. 6, no. 1 (March 1972), pp. 91-111. Also F. Fröbel *et al.*, 'The Tendency towards a New International Division of Labor', *Review*, vol. 1, no. 1 (Summer 1977), pp. 73-85. Transnational capital is a differentiated entity with common but also varying needs. See Robin Murray's list, however, of the economic functions that all capital will prompt, plus his distinction between extended capitals with primarily intra-national requirements and those with needs of a truly inter-national kind: 'The Internationalization of Capital and the Nation-State', *New Left Review*, no. 67 (May-June 1971), pp. 84-109.

53. A.G. Frank, 'Long Live Transideological Enterprise! The Socialist Economies in the Capitalist International Division of Labor', *Review*, vol. 1, no. 1 (Summer 1977), pp. 91-140.

54. Hymer, 'The Internationalization of Capital', p. 101.

55. Ibid., pp. 103, 105. Also S. Hymer, 'The Multinational Corporation and the Law of Uneven Development' in J. Bhagwati (ed.), *Economics and World Order* (Macmillan, New York, 1972).

56. R. Sklar, 'Postimperialism: a Class Analysis of Multinational Corporate Expansion', *Comparative Politics*, vol. 9, no. 1 (October 1976), pp. 75-92.

57. H. Magdoff and P. Sweezy, 'Notes on the multi-national corporation' in K. Fann and D. Hodges (eds.), *Readings in US Imperialism* (Porter-Sargent, Boston, 1972). Cf. A. Emmanuel, 'The Multinational Corporations and Inequality of Development', *International Sociel Science Journal*, vol. 28, no. 4 (1976), pp. 754-72.

58. Sklar, 'Postimperialism', p. 85.

59. For a vicarious sense of the perspectives such collusion can engender see Ch. 1, 'The Barbecue' in A. Sampson, *The Sovereign State of I.T.T.* (Fawcett

World, New York, 1974).

60. S. Huntingdon, 'Transnational Organisation in World Politics', *World Politics*, vol. 25, no. 3 (April 1973), pp. 233-368. Cf. here R. Gilpin, 'The Political Economy of the Multinational Corporation: Three Contrasting Perspectives', *American Political Science Review*, vol. 70, no. 1 (March 1976), pp. 184-91. Gilpin distinguishes a Liberal concept of political economy (harmonious, firm-centric, globalist and economistic) from a Marxist (conflictual, class-centric, economically determinist) and mercantilist one (conflictual, state-centric, politically determinist). The distinctions I have drawn are roughly similar. I do not, however, share Gilpin's mostly 'mercantilist' conclusions.

61. J. Galtung, 'Conflict on a Global Scale: Social Imperialism and Sub-Imperialism — Continuities in the Structural Theory of Imperialism', *World Development*, vol. 4, no. 3 (March 1976), pp. 153-65.

62. The conclusion I make here is contested at length in A. Giddens, *The Class Structure of the Advanced Societies* (Hutchinson, London, 1973), especially pp. 252-4. Also J. Goldthorpe, 'Social Stratification in Industrial Society', *The Sociological Review*, Monograph No. 8 (1964).

63. V. Melotti, *Marx and the Third World* (Macmillan, London, 1977), Ch. 2, 'Bureaucratic Collectivism'. Melotti designates this concept to describe a completely new kind of socio-economic formation, characterised by (1) the class ownership of property; (2) a planned economy; (3) the extended reproduction of use-values (rather than exchange values); (4) planned exploitation of surplus product; (5) centralised political power.

64. T. Cliffe, *Stalinist Russia: a Marxist Analysis* (Michael Kidron, London, 1955); M. Djilas, *The New Class* (Frederick A. Praeger, New York, 1957).

65. Parkin, *Class Inequality and Political Order*, p. 21.

66. The literature is extensive, but see S. Lall, 'Is "Dependence" a Useful Concept in Analysing Underdevelopment?', *World Development*, vol. 3, nos. 11 and 12 (1975), pp. 799-810. More generally, there is J. Caporaso, 'Dependence, Dependency, and Power in the Global System: a Structural and Behavioral Analysis', *International Organisation*, vol. 32, no. 1 (Winter 1978), pp. 13-43 and the whole of the rest of that special issue.

67. A. Mack, 'Theories of Imperialism: a European Perspective', *Journal of Conflict Resolution*, vol. 18, no. 3 (September 1974), pp. 516-17.

68. P. Baran, *The Political Economy of Growth* (Monthly Review Press, New York, 1957).

69. Of his many writings, see particularly A.G. Frank, *Latin America: Underdevelopment or Revolution* (Monthly Review Press, London, 1969); *Dependent Accumulation and Underdevelopment* (Macmillan, London, 1978).

70. T. Dos Santos, 'The Structure of Dependence', *The American Economic Review*, vol. 60, no. 2 (May 1970), pp. 231-6.

71. S. Amin, 'Accumulation and Development: a Theoretical Model', *Review of African Political Economy*, no. 1 (1974), p. 9.

72. Ibid., p. 23.

73. Galtung, 'A Structural Theory of Imperialism'.

74. Mack, 'Theories of Imperialism', pp. 526-7.

75. A. Emmanuel, *Unequal Exchange* (Monthly Review Press, New York, 1972).

76. A. Emmanuel, 'Myths of Development versus Myths of Underdevelopment', *New Left Review*, no. 85 (1974), p. 77.

77. Emmanuel, *Unequal Exchange*, p. 378.

78. O. Sunkel, 'Big Business and "Dependencia": a Latin American View', *Foreign Affairs*, vol. 50, no. 3 (April 1972), p. 520.

79. Frank, 'Long Live Transideological Enterprise', p. 227.

80. For opposing conclusions about the empirical importance of 'dependency

theory' see C. Chase-Dunn, 'The Effects of International Economic Dependency on Development and Inequality: a Cross National Study', *American Sociological Review*, vol. 40 (1975), pp. 720-38 (for); and R. Kaufman *et al.*, 'A Preliminary Test of the Theory of Dependency', *Comparative Politics*, vol. 7, no. 3 (April 1975), pp. 303-30; R. Vengroff, 'Dependency, Development and Inequality in Black Africa', *The African Studies Review*, vol. 20, no. 2 (September 1977), pp. 17-26; T. Smith, 'The Underdevelopment of Development Literature: the case of dependency theory', *World Politics*, vol. 31, no. 2 (January 1979), pp. 247-288. Of the theorists, A.G. Frank in particular has been accused of going to political extremes; e.g. A. Nove, 'On Reading Andre Gunder Frank', *Journal of Development Studies*, vol. 6, nos. 3 and 4 (April/July 1974), pp. 445-55. Frank's very extremism helped establish the general position, however: see A. Foster-Carter, 'From Rostow to Gunder Frank: Conflicting Paradigms in the Analysis of Underdevelopment', *World Development*, vol. 4, no. 3 (March 1976), pp. 167-80. The paradigm conflict described is largely what prompted the more general revision of paradigms now occurring in the study of world affairs, and the recovery, in the West at least, of the perspective of historical materialism.

81. F.H. Cardoso, 'Dependency and Development in Latin America', *New Left Review*, no. 74 (July-August 1972), pp. 88-95.

82. A. Hodgart, *The Economics of European Imperialism* (Edward Arnold, London, 1977), p. 78.

83. G. Arrighi, 'International Corporations, Labour Aristocracies and Economic Development in Tropical Africa' in R. Rhodes (ed.), *Imperialism and Underdevelopment* (Monthly Review Press, New York, 1970); P. Evans, 'Industrialization and Imperialism: Growth and Stagnation on the Periphery', *Berkeley Journal of Sociology*, vol. 20 (1975/6), pp. 113-145.

84. Cardoso, 'Dependency and Development', p. 93.

85. See the work of A.G. Frank. Also B. Hoselitz, 'Interaction between Industrial and Pre-industrial Stratification Systems' in N. Smelser and S. Lipset (eds.), *Social Structure and Mobility in Economic Development* (Aldine, Chicago, 1966).

86. E. Laclau, 'Feudalism and Capitalism in Latin America', *New Left Review*, no. 67 (May-June 1971), pp. 30-2. The complexities are well sketched by T. McDaniel, 'Class and Dependency in Latin America', *Berkeley Journal of Sociology*, vol. 21 (1976/7), pp. 51-88.

87. R. Avakov and G. Hirsky, 'Class Structure in the Underdeveloped Countries' in T. Thornton (ed.), *The Third World in Soviet Perspective* (Princeton University Press, New Jersey, 1964); A. Hoogvelt, *The Sociology of Developing Societies* (Macmillan, London, 1976), Ch. 5, 'The Transformation of Indigenous Social Structures under Colonialism'; Samir Amin, *Unequal Development*, an essay on the social formations of peripheral capitalism (The Harvester Press, Sussex, 1976), Ch. 5, 'The Contemporary Social Functions of the Periphery'; P. Waterman, Work-'Workers in the Third World', *Monthly Review*, vol. 19, no. 4 (September 1977), pp. 50-64.

88. R. Cohen, 'Class in Africa: Analytical Problems and Perspective', *The Socialist Register* (Merlin Press, London, 1972).

89. Ibid., p. 248.

90. Amin, 'Accumulation and Development', p. 333.

91. Ibid., pp. 333-69.

92. Cf. the optimism evinced by E. Krippendorff, 'Towards a Class Analysis of the International System', *Acta Politica*, vol. 10 (January 1975), pp. 6, 8, 10. Also R. Sandbrook, 'The Working Class in the Future of the Third World', *World Politics* vol. 25, no. 3 (April 1973), pp. 448-78; R. Cohen, 'From Peasants to Workers in Africa' in P. Gutkind and I. Wallerstein (eds.), *The Political Economy of Con-*

temporary Africa (Sage, Beverly Hills, 1976) for more on the 'chains' of proletarian-isation and peasantisation. The persistence of pre-capitalist components, 'at once the measure of the continent's underdevelopment and also its cause and its continually reproduced result' (L. Cliffe, 'Rural Political Economy in Africa' in Gutkind and Wallerstein, *The Political Economy of Contemporary Africa*, p. 125), is intrinsic now to the contemporary system. Peasants, variously abused by both capitalist and socialist development strategies that would serve 'revolution' and the state (and not so incidentally, its bureaucratic and political 'servants'), resist the 'primitive accumulation' techniques that all too often deny their own initiative and their own experience and material needs (Gavin Williams, 'Taking the Part of the Peasants' in Gutkind and Wallerstein, *The Political Economy of Contemporary Africa*). Thus, in discussing Tanzania, Williams concludes (p. 141):

> The strategy of *ujamaa* aimed to prevent the development of privileged capitalist classes in the urban and rural areas and to end dependence on foreign corporations by vesting control of industry and marketing in the state and by developing cooperative production in agriculture. It has become a program for herding people unwillingly into 'development villages', imposing futile colonial regulations, handing land and profits to US agribusiness, recruiting farmers to produce tobacco on a scheme sponsored by the World Bank, and begging the United States for food aid. It proceeded from the assumption that the benefits of cooperative production are self-evident and need only to be demonstrated to the peasants. Since these promises could not be validated in practice, cooperation could only be implemented by bureaucratic direction. Bureaucrats, however, require sustenance from the workers and peasants they direct. They have an interest in extending the country's resources. They inherited from the colonial era attitudes which defined them as the bearers of expertise and defined opposition to their plans as evidence of peasant ignorance and backwardness. When the party no longer speaks for the people against bureaucratic oppression, it becomes a servant of that bureaucracy, whose task is to persuade, cajole, and bully the people to adapt to the commands of the state.

93. See R. Stavenhagen, *Social Classes in Agrarian Societies* (Anchor, New York, 1975); O. Sunkel, 'Transnational Capitalism and National Disintegration', *Social and Economic Studies*, vol. 12, no. 1 (1973), pp. 137-71; S. Bodenheimer, 'Dependency and Imperialism: the Roots of Latin American Underdevelopment' in Fann and Hodges, *Readings in US Imperialism*.

94. 'Patterns of Development of the Modern World System', *Review*, vol. 1, no. 2 (Fall 1977), p. 112; the following discussion draws directly on this research proposal, plus earlier material by its main exponent, Immanuel Wallerstein. For a preliminary critique, see T. Skocpol, 'Wallerstein's World Capitalist System: a Theoretical and Historical Critique', *American Journal of Sociology*, vol. 81, no. 5 (March 1977), pp. 1025-90. See also his collection of essays, Wallerstein, *The Capitalist World-Economy* (Cambridge University Press, 1979) as well as B. Kaplan (ed.), *Social Change in the Capitalist World Economy* (Sage, London, 1978); and the original statement of this pattern in terms of the world-economy by F. Braudel, as summarised in *Afterthoughts on Material Civilization and Capitalism* (The Johns Hopkins University Press, Baltimore, 1977).(On 'determination in the last instance' it is worth citing the position adopted by L. Althusser and E. Balibar, *Reading Capital* (Pantheon Books, New York, 1976): 'In difference structures *the economy is determinant in that it determines which of the instances of the social structure occupies the determinant place.* Not a simple relation, but rather a relation between relations; not a transitive causality, but rather a structural causality (p. 224) . . . The phrase 'in the last instance' does not indicate that there will be some ultimate

time or ever was some starting-point when the economy will be or was solely determinant . . ."the last instance never comes", the structure is always the co-presence
of all its elements and their relations of dominance and subordination — it is an 'ever-
pre-given structure"'. . . ' Evasive?)

95. Ibid., pp. 112-13. See Wallerstein's discussion of the stages in the system's
evolution in 'The Rise and Future Demise of the World Capitalist System: Concepts
for Comparative Analysis', *Comparative Studies in Society and History*, vol. 16
(1974), pp. 406-12: emergence (1450-1640); consolidation (1650-1730); emergence
of industrial capitalism; and the consolidation of the industrial capitalist world
economy from 1917 on.

96. I. Wallerstein, 'Dependence in an Interdependent World: The Limited Possibilities of Transformation within the Capitalist World Economy', *African Studies
Review*, vol. 17, no. 1 (April 1974), p. 4; 'Semi-peripheral Countries and the Contemporary World Crisis', *Theory and Society*, vol. 3, no. 4 (Winter 1976), pp.
461-83.

97. Wallerstein, 'Dependence in an Interdependent World', p. 7.

98. S. Amin, *Accumulation of Capital on a World Scale*, vol. I (Monthly Review
Press, New York, 1974), p. 4.

99. 'Patterns of Development of the Modern World System', pp. 117-18.

100. Ibid., p. 129.

101. I. Wallerstein, 'Introduction: the Study of Social Change', *The Modern
World System* (Academic Press, New York, 1974).

102. I. Wallerstein, 'The Present State of the Debate on World Inequality' in
Wallerstein (ed.), *World Inequality* (Black Rose Books, Montreal, 1975), p. 16.

103. Within this context one can see the recrudescence of ethno-nationalism in
industrialised states as an experience of class consciousness of lower caste-class
groups in societies where the class terminology has been pre-empted by nation-
wide middle strata organised around the dominant ethnic group (ibid., pp. 23-4).

'Ethno-nationalism', in Wallerstein's language, denotes attempts to alter the distribution of goods by appealing to such 'status' identification as kinship, language,
race, religion or citizenship.
'Ethno-national consciousness is the constant resort of all those for whom class
organisation offers the risk of a loss of relative advantage through the normal workings of the market and class-dominated political bargaining' ('Class-Formation in the
Capitalist World Economy', *Politics and Society*, vol. 5 (1975), pp. 372-3).

104. Wallerstein, 'The Rise and Future Demise of the World Capitalist System',
p. 348. Capitalism is defined here as 'production for sale in a market in which the
object is to realise the maximum profit' (ibid., p. 400). This way Wallerstein, somewhat speciously, avoids or resolves debates about 'free' labour, 'merchant' capital
and its 'internationalisation'. See elsewhere, however, his more general assertion
that: 'The usefulness of capitalism as a term is to designate that system in which
the structures give primacy to the accumulation of capital *per se*, rewarding those
who do it well and penalizing all others, as distinct from those systems in which
the accumulation of capital is subordinated to some other objective, however
defined . . . Earlier there had been capitalists. There had even been embryonic or
proto-capitalist systems. But there had not yet been . . . a capitalist *system*', Wallerstein, *The Capitalist World-Economy*, p. 272. 'We may thereupon designate as the
bourgeoisie those who receive a part of the surplus value they do not themselves
create and use some of it to accumulate capital (p. 285) . . . the proletariat . . .
[as] those who yield part of the value they have created to others' (p. 289). Cf.
K. Marx, *Capital*: A Critique of Political Economy (J.M. Dent, London, 1930),
vol. 2, p. 580: 'Capital . . . is the command of unpaid labour', and p. 635: 'The
capitalist process of production regarded as a comested whole, or as a process of

reproduction . . . produces, not only commodities, not only surplus value, for it also produces and reproduces the capitalist relation itself . . . on one side the capitalist, and on the other the wage worker.'

105. G. van Bentham van der Berghe, 'The Interconnection between Processes of State and Class Formation: Problems of Conceptualisation', Institute of Social Studies, The Hague, Occasional Paper no. 52 (1975).

106. 'Afterward to the Second Edition', *Accumulation of Capital on a World Scale*, vol. 2, pp. 603, 605. Because of the 'work' involved, he elects not to discuss the subject, which is a pity.

107. Tilly, *The Formation of National States*, p. 72. The historical connection, we may note,

> had two sides: (1) the expansion of capitalism freed the resources which state-makers captured, for national ends . . . and (2) the growth of cities and of industrial production . . . produced profitable markets for big agricultural producers . . . incentives for landlords to hasten the creation of a docile land-poor labor force and conditions for political alliance between great landlords and aspirant state-makers.

Meeting the interests of bureaucracies, armies and political machines meant intense pressure on sources of revenue. The conflicts between the aristocracy, the bourgeoisie and an increasingly organised labouring force further heightened the need for, and thus reinforced, centralised state power. We should not lose sight of another great shaping influence – that of war, and, indeed, for European states international conflicts and their political resolutions have had profound effects.

108. D. Senghaas, 'Introduction', *Journal of Peace Research*, vol. 12, no. 4 (1975), p. 252.

109. I. Horowitz, *Three Worlds of Development; the Theory and Practice of International Stratification* (Oxford University Press, New York, 1966), pp. 50-5.

Part III: SOCIAL ORDERING AND SOCIAL CHANGE

6 INDUSTRIALISATION, URBANISATION, BUREAU-CRATISATION

The social structures most characteristic of our age — those of 'state' and 'class' — are the tangible expression of very general forces at work in the world, and though I have noted such forces in a rather cursory fashion above, in this final section I would like to look at them in more detail. I will then conclude with a discussion of the ordering implications of international law, and a brief study of the sources of global conflict in the context of a world society and the world system as a whole.

The image of a social 'force' is a rather mechanistic one. I would not wish to invest any instance of such an idea with independent motive power or autonomous resolve. I remain mindful of the fact that the concept can only summarise our understanding of specific human behaviours that, occurring *en masse*, generate sets of events or a social process we label as a movement or an institution or a structure that we consider significant in some way. There is no *extrinsic* principle that can be called upon to explain the social dynamics of ordering and change. Where we take recourse to 'climate', for example, or 'geography' to specify a cause, we have still to account for the mediating presence of human groups; the social environment can only find expression through society itself, through patterns of socialisation and the diverse ways in which we live. *Intrinsic* principles, on the other hand, excepting the crudest kind of instinct theories, account for social interaction as a matter of course.

What aggregate behaviours are the most significant in contemporary terms? Here I would argue that state formation and class formation are shaped most directly by three basic global trends, those, that is, towards further industrialisation, urbanisation and bureaucracy. Industrialisation not only includes the development of industry but also the mechanised use of agricultural resources and the steady erosion of subsistence cultivation in favour of larger and nominally more productive ways of growing fibres and food. Precisely what is it that suffers change, and how and in whose interests do these processes proceed? We also observe a concomitant trend for people to come to cities and towns on a permanent or intermittent basis to offer their labour for wages, expanding thereby the ranks of an incipient proletariat in urban centres that are unable adequately to provide for them. One universal response has been to extend the process of decision-making and administration through organisational structures of all kinds. This development has led to the proliferation of bureaucratic methods of institutional control; ordering devices that have come to assume international dimensions.

Industrialisation

'Industry'—the manufacture, typically in factories, of standardised commodities by a progressively more automatic and specialised range of machines—draws on new and now quite spectacular sources of energy to multiply the human capacity to produce what it needs and what it desires. Where 'industry' has come to prevail, economic growth and the increase in *per capita* income show a dramatic increase,[1] and the effects have been revolutionary indeed. Since we live in the midst of this so far self-sustaining enterprise, we may all the more readily appreciate how recent and radical it really is.

Though never predetermined, it was far from accidental. The process has had very extensive socio-cultural roots. The concept of the machine, for example, was a familiar one for many hundreds of years before the key inventions were made that we normally associate with the transition to the modern age; likewise the mental and commercial forms that provided the all-important context in which such industry could take hold and proliferate. Lewis Mumford identifies three separate waves riding this deep tide, overlapping and interpenetrating each other. The first begins somewhere about the tenth century; the second comes to a crest in England in the eighteenth, and is the one we normally designate as the Industrial Revolution; and the third streams around us today[2]—contemporary technology finding global purchase, and the regions already industrialised generating further innovations to add to those already extant. In terms of effects it was the second wave that broke the banks, as witness the subsequent and quite unprecedented flood of goods and services, both productive and destructive, flowing from the states that succeeded in so transforming themselves. There was also the rapid increase in population and life expectancy, the massive immigration from country to country and the shift away from the land, the vastly magnified power to transport people, material and ideas around the world, the burgeoning sciences and technologies, the piling up of pollutants, the rapidly growing consumption of resources, plus pervasive changes in patterns of education and of human expectations in general.

Historians nominate Britain as the original source of the industrial inspiration. The critical technological advances occurred there in the manufacture of cotton, under permissive circumstances that were finally to break the 'circular link between poverty, the absence of industry, and a pattern of consumption that reconciles need with means and confines means to need'.[3] The 'pressure of demand', both at home and more importantly abroad, was an impelling one, but so were the factors in supply: a relative measure of domestic prosperity (enough at least to allow enterprising individuals to make the initial investments required),[4] a sufficient agricultural surplus, appropriate raw materials, a vigorous entrepreneurial ideology plus ingenious mechanics looking for profitable ways to serve the large markets within the country and without it. More intangible ingredients – the rationalistic capacity to accommodate change for example, and the egalitarian propensity to promote those showing competitive personal merit or skill as much as privileged familial or propertarian connections – were no less important. Indeed in this last respect: 'achievement has remained, so far, the cardinal social virtue of the citizens of industrial societies',[5] a value enhancing both social mobility and the value of universal education in turn.

Mechanical production in Britain was closely associated with the concept and practice of *capitalism*, in this context the private ownership and private control for profit of the factories that made the goods, and both capitalism and industrialism served to secure a liberal outlook that has remained the ideological foundation of this sort of industrial society to the present day. The notion of an individualised, basically passive, yet self-interested and psychologically leisure-seeking populace lay at the heart of the doctrine of *laissez-faire* and the feeling that left to their own devices those commanding capital or labour would in their selfish way automatically facilitate progressive market arrangements beneficial to all. The Industrial Revolution placed the capitalist class in a position of great economic and political power, and they kept their belief systems beside them, justifying and explaining in classical liberal terms the nature of the new age.[6]

Many resisted this view in the light of a more socialistic one, and none more so than the Marxists. They defined capitalism not only in terms of the profit-seeking of privately endowed capitalists, but also as a function of a market in commodities where not only goods but 'free' labour too was sold, for money, by those who did not own the means of manufacture. They decreed it a 'mode of production', marked by

> three essential features: (1) the whole of social production takes the form of commodities; (2) labour power itself becomes a commodity, which means that the producer, having been separated from the means of production, becomes a proletarian; and (3) the means of production themselves become commodities . . . they become capital.[7]

In this sense, 'until the Industrial Revolution the capitalist mode of production did not yet really exist'.[8] It came to the fore only when the level of development of the productive forces was

> sufficiently advanced . . . to be no longer simple enough to be manageable by the individual producer . . . Industrial workers cannot make their own factories. Consequently, the center of gravity of the means of controlling society shifts from domination of the *natural* means of production to domination of those means of production that are themselves *products* – equipment, machinery, plant.[9]

The exclusive appropriation of the secondary means by one class, the bourgeoisie, was a further feature of this process, and though we find such ownership occurring throughout history in individual or family form, it can be collective too.[10] This allows us to extend the notion of 'private' possession and control from that of separate persons to that of groups.

Industrialisation has proved compatible with quite different sociopolitical and economic belief systems, however, not just capitalistic ones. And though it is possible to specify, as I have done earlier, particular attributes common to any and all industrial societies, attributes that those who seek the industrial estate often strive to emulate in the hope that by observing the forms productive largesse shall come to flow, the process has varied markedly from that first experienced in a comparatively spontaneous fashion by the British. In Germany, for example, unlike the pattern that prevailed across the Channel, critical assistance was supplied by investment banks; while for a 'rushing laggard'[11] like the Soviet Union we find the role of the private entrepreneur that was intrinsic to the original experiment usurped altogether by the state. Pursuing this point in greater detail Barrington Moore has identified historically three main roads to the industrial destination. Thus we observe 'bourgeois revolutions' taking place in England, France and America, where economically independent traders and manufacturers established a democratic urbanised capitalism that came to co-opt or to usurp, wherever there was one, the power of the landed nobility; 'reactionary' revolutions staged from above and most characteristic of Germany and Japan, where the bourgeois ingredient was far less prominent and a capitalistic Fascism.the typical result; and thirdly, Communist, peasant-based revolutions exemplified by Russia and China.[12] Though nominating one main pattern in each case, elements of the others, he argues, can also be found as subordinate themes. The advent in India of parliamentary democracy unaccompanied by capitalist or Communist reconstruction Moore considers a salutary anomaly. One singular factor remains: 'At bottom all forms of industrialisation so far have been revolutions from above, the work of a ruthless minority.'[13]

We can discern the influence of each upon the others in the temporal sequence in which they occurred. The speed of the process has also varied. Any sense that industrial transformation can be realised within one generation, however, seems for much of the world to be spurious, particularly since the global sectors attempting such a feat now do so in the face of those already organised in this way, and from individual base-lines already heavily conditioned by the prior impact of the industrial revolutions that have occurred elsewhere. The world market is an established arena of exchange, and its ground rules are those laid down by its innovators:

> the fact that it is convenient to identify the international economy as a separate unit of analysis is a distinguishing feature of the modern period in world history. It constitutes a third dimension of growth. For in any one country growth depends on the opportunities presented by the international environment in which it finds itself as on the factors of production (people and things) within its national borders.[14]

For poor, non-industrialised countries, the problems they confront because of the global presence of rich ones are severe.[15] Technological progress made in the world's 'advanced' sectors, in the control of epidemic diseases for example, have been transferred without the sort of changes in productive infrastructure that induce those kept alive to restrict family size. Population pressures have become acute, and even a comparatively rapid rate of economic growth, particularly where much of the wealth produced is co-opted by an elite minority, is tantamount in terms of mass welfare to running with a severe limp on one spot. The unemployed tend to stay that way, their plight exacerbated by the capital- rather than labour-intensive nature of the industrial plant which poor state regimes and their diverse transnational partners import. A surfeit of labour cannot always be considered a potential resource either, since to be effective as productive entities workers not only have to be taught the skills the machines require but also provided with the organisational supports that make their manufacturing effective; all of which takes money, and often more of it than a more capital-intensive enterprise takes—hence the preference. The notion of organisational supports raises the issue of

Northern-style educational and other social service schemes, as well as
Northern-inspired economic concepts and political forms, which can
prove inappropriate in a poor state context. This is particularly so
where capitalist-inspired regimes have preserved existing inequalities and
generated new ones. Meanwhile the rich states have continued the development of their global industrial interests and their technological innovations,
tipping the terms of trade more and more against poor state products,
their very prosperity a potent inducement for investment capital to
remain where it is rather than move into peripheral global sectors, and
drawing in from all over the world skilled personnel with modern qual-
ifications, a process that inevitably raises the cost to poor states of keeping for themselves those whose capacities they may need most.

Industrialisation as the engine of global economic progress has thus
proved a most uneven affair. Some would see the contemporary incidence
of it as 'fundamentally different' from the old.[16] The conditions that are
necessary and sufficient for 'machinofacture'[17] to spread are not universally
manifest, often in large part because of the unbalanced progress of global
industrialisation itself and the capitalistic context in which, on a world
scale, it largely proceeds. And significant parts of the world may be
destined for a protracted period of time to receive most of their industrial
goods from those who make them, in return for whatever they can supply
in terms of mineral and agricultural resources.[18] A structuralist analysis
of the world system would consider this uneven quality as actually *necessary* for it to function in its present fashion, ensuring profit for those
who command the world's stock of capital and who seek to maximise
their returns in the short run. If this is so, the prospects for the poor are
daunting indeed. It becomes problematic 'whether the countries that
industrialized became rich because they industrialized or whether they
industrialized because they were rich'.[19]

A planned world economy that took rational account of the long
term would, one suspects, proceed rather differently. The world economy has grown in a piecemeal, comparatively unplanned way, however,
and the traffic between states in technology, goods, finance and raw
materials reflects its skewed expansion. Self-regulating in important
respects, it thrives on the institutional separation of economics and politics.[20] Land, labour and money — the elements of industry — are treated
as commodities, which they are not, but the fiction is an effective one
for organising their supply; and 'society' (the world one in this case) in
accommodating the mechanism of the market becomes thereby an
'accessory' to the economic system that prevails there. The defence of
the human community against the adverse effects of 'commodification'

has had to proceed on a state-by-state basis, and except where the
system itself comes under attack, national self-interest tends to prevail.
A world market like this one is antipathetic in fact to any sustained
social sense, except among those who receive the bounty and the
benefits of the exchanges involved.

Though industry is still heavily concentrated in only a few sectors of
the global economy and the main expansion in trade continues to be
that between states already much 'developed' in this regard,[21] industrial
production *has* been established elsewhere, usually beginning with uncom-
plicated techniques for making improved wares for local use that substitute for imports, extending later perhaps to processing works for
agricultural products and minerals, and lastly to the means for manufacturing capital goods and complex consumer durables. We must keep
this in perspective: 'When compared with the developments in western
Europe and North America, the economically underdeveloped areas of
Latin America, Eastern Europe, Africa and Asia have *relatively* less
industry today than they had a generation ago.'[22] Industrialisation of
peripheral and semi-peripheral states, where it takes place at all, still
proceeds more slowly in terms of productive output than that occurring
in the core. Its effects are notable nevertheless and 'industrialisation is
now . . . an integral part of underdevelopment.'[23]

There is considerable debate then as to whether, in its capitalist form
at least, it can make the decisive contribution to poor state progress it
portends. Established typically in only a few areas of local poor state
economies, the hoped-for multiplier effects have often been far less
significant than a self-generating level of development would require,
and hence an increasingly more urban population finds increasingly less
work.[24] Pluralists are apt to consider this the product of inflexible traditions and social institutions, of a cultural incapacity to countenance
change or to raise the necessary capital. Poor states were poor before
'industry' was invented, they say, and neither their original nor their
continuing poverty can be attributed in the first instance to the dis-
torting effects of the outside world. There is some comfort perhaps
to be drawn from Alexander Gerschenkron's thesis that 'backwardness' confers developmental advantages of its own[25] – the more retarded
a country's industrial development stands in relation to that of others,
the more 'explosive' the process will be when it does occur and the
more directed and the stronger the drive then is towards large-scale
enterprise. However, the Malthusian logic of a population growth that
far exceeds any expansion in productive capacity is seen to be almost
inexorable. Structuralists on the other hand tend to consider the inter-

national environment, particularly the sort of industrialisation that is externally induced, as a negative, if not outright exploitative, influence.[26] All the above only confirms, from their point of view, the 'absurdity of accumulation' as a way of securing socio-economic development.[27] As colonies, poor states exported raw materials and imported finished goods, and industrialising them was very much a secondary consideration for imperial regimes. Two major wars, a world-wide depression, and the fact of decolonisation has served to stimulate domestic manufacture, a trend that has continued and sometimes at rates higher than those in the rich states. *Per capita*, however, the picture is still one of severe disadvantage. Domestic class differences and the variations within regions remain very wide.[28]

To recapitulate: industrialisation as a global event is very recent. It has been a conspicuous part of the life of many states only since World War Two. Before then most of today's poorer countries were still colonies anyway, so it is often difficult to foresee what its general consequences will be. On the whole, however, the sort of industrialisation taking place, contingent on rich-state technology, has had a limited effect in expanding domestic markets or modernising rural and traditional arenas. Banking, finance, capital goods manufacture and processing industries, retailing and mining and even agriculture; all have been deeply penetrated by foreign concerns. These tend to exercise their own influence and controls at the expense of local entrepreneurs, and seriously compromise what room for manoeuvre ruling elites may possess. The latter may not, of course, choose to exercise any more than their caretaking functions on behalf of external investors. Development— capitalist *or* socialist—becomes a dependent enterprise, which immiserates as many if not more than it maintains. The industrial sector, where it is constituted as an appendage to the international economy, does provide material benefits for those who work for it. They are few, though, and the populace on the margins receive little of the return, where they are not in fact made worse off by the process as a whole.

The pattern is reflected in that of international trade. Taken as a whole, two-fifths of peripheral state exports are in the form of minerals and oil, two-fifths in agricultural products (mostly from plantations), and less than one-fifth are processed goods or manufactures. Poor states tend to trade these among themselves.

Thus three-quarters of the periphery's exports come from modern high-productivity sectors that are the expression of capitalist development in the periphery—to a large extent the result of investment of

nearly 80 percent of its trade with the center, whereas . . . 80 percent
of the foreign trade of the central countries is carried on among themselves . . . industrial products being exchanged for other industrial
products.[29]

Establishing a capacity to substitute for imports has not changed the
extrovert nature of peripheral economies and the sort of global specialisation that reserves to the countries of the centre the most advanced
means of manufacture. The consequences are far-reaching and implicate
much more than 'industry' as such. Thus:

> The distortion toward exporting activities in the allocation of both
> financial resources . . . and human ones . . . gives extraversion a qual-
> itative dimension and asserts the dominance of the exporting sector
> over the economic structure as a whole, which is subjected to and
> shaped by the requirements of the external market.[30]

Ostensibly successful manufacturing countries like South Korea, Taiwan
and Singapore still suffer severe dependence effects. Increasingly they
must import food and other goods, their profits accrue to considerable
extent elsewhere, their workers are disciplined both directly through
repressive legislation and indirectly by fear of unemployment, and their
elites remain culturally compromised and committed to the system as
it stands (though well placed to reap the considerable benefits of their
globally subordinate status).

One response to radical disappointments with the sort of global
industrialisation achieved so far has been a sharpened awareness of the
importance of agriculture and the role played by the agrarian surplus in
feeding urban workers, providing investment capital, and in sustaining
the demand for the development of manufactures. The Chinese experience
has proved salutary in this respect. Many poor states, already burdened
by a notable incidence of urban unemployment, require a more efficient
agriculture as much as an industrial base. Few have the power to repat-
riate urban fringe dwellers back to the countryside; most also lack the
will to effect the sort of social reform that would increase agricultural
efficiency. There is a developmental impasse that is typically resolved
by imports, inflation and a deteriorating balance of payments. For those
countries that have come to rely on their primary produce for export,
the problems are more serious again. As the victims of any long-term
decline in the terms of trade, they have to sell abroad in increasing
amounts to buy the same foreign goods they need. Industrialisation here

would appear a logical remedy. Even where a ruling regime is no comprador creature and stands prepared to ignore the vested domestic and foreign interests that benefit from and hence defend such production, the socio-economic effort involved in developing a broad-gauge and efficient industrial capacity may be prohibitive.

Radical analyses tend to be pessimistic and rather grim. 'The tragic fact of the matter is that the poor bear the heaviest costs of modernization under both socialist and capitalist auspices. The only justification for imposing the costs is that they would become steadily worse off without.'[31] Those who remain impressed, implicitly or explicitly, by the reformist logic of industrialism look to a gradual, if uneven, transformation to accommodate global demand. Demand is a function of patterns of desired consumption, though, and as larger numbers of poor state citizens look to factory-made goods for their material satisfaction, it grows more and more of a challenge simply to subsist. 'Intermediate technology' remains the Cinderella of the global productive system, since it is the life-style of the prince that most influences what would-be commodity users desire.

The conditions under which industrialisation must now proceed, such as growing populations fed on imported foodstuffs, a paucity of skilled workers, neo-mercantilist exclusion by other countries—rich and poor alike—of foreign manufactured goods, inhibitions on the development of an indigenous capacity for technical innovation because of the low level of domestic production and the dominance of what does exist by external concerns; none of these are conducive to rapid progress. Capital remains scarce, while the need for it has grown out of all proportion. In this last instance, one approximate calculation has suggested that

> the average cost of total capital in a single characteristic, industrial operation in France in the nineteenth century was roughly the same as six to eight months wages for the average worker; in England it had been even less; the corresponding cost for underdeveloped countrie is . . . almost 30 years.[32]

And while the historical record continues to sanction the ambition to make a modern manufacturing nation out of a non-industrialised one in a generation or two, with all the advance in standards of living that is meant to accrue, poor states are mostly too small to effect economies of scale, too 'backward' to compete successfully with advanced states even where they are allowed to do so, and too dependent to become much more than international mendicants in a world economy that works overwhelmingly for the long-established rich.

The problem lies, perhaps, as Marx early indicated, in the fact that the whole modernising process has remained incomplete; to be successful, that is, it may need to effect a total change in the whole order of society, in its political and bureaucratic machinery and the socio-economic base on which it is built. It is not for nothing that Marx condemned the stagnant and degraded character of 'primitive' rural life, for example, and its capacity to transform 'a self-developing social state into never changing natural destiny'.[33] And while condemning the destructive effects of imperialism, in a back-hand way he specifically sanctioned it, since world capitalism and universal industrialisation are the necessary precursors, in this sense, to a proletarian revolution and a changed and 'better' world. Perhaps they still are, though many today would choose not to live where this is so.

Urbanisation

'The city once was like a cloud, not larger than a man's hand; it is now the tree that overshadows the world.'[34] The image is apt, since in many ways the most visible process to have accompanied that of industrialisation has been the global growth in the number and the size of urban centres and towns. A direct consequence of the heightened human capacity to produce goods and control the environment, 'industry' and the 'city' are clearly cognate. 'Urbanisation' would appear an integral aspect of contemporary 'development', and an industrial state that is not highly urbanised, or a rural one that is, remains so far in the realm of the imagination. They are not the same, though. Urbanisation must be seen as a singular social activity (of several sorts) before we can establish what it shares with industrialisation, and what it conveys apart.

On the one hand, urbanisation can be described as an increase in the sheer number of people who live in large, heavily settled geographic domains, or as a rise in the ratio of town to farm and village dwellers. It has also been defined in terms of the tendency for economic enterprise to aggregate in single places, for the proliferation of 'urbane' systems of social relationships, or as the trend towards the progressive inculcation of the psychological concept of what it means to be an urbanised being.[35] On the other hand, we can eschew the concept altogether and adopt an alternative ideology that talks, as the neo-Marxists do, in terms of the 'social production of spatial forms',[36] and urban systems as a manifestation of socio-economic class.

Urban conclaves are not new. However we define them they have been in evidence for several thousand years, decisively extending the potential variety and quality of social affairs. Historically, they occur as spiritual or economic entities – consuming, producing, or trading goods and values in turn – or as politico-administrative ones that offer fortified protection, or as all three depending upon how they arose and how they subsequently developed.[37] In their non-industrial form they manifest many shared features[38] that in many cases have persisted into the present day. Centred physically, for example, upon their focal pursuits and the homes of the ruling class, they tend to fall into discrete occupational or ethnic areas, the urban perimeter being the province of the poor and those beyond the social pale. In his study of post-war Popayan, a Columbian city then comparatively innocent of 'industry', Andrew Whiteford described the three classes he found there. They clearly displayed this age-old pattern. The aristocrats lived in grand antique houses near the main plaza and were all well placed politically, affluent and property-owning, 'highly literate, worldly wise, and proud'.[39] There was a middle class, geographically more dispersed, which one of its number described as having 'enough to eat but not to waste', dressing 'well but not with style', building 'nice homes which are not fancy' and living in comfort 'without pretension'[40] in a fashion immediately recognisable over the whole communal spectrum as appropriate to their station. On the urban outskirts were the barrio dwellers – the labouring poor. The Mexican city of Queretaro, chosen to complement this analysis, possessed a similar profile. As a consequence of the country's revolutionary heritage, though, recognition of the concept of class was less in evidence there. 'Modernisation' had also generated a more substantial bourgeoisie, and had notably affected styles of life in general.

Before looking a little closer at the impact of contemporaneity, and whether we can posit a distinction between industrial and non-industrial cities and towns, it might be useful to detail, however crude the picture, the relevant shifts in population that have been observed on a world scale and the gross demographic contours of the phenomenon as a whole.

The earliest 'cities' were never as large as those we take for granted now. With improvements in the technology of food production, transport, disease control, communications and manufacture, it became feasible to sustain large numbers of people who did not directly generate an agricultur surplus of their own. With the advent of 'industry' and mechanised agriculture, this capacity became a generative factor in its own right. By 1950 the proportion of people living in cities was greater than that establis ed for 'any particular country prior to modern times and many times higher than that formerly characterising the earth as a whole'.[41] By 1970 one-quarter of humankind could be found in settled centres of 100,000 inhabitants or more.[42]

On the above figures the world's population is still predominantly rural. Though demographers bicker about what statistical line to choose between 'country' and 'non-country', and how effective it is in discriminating between the two,[43] three-fifths of all Earth's people still live 'on the land', and though big urban centres are more and more a general feature of the world 'the actual situation is still predominantly one of rural villages and small towns'.[44] If we consider just the amount by which the numbers living in cities has increased,[45] though this has grown at a faster rate than that of the world's total population, it is not inordinate when placed in perspective. This said, the increase in the sheer numbers living in urban environments must be considered as a figure without precedent. Interestingly enough, this seems to have been – for the last generation at least – as much a process generated from within as a consequence of rural-urban drift. Demographically it is the increase in births over deaths in the cities themselves that is the 'principal factor' contributing to urban growth on a world scale.[46]

The differential picture is more complex. In the rich states the outflow from the country to the towns still outstrips 'anything previously known in their history'[47] and their rural numbers are declining overall. The migration occurring in the poorer countries does less on the other hand to deplete the growing population outside the towns. While the former move closer to an end to their entire rural populations, the latter grow in both sectors, and the movement to the cities and towns, though sufficient when added to the natural increase already occurring there to cause their rapid and visible expansion, is less significant with respect to the number of those who remain behind.

If we consider the proportion of people living in cities as opposed to the country – the *ratio* of the urban populace to the rural one – it is, however, changing radically on a world scale; so radically in fact that: 'If the proportion urban were to continue to rise at the 1950-1970 rate, over 50 per cent of the human race would be living in urban places by 1987, and 100 per cent would be living in such places by 2031.'[48] This is not as silly as it sounds since it would be quite feasible, if ways could be found to make food and fibres by artificial means that did not rely on plants, to contemplate a world where virtually everyone lived in cities and towns. The suburban spread of the megalopolitan centres of the industrialised global core, possible now because of the productivity of modern modes of agriculture and the capacity of contemporary transport and communications to service decentralisation, may mean for some countries at least

> urbanization in the sense of emptying the countryside and concentrat-
> ing huge numbers in little space will reverse itself—not, however, in
> the direction of returning people to the farm but rather in that of
> spreading them more evenly over the land for purposes of residence
> and industrial work. Rurality would have disappeared, leaving only a
> new kind of urban existence.[49]

Whatever the disposition of the end product, world urbanisation cannot continue at the present rate beyond the next two generations; we
live at present at the peak of a most extraordinary event, with consequences that few pretend to foresee. Presumably the global trade that
makes conurbation possible will continue to grow since, as Kingsley
Davis argues, 'the hinterland of today's cities is the entire world.'[50]
Except in those parts where, from ideological predilection, a specific
attempt is made to reduce the discontinuities between country and
town, domestic structures will be rearranged more and more to support
settled centres.[51] It remains imponderable just how urban areas will
develop as the quantitative increase places qualitative pressures upon
their social, economic and ecological structures.

How do we explain this whole quite extraordinary enterprise? A city
or a town is a tangible artifact and we walk about it describing this facet
or that, admiring or condemning the economic and political, the sociological, cultural or ecological planes. We look for changes over time, high-
lighting the patterns we observe, even projecting them into the future.
But we can only really understand the picture an urban centre presents
if we approach each such entity 'as a vantage point from which to capture some salient features in the social processes operating in society as
a whole . . . [as] a mirror in which other aspects of society can be reflected',[52] as the dynamic expression of more general relationships that
cities and towns shape in turn and work upon to independent effect.

As one expression of *industrialised* economies, for example, cities
and towns collect a large work-force in a comparatively compact venue.
Land is used intensively for residential, road, shop, office or factory
sites and many people are sustained conveniently in one place, however
dispersed that 'place' may be. Once it has occurred, this fact generates
its own influence on the process of socio-economic change. Not all urban
centres have arisen to serve such a purpose, however. 'There is nothing in
industrialization itself', for example, 'that will account for the growth of
the giant capitals of Europe, which have remained essentially administrative

financial, commercial, and "cultural" in character.'[53] The locational merits of particular sites plus the many advantages associated with having factories close together have forged a clear link between the two processes, though, a link which remains tight and fast.

More fundamentally, any urban area must realise the production and distribution of those goods and services that allow it to survive or it simply ceases to do so. Over a certain somewhat indeterminate size, depending partly at least upon predisposing cultural factors (that are in turn open to change as urbanisation proceeds), this requires an increasingly divided and specialised body of labour, and an increasingly elaborate system of social management. It also requires an, again imprecise, modicum of 'industry' and a contemporary capacity for transport and communications. In the developed capitalist countries the market has governed much of this provision. The reciprocal and general interdependence of its individual citizens, though they remain indifferent to one another, meets the need for the ever more complex networks which integrate the whole. The market is complemented by a more or less decisive state component, the latter being used to provide basic services or to secure corporate enterprise. In rich socialist states the market is scarcely free in a like sense at all, and production and distribution are bureaucratically planned under the aegis of party directives. Each sort of polity has evolved characteristic class hierarchies that are reproduced in the cities and towns, underpinning in turn the particular system that prevails and persists. The cities become the 'pivot' around which a 'given mode of production' is organised, a 'centre of revolution against the established order, and . . . a centre of power and privilege (to be revolted against)'.[54]

Urban centres are founded upon the 'extraction and concentration of a social surplus product',[55] which is used in a selfish fashion either to support diverse cultural pursuits, or in a more general way to further a larger society's growth and development in both its rural *and* urban dimensions. We can distinguish, thus, the cities that consolidate and extend a country's productive capacity from those that consume what the hinterland supplies, providing only marginal return. In rich states cities are crucial to industrial production and to the flow of goods and services that stimulate it. Under the capitalist economies in particular, growth depends upon people's propensity to consume, and much of their social life is dominated by the need to preserve and extend the consumption patterns that generate further capital income.[56] We can distinguish too between centre and peripheral forms, between the urban conclaves of the developed North and the dependent ones of the poor South, that act as conduits, directing the outflow of profits and resources and helping in their own way to channel the 'massive global circulation of surplus value in which contemporary metropolitanism is embedded'.[57] Market exchange regulates this process of circulation to the advantage of established urban centres, evolving a hierarchy of wealth and prestige that is appropriate to the difference in industrial power. The peripheral countryside looks more and more to regional cities and towns, and these look in turn to national centres and thence to the great metropoles of the North. 'City, suburb and rural areas are now incorporated within the urban process,'[58] while the quality of urban life conditions more and more a homogeneous human culture familiar to all.

This is a very diffuse outcome, and indeed, as cities and towns have grown in importance their discrete and singular functions have grown more complex and less determinate as a result. In this sense the emergenc of industrial society has done nothing to strengthen the city but has spelled instead 'its virtual disappearance as an institutional and relatively autonomous social system organised around specific objectives . . . Urban diffusion is precisely balanced by the loss of the city's ecological and cultural particularism.'[59] This is most evident in poor countries where urbanisation takes place unsupported by the sort of socio-economic development that has occurred in industrialised states. The large, un-planned, ill-serviced cities we find on the global periphery and semi-periphery are a unique phenomenon. Rather than examples of 'pseudo-urbanization',[60] however, as the process has been called (which suggests that these conclaves are somehow spurious or false when they are far too much in evidence for such a connotation to be appropriate) or as cases of 'over-urbanization' which is the more common expression[61] (and is closer to defining their key feature: diffuse form without a Northern-style structure) we might do well simply to accept the advent of a dif-ferent sort of process, one characterised by maximal aggregation and min imal integration *at the same time*. The levels of local or *sub*urban organisati can be very high in such places, in shanty settlements just as much as in those areas where the bourgeoisie live or that once belonged, as they may still do, to foreign administrators and merchants. The general urban fram work is typically skeletal though, with an *ad hoc* quality rich-state cities have mostly planned away.

How much this particular phenomenon has to do with industrialisatio is unclear, since poor-state cities have continued to grow, not, as in the global North, because of industrialisation, but regardless of their failure to do so.[62] Those unable to find employment in the factories of the limited secondary sectors of the urban economy have pursued tertiary occupations in its more traditional, labour-intensive 'bazaar' ones, which are linked more closely anyway to the peasant population of the country-side from which immigrants come.[63] (The expansion of tertiary and service activities is a typical feature of rich-state urban centres too, but the processes are not comparable since they express different trends – the one towards enhanced manufacturing efficiency and affluence, the other a sort of pseudo-employment for the dispossessed that is seemingly very elastic in its capacity to absorb those without work.) The political effect is, among other things, to defuse the revolutionary potential a densely settled, self-conscious, and occupationally ambitious under-class like this might otherwise be assumed to bear.[64] Only where capitalist production methods have impinged to such an extent that the traditional structures have begun to fail does one see open unemployment of an urban lumpen-proletariat on a mass scale. Here, where the buffering effects of the trad-itional forms are breaking down, social polarisation does occur. A co-herent group or class response, even one of an ethnic or tribal kind, must still overcome, however, the 'highly individual needs of the very poor plus their distrust and lack of organisational experience'.[65] When we add in the contemporary technology of repression and the way the small numbers of people who command it can marshall the larger numbers who do not, it is no wonder that urban revolution is rare.

The existence of an intermediate zone undermines somewhat the sense of a discrete rural-urban divide. The contrast is easily overdone: 'there is no magic in urban residence . . . living in cities neither triggers the economic or social changes associated with urban areas nor delivers basic health amenities to a large part of the population.'[66] When we count out the local bourgeoisie, rural-urban contrasts in labour patterns and in individual prosperity remain small. The young males who move directly into megalopolitan slums, or indirectly via 'relay' towns, are prompted to do so by the limited opportunities open to them on the land, and by an optimistic perception of the city as a positive alternative that can be largely a psychological illusion. Despite the self-evident affluence of its elites, wealth remains unrealised for the urban mass. The poverty of the cities and towns is not so far removed in fact from that of the countryside. It is oppressive because it is so concentrated, but we should not lose sight of the equivalent hardships of rural life just because, except for the more conspicuous disasters or famines, deprivation is less apparent there.[67]

Rural/urban differences and inequalities remain important, however. The greater the economic capacity a 'developing' country comes to have, the more likely in practice it is to direct its human and material resources towards urban welfare rather than that of the state as a whole.[68] There

seems to be one typical pattern, for example, whereby the settled centre
that were established under imperial control to service mines, plantation
or commercial ports persist after 'independence' as the physical foci of
power for the emergent indigenous elites. Subsequent economic activity
flows through these administrative gateways, often no further than the
suburbs of the bourgeoisie, whose preferred life-style prompts them to
co-opt whatever resources do exist for themselves. In West Africa, for
example, which at the moment has one among the highest regional
rates of urban growth in the world as well as some of the poorest people
the port cities, which were the trading and administrative centres of the
colonial powers—since they already possessed at least some sort of
aggregate labour force as well as rudimentary services and a Westernised
'feel'—saw the siting of what post-independence industrial developmen
has taken place, and a rapid growth in importance and appeal. 'West
Africa continues to look down the track towards these big coastal cities,
modes of exchange in a world trade system',[69] though they are geographically 'eccentric' in the context of the separate states themselves.

Michael Lipton has documented the 'urban bias' of poor state develo
ment policies in some detail; it is not an elevating tale. Nor is the telling
likely to have much effect, since except for the commune-conscious
Chinese, poor countries are likely to remain, for the foreseeable future,
'so structured as to provide rural people with inefficiently and unfairly
few resources'.[70] The 'state' all too readily becomes the creature of
urban requirements; the city is no longer 'lost in the nation' but rather
the nation is 'created by the city as a projection of itself', and usually to
imperialistic effect.[71]

This rural-urban dichotomy has an important cultural dimension,
since the presence of growing numbers of people in settled aggregates
does seem, regardless of the particular context, to enhance personal
anonymity and impersonal relationships, occupational specialisation an
the division of labour, and social heterogeneity and the importance of
formal rules that discriminate the functional status of individuals rather
than their personal ones. Cities not only permit such qualities, to a certain
extent they seem predicated upon them.[72] In individual terms the
impact of urban values is said to contribute in a decisive way to a 'modern' outlook,[73] though this will remain contingent upon the range of
educational and occupational opportunities the urban environment
provides, and the economic advantages these can secure in turn.

In more general terms cities, if they are not solely concerned with
commerce, manufacture or administration, may serve to consolidate
and systemise the 'little traditions' of the countryside—to use Robert

Redfield's expression—and make of it something more explicit and per-haps more durable. This 'orthogenetic' role they share with that of 'heterogenetic transformation'—the cultural transmission, for example, to indigenous peoples of the market values of the capitalist world economy and of technological rationality.[74] These values may win only limited acceptance, stimulating attempts to recover traditional mores that do not sanction such Northern predilections for 'hard work, enter-prise, a favourable view of social change and a central faith in material prosperity'.[75] Cities and towns do tend to realise in built form, however, the broad social currents that swirl through the world. The individual eddies they make can prompt a particular, often quite idiosyncratic expression of them, but the homogenising force seems to be the stronger in the long run.

To summarise: pluralist analysis treats the difference between country-side and town as the inevitable outcome of the developmental process, to be managed by public policies within the general rubric of market enterprise. In the interests of industrial efficiency, measured in terms of capital accumulation and profit, society is so organised to specialise functions and differentiate the one realm from the other. 'From a socio-ecological standpoint', city growth 'is simply the concentration of differentiated but functionally-integrated specialisms in rational locales.'[76] Market competition will promote manufacturing that is aggregated or dispersed as the desire to minimise the costs of production dictates. Close settlement provides a market for the services that those who work there need, and so on. From this point of view any division between rural and urban affairs becomes less and less important as 'urbanization' becomes the dominant influence overall.

The 'practical question of who gets what, who determines who gets what and what determines who determines who gets what'[77] is answered most clearly, however, by placing urban growth, as structuralists do, in the context of a world capitalist economy. As populations grow and as money and the market ethic spreads, so spatial forms emerge, more consequence than cause, that circulate capital and goods and disseminate knowledge and information in a readily usable form.

We are dealing at large not with the transition from a rural to an urban world (though we can trace important changes in terms of this dichotomy) but with the subjugation of diverse social subcultures by one common culture that is socially transcendant and politically and economically most acute.[78] This one culture resonates with European values. It displays certain features, however, even if in only a rudimentary way, that stand apart from any value scheme as such—that seem typical of human agglomerations of any 'significant' size — and it extends them to the countryside beyond. The most important of these features is 'bureaucracy'. Without at least the semblance of same, no numerous human enterprise with a common end would be possible. Wherever mass collective action is sustained on a daily basis, it is by something resembling bureaucratic means. There is urbanisation without industrialisation, but bureaucratisation is common to both.

Bureaucratisation

Bureaucracy — that 'giant power', as Balzac put it, 'wielded by pygmies' — is a conspicuous feature of any and every political society;[79] even the most rudimentary among them now employs something of its typical administrative means to co-ordinate and rule. It has come to characterise many other sorts of organisations beside, and *bureaucratisation* — the progressively more extensive and intensive use in the making and the implementation of decisions of a social instrument that is centralised, regularised, disciplined, secretive, impersonal, hierarchic, 'rational' and nominally 'efficient' — stands beside industrialisation and urbanisation as a defining factor of contemporary social change. Not only does government, and indeed complex organisations in general, grow more bureaucratic; world society at large has come to assimilate the sort of values and attitudes such an ethos informs.

The problems involved in effectively realising the dictates of ruling elites have proved perennial ones. Many leaders of antique polities evolved elaborate systems staffed by officials (variously selected and rewarded) to implement their directives and to manage affairs of state — those of ancient Egypt, China and Rome being conspicuous examples. It is not always a simple matter in such cases discriminating administration as such from the capacity to govern, those wielding the subordinate means often seeming to pre-empt the preferred ends of their political superiors. The history of the phenomenon is deep and diffuse, however, and though its boundaries are often difficult to define, it is immediate and real. In analytic terms, it has drawn the attention most notably of Max Weber, who clearly recognised the ubiquitous qualities of bureaucracy and its enormous potential effects.

Weber characterised bureaucracy as the sort of organisation that observes defined and recognised spheres of competence (as laid down by established regaulations). Each individual office is strictly arranged by its ranked grade, and the work-load is systematised and co-ordinated by means of written files. Office-holders are required to discriminate between their private and professional affairs, undergo specialised

education or technical training, accept employment as a primary and
not a secondary working commitment, and learn the rules on which
their post and that of those around them is run. Office-holding takes on
a sense of vocational enterprise, served by the sense of security that sal-
aries, pensions and tenure endow. Under circumstances like these, the
compromised character, typical of more personalised and less impartial
modes of administration, is much reduced.[80]

In offering such a description Weber was aware that not all the listed
attributes would be present in any particular case, but the syndrome did
give us, he felt, a yardstick of use in measuring the world. Bureaucracy
also relied, in his view, on the general acceptance of the 'rule of law', on
known regulations and established and recognised processes for revising
them, and it served thus to legitimate the notion of legal authority itself. Above all, it seemed to him a rationalising device and an immensely
successful one: 'Everywhere its origin and its diffusion have . . . had
"revolutionary" results . . . Precision, speed, unambiguity, knowledge
of the files, continuity, discretion, unity, strict subordination, reduction
of friction and of material and personal costs—these are raised to an
optimum point . . .'[81] The result is a form of organisation that is, in a
'purely technical' sense at least, superior to any other; it stands to the
rest 'exactly as does the machine with the non-mechanical modes of
production'; 'fully developed' it is the administrative homologue—reliable,
repetitive and tireless—of factory manufacture.

One critical question follows: does it work? Does 'efficient' administration—the ostensible product of the 'pure' and 'full' form of bureaucracy, as Weber described it—necessarily flow from this one list of
attributes, or might there not be inconsistencies, or alternative features
with the same or superior effect? 'Efficiency' itself is an elusive criterion.
On the one hand we have the sort of Parkinsonian principle that 'work
expands so as to fill the time available for its completion,'[82] with staff
proliferating regardless of their load, and bureaucratic forms being used
to frustrate, where they are not actually a substitute for, the achievement
of the administrative purpose. On the other hand, the indices we use to
determine 'efficiency' will tend to be value-laden ones. And where bureaucratic forms achieve other social purposes than those of administration
alone, we need to assess very carefully what it is that 'efficiency' means.
If we accept that the 'basic question is how best to co-ordinate human
activities in order to make a highly rational unit, and at the same time
maintain social integration, the normative commitments of participants,
and their motivation to participate',[83] we find the latter often intruding
upon the former, partially or completely but not *necessarily* excluding

it. 'Getting things done' extends to much more here than the official end the organisation serves, though this need not always be incompatible with its ultimate function. Thus one study on the Mexican Ministry of Hydraulic Resources came to the conclusion that 'government agencies *can* operate efficiently within a structure which on the surface appears to be inefficient' (in the narrow sense of task effectiveness). The presence of 'formalism, role overlapping, personalism, patronage, and institutionalised bureaucratic politics' (which may look inefficient in the narrow sense but serve broader social purposes) did *not* exclude in practice the performance of the designated technical tasks.

The nature of the organisational function itself is not neutral. Security roles like administering 'justice' or maintaining law and order are of a different kind, it has been argued, from those of distributing social welfare or implementing programmes designed to encourage material 'development'. Separate tasks will implicate separate sorts of technical capacity, separate ways of acting and thinking and separate techniques for influencing those dealt with.[84] This is complicated in the case of ex-colonies where the administrative burden was originally one of imperial control. Indigenous bureaucrats tend to be elitist, overbearing, intolerant and dictatorial. These qualities are not always well found in a post-independence environment, particularly where the emphasis is moved towards service in association with rule.[85] In addition, a European-style preoccupation with regulations and rules, whilst enforcing a regard for what might be 'just' and 'fair', has often to be tempered (particularly where the ruling elite seeks legitimacy and trust) with indigenous notions of kin obligation or communal equity.

Regardless of whether it works: 'Everywhere the modern state is undergoing bureaucratization.'[86] There have been common conditioning factors like the global advent of a money economy, for example, which is germane to the process of bureaucratisation since 'bureaucracy as a permanent structure is knit to the one presupposition of a constant income for maintaining it.'[87] Again, though it has no necessary effect, large populations in complex aggregates predispose bureaucratic administration. Affluence is instrumental too. In this respect 'bureaucratisation is a function of the increasing possession of goods used for consumption,' higher standards of living making for an 'increasing subjective indispensability of organised collective, inter-local and thus bureaucratic, provision for the most varied wants, which previously were either unknown or were satisfied locally or by a private economy'.[88] To the above we can add the communal preference for order and hence for a force of police, for the provision of social welfare, and for ever more elaborate systems of communications and transport.

'The peculiarity of modern culture,' Weber said, by which he meant the culture of the capitalist market economy,

> and specifically of its technical and economic basis, demands . . . 'calculability' of results . . . The more complicated and specialised modern culture becomes, the more its external supporting apparatus demands the personally detached and strictly 'objective' *expert* in lieu of the master of older social structures, who was moved by personal sympathy and favor, by grace and gratitude[89]

or the client-patron nexus that still prevails in much of the peripheral world; the more it requires individuals who are prepared to school themselves to the 'habitual . . . mastery of single yet methodically integrated functions', to conditioned compliance, to the discipline of 'precise obedience within . . . habitual activity'[90] and the mental set such discipline demands.

The values implicit in the cultural package the global North provides are pervasive and importunate ones. This said, they are still a good distance from displacing local mores altogether, and in many cases a conscious attempt is made to resist such influences at the same time as they are accorded intimate embrace. And though the informal approach of an earlier age persists in the global centres themselves, regardless of the 'irrational' influence this may have on the process of impartial administration, the difference between the metropolitan context and that of the periphery remains marked, with semi-peripheral states displaying mixed characteristics in between. In general, bureaucracy in peripheral countries still bears the greater influence of non-legal characteristics — the persistence of patronage, for example, that flows from family, class, kin and ethnic identification; heterodox patterns of authority; an acute awareness of prestige and rank; highly personalised systems of interaction; widespread graft and corruption; and the selective and general neglect of the social mass.

Factors like these promote a less precise line between politics and administration. Where the state bureaucracy participates in a decisive way in planning industrial and agricultural production, it tends to become

> a state bourgeoisie; that is, it takes over, by controlling the economy, part of the surplus generated in the country. This bureaucracy nonetheless remains dependent in so far as the economy itself is dependent

and as domination by the center makes it possible for the latter to appropriate the main part of the surplus for itself.[91]

In a socialist state like China the civil bureaucracy remains subordinate to the Communist Party and to the declared desire for developmental independence, and Amin's observation quoted above does not apply. The line between politics and administration is no less obscure however, particularly as the Communist Party constitutes a complex bureaucracy in its own right. It is the party, furthermore, that decides the criterion of appointment to state administrative office, and its own members who tend to win such award.[92]

The notion that bureaucratisation is inevitable owes much to the ideology of industrial society and to the rather deterministic notion that contemporary technology will tend to define characteristic social structures that will employ in turn the sort of bureaucratic administration common in the developed global North. Convergence theorists treat bureaucracy, like stratification, as a functional requirement of any society that seeks to industrialise, since industrialism denotes common social aspirations that prevail regardless of any other intervening belief.[93] Industrialism predisposes 'rationality', they say — the precise, explicit, economically calculable and legally disciplined attempt to enhance human production by the most efficient available means. 'Bureaucracy' is the concomitant endeavour to rationalise social organisation. Industrialisation, however, like modernisation in general, involves the normative hegemony of transatlantic values, and bureaucratisation is one important expression of and vehicle for such values. Separating out the organisational aspects of bureaucratisation from its behavioural ones allows us to identify what seem to be universal institutional practices — centralisation, for example, and the award of specialised offices to those deemed suitably trained[94] — but even ostensibly neutral features like these can carry within them normative standards and beliefs such as the desirability of 'achievement motivation' and the Protestant ethic that Weber discussed. These are partial norms, and may not be globally apposite at all.

'Rationality' depends upon culturally particular concepts about what seems 'reasonable', which modifies in reality that 'rationality in *things* which is derived from their very nature and which imposes itself upon the human who tries to deal with them . . . the *necessita* inherent in the situations with which the person in politics is confronted'.[95] While individual statesmen may all pursue such general aims as economic growth through industrialisation, this may equally rationally be achieved by means of personalised capitalistic competition as by communal socialist command. The choice of means is ideologically determined, and not implicit in the general goal. To the extent that it affects the sort of bureaucracy that results, it becomes an empirical question just how much the sort of bureaucracies states develop as they industrialise do have in common, and how much they differ. To the extent that there is a single logic to the process, whatever its source, they will tend to converge; where this logic is significantly modified to accommodate other political preferences, they will not.

This debate has significant consequences for that between capitalists and socialists, since acceptance of 'convergence' and the march of 'rationality' defined in European terms transcends both sets of proponents. Weber argued that socialism would carry through in the economic realm the sort of process apparent in politics: 'The state . . . [having] "nationalised" the possession of arms and of administrative means . . . [S]ocialization of the means of production would merely subject an as yet relatively autonomous economic life to . . . bureaucratic management';[96] the state would become truly totalitarian, the daily purveyor of 'mechanism, depersonalization, and oppressive routine'.[97] The 'metaphysical pathos', as Alvin Gouldner called it, of this point of view,[98] lies in the way in which it encourages a sense of ideological surrender and political *ennui*. To accept such a perspective is to accept the notion that beyond both pluralistic competition and class struggle lies a basic omniscient outcome—that of bureaucracy.

Unlike Weber, Marx saw capitalism as a fundamentally compromised construct, and bureaucracy not as an organisational device but as an expression of class rule: 'the image of prevailing social power [though] distorted by its claim to universality'; the 'institutional incarnation of political alienation'.[99] He reserved the term to refer to state administrators whose more immediate concern with career prospects (the 'materialism of dumb obedience' and the administrative appropriation of the communal estate) seemed the real purpose behind their commitment to public affairs. Bureaucracy in this sense was destined to disappear once social revolution had transcended class society and replaced it with 'mere administration'.[100] In practice, bureaucracy still prevails under present-day socialism, ostensibly as a temporary instrument serving transitional ends. The fact that the transition has become a protracted one, and that state bureaucracies and bureaucratic methods have become progressively more entrenched there has largely served to negate the realisation of Marx's optimistic vision. It is something of which he would not have approved, opposed as he was to discrete and exalted administrators and to the pernicious effects of the functional division of labour and the hierarchy of institutions upon which administration feeds.

Such Weberian pessimism may well be ultimately misplaced, however. Whatever the choice of the values deemed necessary to realise the productive potential of contemporary technology and the material progress it makes possible, such progress does require a heightened capacity to manage and administer what is involved. But the opportunity is not lost, thereby, for the sort of consultation and co-operation that runs against Weber's monocratic 'Prussian enthusiasm' for military hierarchies.[101] A bureaucracy built along co-operative lines 'may well be by comparison a higher type . . . a "more fully developed" form of administrative organisation, not only in terms of humanitarian values, but also in terms of "results"',[102] and this need not and has not been neglected simply because one theorist so decreed. There have been diverse attempts in Europe and America to mitigate the worst features of bureaucratic excess (bureaucracy in the deprecatory sense as Frank Kafka depicted it, or the less surreal and more familiar phenomenon of the arbitrary, corrupt or bloody-minded official, retreating behind the rigid application of ridiculous rules to frustrating and non-functional effect). Attempts have been made to provide a more congenial environment for those who practise organisational skills, to enhance their flexibility and meet desires for democratic reform. 'The main task of management' in this respect 'is not to lay down rules on how to do the work but to maintain conditions in which adjustments spontaneously occur when new problems arise and to protect these conditions from bureaucratic processes of ossification';[103] to avoid, that is, the cybernetic disaster of complex organisations that remove themselves, in large part simply because of their capacity to reduce the realm of uncertainty, further and further from reality to the point where they are finally incapable of revising what they do in the light of their mistakes.[104]

This is to accept the human capacity to shape bureaucratic routines to idiosyncratic ends, as well as those, socially derived, that originate from outside the organisation, and to work with that capacity rather than against it — a point particularly important where the routines are comparatively alien to domestic experience, as I have already discussed in the context of 'developing' states. It also reinforces a general change that seems to have occurred over time away from the emphasis upon organisational discipline and coercion towards more diffuse and personally relevant ways of ensuring the uniform, regular and compliant individual practice that *is* bureaucratic performance.

We may conclude, then, that though bureaucratisation as a specific means of rationalising organisational structures and directing the individual behaviour that takes place within them continues to spread, it is still highly susceptible to reform within each local arena. While it promotes European rationalism as a scheme of values and a way of life, it remains open to the sort of humane subversion that can go some distance at least to mitigating its less beneficial influence. How far should we encourage this? Should we oppose bureaucratisation altogether? In 'developing' states the process of acculturation has not stopped administrative institutions from proliferating. These have developed their own interests as well as a material stake in the sort of growth that secures the income of their incumbents and the privileged consumption patterns this income allows. The retrograde consequences for the general populace are very evident. The crudely drawn but familiar picture of arbitrary, urbanised, patronising, elitist, personalist and parasitic administrators that so often prevails points up the strengths of the bureaucratic style Weber depicted. It would do well, in our honest appreciation of cultural differences and of the problems that abound in poor states, not to lose sight of what is of merit in the 'European' values bureaucratisation was elaborated to try to sustain. The process is proving too important, however, not to come to universal fruition in unexpected ways that no European is likely to predict.

Notes

1. An industrialised country is one in which a 'reasonable' amount of its productive output is derived from 'industry'; a majority proportion of which is in manufactured goods; having a manifest effect on the populace at large and some more specific influence on the employment of the available labour force. See R. Sutcliffe, *Industry and Underdevelopment* (Addison-Wesley, London, 1971), Ch. 2.1, 2.2, who gives the fudged values implicit in this composite definition a more specific quantitative construction, i.e. a country where at least 25 per cent of the gross domestic product arises in the industrial sector (60 per cent or more of which is in manufacturing) and where a minimum of 10 per cent of the population is employed there, is by his reckoning 'industrialised'. For a brief discussion of the history of the concept of an 'industrial revolution' see G. Clark, *The Idea of the Industrial Revolution* (Jackson, Glasgow, 1953).

2. L. Mumford, *Technics and Civilisation* (Routledge and Kegan Paul, London, 1943), p. 109, where he outlines his eotechnic, paleotechnic and neotechnic phases.

3. D. Landes, 'Technological Change and Industrial Development in Western Europe, 1750-1914' in H. Habakkuk and M. Postan (eds.), *The Cambridge Economic History of Europe*, vol. 6 (Cambridge University Press, London, 1966), p. 357. Also C. Cipolla (ed.), *The Fontana Economic History of Europe*, vol. 3, 'The Industrial Revolution' and vol. 4, 'The Emergence of Industrial Societies' (Fontana, London, 1973); A. Thompson, *The Dynamics of the Industrial Revolution* (Edward

Arnold, London, 1973).

4. 'It was the flow of capital, more than the stock, that counted in the last analysis; so much for the Marxist preoccupation with primitive accumulation' (Landes, 'Technological Change', p. 310). Also A. Gerschenkron, *Economic Backwardness in Historical Perspective* (Harvard University Press, Cambridge, Mass., 1962), pp. 45-6.

5. R. Dahrendorf, *Class and Class Conflict in Industrial Society* (Routledge and Kegan Paul, London, 1959), pp. 68-71.

6. E. Hurst, *Property and Prophets: the Evolution of Economic Institutions and Ideologies* (Harper and Row, New York, 1975), p. 155.

7. S. Amin, *Unequal Development* (The Harvester Press, Sussex, 1976), p. 60. Cf. K. Polanyi, *The Great Transformation* (Rinehart, New York, 1944), pp. 40-2, who sees the advent of a self-regulating market society governed by monetary transactions for gain not subsistence as a 'radical transformation', and the direct consequence of the application of machine production to a commercial society.

8. Amin, *Unequal Development*, p. 31.

9. Ibid., pp. 59-60. Marx himself did not consider machinofacture to have made much of a difference to the basic bourgeois propensity to appropriate surplus value; see *Capital*, Ch. 13, 'Machinery and Large-Scale Industry'.

10. The simple fact is that the institutional apparatuses of production and exchange do not lend themselves, given their present structure, to control and ownership by the associated producers within real living and working communities. They lend themselves solely to institutional control and ownership by state apparatuses that perpetuate, along with the social division of jobs, the stratification of society into classes and, in particular, the existence of a bureaucracy that keeps the proletariat in a state of dependence and subordination as total as under capitalism (A. Gorz (ed.), *The Division of Labor* (Humanities Press, New Jersey, 1976).

11. Landes, 'Technological Change', p. 594.

12. B. Moore, *Social Origins of Dictatorship and Democracy* (Penguin, Harmondsworth, 1967), pp. xii-xiv, Chs. 7-9.

13. Ibid., p. 506.

14. W. Cole and P. Deane, 'The Growth of National Incomes' in Habakkuk and Postan (eds.), *Cambridge Economic History of Europe*, p. 52.

15. I draw here on the list that P. Streeten gives in 'The Frontiers of Development Studies: Some Issues of Development Policy', *The Journal of Development Studies*, vol. 4, no. 1 (October 1967), pp. 3-8.

16. E.g. G. Soares, 'Economic Development and Class Structure' in W. Faunce and W. Form (eds.), *Comparative Perspectives on Industrial Society* (Little, Brown, Boston, 1969), p. 138.

17. S. Lilley, 'Technological Progress and the Industrial Revolution, 1700-1914' in Cipolla, *Fontana Economic History of Europe*, vol. 3, p. 187; K. Marx, *Capital* (J.M. Dent, London, 1930), vol. 1, p. 396.

18. J. Jewkes, 'The Growth of World Industry', *Oxford Economic Papers*, new series, vol. 3 (1951), pp. 1-15.

19. W. and H. Woodruff, 'Economic Growth: Myth or Reality', *Technological Culture*, vol. 7 (1968), p. 472.

20. Polanyi, *The Great Transformation*, pp. 71-6.

21. A. Maizels, *Industrial Growth and World Trade* (Cambridge University Press, Cambridge, 1963). The empirical trends identified there have persisted.

22. W. Woodruff, *Impact of Modern Man: a Study of Europe's Role in the World Economy 1750-1960* (Macmillan, London, 1966), p. 198. Cf. W. Leontief *et al.*, *The Future of the World Economy* (Oxford University Press, New York, 1977).

23. G. Kay, *Development and Underdevelopment: a Marxist Analysis* (Macmillan, London, 1975), p. 125.

24. W. Baer and M. Herve, 'Employment and Industrialisation in Developing Countries' in R. Jolly *et al.*, *Third World Employment* (Penguin, Harmondsworth, 1973).

25. A. Gerschenkron, *Economic Backwardness in Historical Perspective* (Harvard University Press, Mass., 1962), especially 'Reflections on the Concept of "Prerequisites" of Modern Industrialisation'.

26. Note here the debate between B. Warren, 'Imperialism and Capitalist Industrialisation', *New Left Review*, no. 81 (1973), P. McMichael, J. Petras and R. Rhodes, 'Imperialism and the Contradictions of Development', *New Left Review*, no. 85 (1974), and A. Emmanuel, 'Myths of Development versus Myths of Underdevelopment', *New Left Review*, no. 85 (1974). Exploitation denotes 'the employment of labour at wages lower than would obtain in a free bargaining situation; or in the appropriation of goods at prices lower than would obtain in a free market'. D. Landes, 'Some Thoughts on the Nature of Economic Imperialism' in M. Falkus (ed.), *Readings in the History of Economic Growth* (Oxford University Press, Nairobi, 1968), pp. 379-80.

27. Kay, *Development and Underdevelopment*, p. 130.

28. G. Cukor, *Strategies for Industrialisation in Developing Countries* (C. Hurst, London, 1974), Ch. 5; K. Griffin, *International Inequality and National Poverty* (Macmillan, London, 1978), particularly Ch. 6: 'Poverty in the Third World: Ugly Facts and Fancy Models'.

29. Amin, *Unequal Development*, p. 186.

30. Ibid., p. 203.

31. Moore, *Social Origins*, p. 410.

32. Sutcliffe, *Industry and Underdevelopment*, p. 324.

33. 'The British Rule in India' in S. Avineri (ed.), *Karl Marx on Colonialism and Modernization* (Doubleday, New York, 1968), p. 88.

34. J. Comhaire and W. Cahnman, *How Cities Grew: the Historical Sociology of Cities* (Florham Park Press, New Jersey, 1963), p. 1.

35. C. Tilly, 'The State of Urbanization', *Comparative Studies in Sociology and History*, vol. 10 (1965-1967), pp. 100-13. This is his distinction between demographic, economic, interactional and normative definitions of the process.

36. M. Castells, *The Urban Question: a Marxist Approach* (Edward Arnold, London, 1977), p. 17.

37. M. Weber, *The City* (Free Press, New York, 1958).

38. G. Sjöberg, *The Preindustrial City* (Free Press of Glencoe, Illinois, 1960), pp. 323-8.

39. A. Whiteford, *Two Cities of Latin America: a Comparative Description of Social Classes* (Doubleday, New York, 1964), p. 30.

40. Ibid., p. 31.

41. K. Davis, 'The Origin and Growth of Urbanization in the World', *The American Journal of Sociology*, vol. 60, no. 5 (March 1956), p. 433.

42. K. Davis, *World Urbanization 1950-1970*, vol. II (University of California, Berkeley, 1972), p. 46.

43. 'Over much of the world . . . the problem is . . . to establish a fit of statistical space with physical reality.' Despite megalopolitan commuters, however: 'the discordance between physical and socio-economic space is not yet very considerable . . . concentration remains the predominant feature of urbanization and its true measure' (R. Jones (ed.), *Essays on World Urbanization* (George Philip, London, 1975), p. 6).

44. K. Davis, *World Urbanization*, vol. II, p. 10.

45. 'In 1800 there were about 15.6 million people living in cities of 100,000

or more. By 1950 it was 313.7 million' (Davis, 'The Origin and Growth of Urbanization in the World', pp. 433-4). In a later study Davis gives the 1950 figure as higher again (taking his lower estimate: 406 million) and that for 1970 as 847.3 million (*World Urbanization*, vol. II, p. 15).

46. Davis, *World Urbanization*, vol. II, p. 59.

47. Ibid., p. 308.

48. Ibid., p. 52.

49. Davis, 'The Origin and Growth', p. 437.

50. Ibid., p. 433. On future patterns of international trade see Leontief, *The Future of the World Economy*, pp. 56-9. By the year 2000, Leontief estimates, 14.5 per cent of world gross product will cross national borders as compared to 10.6 per cent in 1970 (p. 56).

51. M. Lipton, *Why Poor People Stay Poor: a Study of Urban Bias in World Development* (Temple Smith, London, 1977).

52. D. Harvey, *Social Justice and the City* (Edward Arnold, London, 1973), p. 16. Also his 'The Urban Process under Capitalism', *International Journal of Urban and Regional Research*, vol. 2, no. 1 (March 1978), pp. 101-30.

53. Landes, 'Technological Change', p. 600.

54. Harvey, *Social Justice and the City*, pp. 203-4.

55. Ibid., p. 233.

56. D. Harvey, 'The Political Economy of Urbanization in Advanced Capitalist Societies: the Case of the US' in G. Gappert and H. Rose (eds.), *The Social Economy of Cities* (Sage, Beverly Hills, 1975).

57. Harvey, *Social Justice and the City*, p. 232; D. Slater, 'Towards a Political Economy of Urbanization in Peripheral Capitalist Societies', *International Journal of Urban and Regional Research*, vol. 2, no. 1 (March 1978), pp. 26-52.

58. Ibid., p. 108; cf. Lipton, *Why Poor People Stay Poor*.

59. Castells, *The Urban Question*, pp. 14-17.

60. A term used by T. McGee, *The Southeast Asian City* (Bell, London, 1967).

61. For a critique of the concept see N. Sovani, 'The Analysis of Over-urbanization', *Economic Development and Cultural Change*, vol. 12, no. 2 (January 1964), pp. 113-22.

62. Jones, *Essays on World Urbanization*, p. 40; quoting McGee. Also Amin, *Unequal Development*, p. 206:

> The distortion of precapitalist agrarian relations and the ruin of the crafts bring about urbanization without industrialization. The low level of the reward of labour, at one pole, and the concentration of capital, at the other, encourage foreign capital to establish modern sectors in the periphery, producing for export

and thus reproducing underdevelopment through 'unequal exchange'.

63. W. Armstrong and T. McGee, 'Revolutionary Change and the Third World City: a Theory of Urban Involution', *Civilisation*, vol. 18, no. 3 (1968), pp. 353-78.

64. J. Nelson, 'The Urban Poor: Disruption or Political Integration in Third World Cities?', *World Politics*, vol. 22 (1969-70), pp. 393-414.

65. Ibid., p. 411.

66. M. Qadeer, 'Do Cities "Modernize" the Developing Countries? An Examination of the South Asian Experience', *Comparative Studies in Society and History*, vol. 16 (1974), p. 272.

67. G. Sjöberg, 'Cities in Developing Industrial Societies: a cross-cultural analysis' in P. Hauser and L. Schnore (eds.), *The Study of Urbanization* (John Wiley, New York, 1965), p. 223. The movement between villages and towns is a

two-way one; interactions arise which can prove highly significant in terms of cultural change. G. Balandier, 'Urbanism in West and Central Africa: the Scope and Aims of Research' in *Social Implications of Industrialization and Urbanization in Africa South of the Sahara* (UNESCO, 1956). See, however, the divergent opinions of P. Morris, 'The Political Economy of Urbanisation: a Comment', *International Journal of Urban and Regional Research*, vol. 1, no. 1 (March 1978), pp. 171-3.

68. J. Gugler and W. Flanagan, 'On the Political Economy of Urbanization in the Third World: the Case of West Africa', *International Journal of Urban and Regional Research*, vol. 1, no. 2 (June 1977), pp. 272-89.

69. Ibid., p. 286.

70. Lipton, *Why Poor People Stay Poor*, p. 46.

71. N. Keyfitz, 'Political Economic Aspects of Urbanization in South and Southeast Asia' in Hauser and Schnore, *The Study of Urbanization*, p. 276.

72. R. Dewey, 'The Rural-Urban Continuum, Real but Relatively Unimportant', *American Journal of Sociology*, vol. 66 (1960-1), p. 65.

73. A. Schraiberg, 'The Modernizing Impact of Urbanization: a Causal Analysis', *Economic Development and Cultural Change*, vol. 20, no. 1 (October 1971), pp. 99-102. Georg Simmel described the mental effects of urban living as pervasive ones: 'spirituality, delicacy and idealism' go by the board; the division of labour means reducing the individual to the status of an instrument, with the subsequent death of personality:

the metropolis is the genuine arena of this culture which outgrows all personal life. Here in building and educational institutions, in the wonders and comforts of space-conquering technology, in the formation of community life, and in the visible institutions of the state, is offered such an overwhelming fullness of crystallized and impersonalized spirit that the personality, so to speak, cannot maintain itself under its impact. On the one hand, life is made infinitely easy for the personality in that stimulations, interests, uses of time and consciousness are offered to it from all sides. They carry the person as if in a stream, and one needs hardly to swim for oneself. On the other hand, however, life is composed more and more of these impersonal contents and offerings which tend to displace the genuine personal colorations and incomparabilities.

The individual has to exaggerate this personal element to remain audible 'even to himself'. K. Wolff (ed.), *The Sociology of Georg Simmel* (Free Press, New York, 1950), p. 422.

74. R. Redfield and M. Singer, 'The Cultural Role of Cities', *Economic Development and Cultural Change*, vol. 3, no. 1 (October 1954), pp. 58-9.

75. Ibid., p. 72.

76. E. Lampard, 'The History of Cities in the Economically Advanced Areas', *Economic Development and Cultural Change*, vol. 3, no. 2 (January 1955), p. 82.

77. R.E. Pahl, 'Stratification, the Relation between States and Urban and Regional Development', *International Journal of Urban and Regional Research*, vol. 1, no. 1 (March 1977), p. 16.

78. M. Castells, 'Is there an Urban Sociology?' in C. Pickvance (ed.), *Urban Sociology: Critical Essays* (Tavistock, London, 1976).

79. H. de Balzac, *Bureaucracy* (1898), p. 84; cited in M. Albrow, *Bureaucracy* (Macmillan, London, 1970), p. 18.

80. H. Gerth and C. Mills, *From Max Weber: Essays in Sociology* (Kegan Paul, Trench, Trubner, London, 1947), pp. 196-204. There has been much discussion of Weber's concept of the 'ideal type'. Suffice to say that in presenting an abstract list of attributes that could be used to identify 'bureaucratisation' – the more of

one, the more of the other—he had no desire to provide a Platonic surrogate for further empirical research. See P. Blau and M. Meyer, *Bureaucracy in Modern Society*, 2nd edn (Random House, New York, 1971), pp. 23-25; F. Riggs, 'Letter to the Editors', *Comparative Studies in Society and History*, vol. 18 (1976), pp. 533-4; C. Friedrich, 'Some Observations on Weber's Analysis of Bureaucracy' in R. Merton *et al.* (eds.), *Reader in Bureaucracy* (Free Press, Illinois, 1952), pp. 27-33.

    81. Gerth and Mills, *From Max Weber*, pp. 244, 214.

    82. C. Parkinson, *Parkinson's Law* or the pursuit of progress (John Murray, London, 1957), p. 9. The facetious formula for this trend is $x = \frac{2k^m + 1}{n}$, 'k' being the number of staff seeking promotions through the appointment of subordinates, 'l' the difference between the ages of appointment and retirement, 'm' the number of man-hours devoted to answering minutes within the department, and 'n' the number of effective units being administered. 'x' is then the number of new staff required each year. The figure 'proves' to be 'invariably' 5.17 to 6.56 per cent for any public department that is not actually at war. Unfortunately Parkinson does not allow for austerity budgets and staff ceilings politically imposed. Ho hum.

    83. A. Etzioni (ed.), *Complex Organisations* (Holt, Rinehart and Winston, New York, 1961), p. 1.

    84. M. Greenberg, *Bureaucracy and Development: a Mexican Case Study* (Heath Lexington, Mass., 1970), p. 138; R. Roy, *Bureaucracy and Development: the Case of Indian Agriculture* (Manas, New Delhi, 1975), pp. 14-16. Also S. Dube, 'Bureaucracy and Nation-Building in Transitional Societies', *International Social Science Journal*, vol. 16, no. 2 (1964), pp. 229-33.

    85. For a brief sketch of the special features of the colonial bureaucracies, see Dube, 'Bureaucracy and Nation-Building', pp. 231-2.

    86. Gerth and Mills, *From Max Weber*, p. 232.

    87. Ibid., p. 208.

    88. Ibid., pp. 212-13.

    89. Ibid., pp. 215, 216.

    90. Ibid., p. 229.

    91. Amin, *Unequal Development*, p. 350.

    92. Developing areas usually possess

not one but usually two or three, bureaucracies—or, at least, different layers of bureaucratic organisation and structure . . . the 'pre-development' layer, which had developed before the attainment of independence . . . [t]he second stratum . . . engendered by the dual impacts of the attainment of independence and of modernization and of establishing new social, political and economic goals . . . [and] the different 'party' bureaucracies which grew out of the leading nationalistic movements which became dominant parties.

S. Eisenstadt, 'Problems of Emerging Bureaucracies in Developing Areas and New States' in B. Hoselitz and W. Moore (eds.), *Industrialization and Society* (UNESCO, 1963), pp. 160-1. Also his 'Bureaucracy and Political Development' in J. La Palombra (ed.), *Bureaucracy and Political Development* (Princeton University Press, New Jersey, 1963).

    93. R. Skinner, 'Technological Determinism: a Critique of Convergence Theory', *Comparative Studies in Society and History*, vol. 18 (1970), pp. 2-27.

    94. C. Friedrich, *Man and His Government* (McGraw-Hill, New York, 1963), p. 465, who defines bureaucracy in terms of the 'taking of measures', and 'carrying on the work', the judicious application, that is, of general principles derived from other than concrete social instances.

95. Ibid., pp. 472-3.

96. Gerth and Mills, *From Max Weber*, p. 49.

97. Ibid., p. 50.

98. Following Arthur Lovejoy; A. Gouldner, 'Metaphysical Pathos and the Theory of Bureaucratisation' in Etzioni, *Complex Organisations*.

99. S. Avineri, *The Social and Political Thought of Karl Marx* (Cambridge University Press, Cambridge, 1968), p. 48.

100. A. Hegedus, *Socialism and Bureaucracy* (Allison and Busby, London, 1976); I. Deutscher, 'Roots of Bureaucracy' in R. Miliband and J. Savile (eds.), *The Socialist Register*, 1969 (Merlin Press, London, 1969); A. Mouzelis, *Organization and Bureaucracy: an Analysis of Modern Theories* (Routledge and Kegan Paul, London, 1967).

101. C. Friedrich in Merton, *Reader in Bureaucracy*, p. 31.

102. Ibid., p. 31.

103. Blau and Meyer, *Bureaucracy in Modern Society*, p. 59.

104. M. Crozier, *The Bureaucratic Phenomenon* (University of Chicago Press, Chicago, 1964), pp. 187, 203. Crozier sees the latter as not unintended but a necessary aspect of a system that requires at least a modicum of conformity from its members. It cultivates an arbitrary outlook, however; practitioners are protected from the insecurities that stem from performing their designated tasks, but they are protected from the 'sanction of facts' too. 'This engenders a secondary kind of anxiety and explains the paramount importance of human relations within a bureaucratic system . . . People escape the lower-middle-class status panic; instead they develop the skimpy outlook of the petty power struggles of a tight social system' (p. 208).

7   THE SOCIOLOGY OF INTERNATIONAL LAW

All societies are predicated upon a collectively realised capacity for ordered behaviour. They can be more or less cohesive. As I have argued already, at one end of the analytical spectrum they approach what would generally be defined as a 'system', where the relations between the individual members are of a comparatively perfunctory, associational sort and the relative intensity of interaction alone demarcates the social boundary. At the other extreme we find what are commonly called 'communities', each bound by a dense network of shared intellectual and moral concerns, and marked off from the rest of the human domain by the coherent character of their beliefs.

The many and varied ways of ordering human behaviour range in like manner along this spectrum, thus corresponding to the different sorts of societies we encounter in the world. Some of these 'control strategies'[1] will be common to all; others will be more or less marginal depending upon whether the society to which they belong approximates that of the 'systemic' as opposed to the 'communal' kind.[2] Thus we can discriminate controls that are (1) blatantly 'coercive' (more typical of 'systemic' societies) such as the overt violence characteristic of riots and mobs, wars and revolutions, and the terror tactics of dissidents or governing groups (as well as less drastic devices like threats, arguments, abuse, ridicule, boycotts and strikes), from those that are (2) culturally derived (and sustain a 'community') such as the appeal to widely recognised authorities, shared feelings, moral precepts and norms, the use of symbols and rituals, appropriate socialisation, assimilation and initiation techniques, stratification and differentiation. To these two broad categories we might add (3) the 'exchange' strategies derived from specific social 'bargains' where punitive sanctions or moral prescriptions are less applicable, (4) 'procedural' strategies such as bureaucratisation, and (5) 'manipulative' strategies that conceal the user's intent, like lies, gossip and rumour, propaganda and humour, magic, staging and performance, and the control of knowledge and information. The classificatory schema summarised above also cites 'coalitional' strategies and 'withdraw' ones. Though catch-alls like these overlap, they do indicate something of the range of ways in which that regular and predictable human response that stable social concourse requires is actually built up. They also suggest just how much of human behaviour may be implicated in this ordering

214

process, and how much an expression of the society they serve these devices will be. Here we find the sociology of law.[3]

Law is one mode of securing social control. The very explicit and precise nature of it can confer a degree of regularity and certainty not shared by other means. The extension of European thought forms and institutional preferences to the world at large has made this particular cultural conception of it, furthermore, an especially important one. In an abstract sense it refers to those rules, established by self-conscious legislative devices or through usage alone, that the members of a society are 'bound' to observe and purvey to the novice. Particular laws will reflect, as they help in turn to craft, the society in which they are found; and they will correspond in one form or another to the categories cited above. Thus in its coercive capacities (as 'hard' law) it represents the 'systematic application of the force of politically organized society'.[4] Even the most arbitrary regime tends over time to transmute its repressive powers into formal ordinances of this sort. We might imagine a society whose overlords can compel automatic obedience by the use of telemetered electrodes implanted in the minds of its subjects, where law as we know it would be irrelevant, but such a science fiction is not a reality, at least not yet. Law appears as less of an imposition at the communalistic end of the social scale, however (as 'soft' law that is, which some would deny is 'law' properly called at all). Some self-regulating human groups are sufficiently cohesive to be governed by customary cultural premisses alone. Where this is not the case communal societies will evolve laws or law-like ordinances[5] though the whole process is a more intimate one in instances like these because of the emotionally immediate ways in which transgressions tend to be dealt with. It need not be less formalised, however, or even less cruel. As an 'exchange' mechanism it will codify conclusions and undertakings that have been mutually agreed—a conception clearly suited to that of the 'contract' or 'treaty'. There will be 'procedural' laws too, and 'manipulative' ones, plus those of 'coalition' and 'withdrawal'.

Considered as such we can readily appreciate how law, its application and adjudication, is not a set of given formulae given in granite, but a social undertaking too. A sociology of law should be a radical pursuit of the political, economic and social roots of formal legal prescriptions, of the social functions they perform and the social structures they help define. The question of 'whose society' we live in leads quite naturally then to that of 'whose law'?[6] As one expression of a world society and the control strategies that prevail there our understanding of international law will reflect our understanding of the international system (or community, or whatever concept we consider most apt) as a whole. Thus a *pluralist* perspective that fastens upon state formation and the primacy of sovereign global groups competing for power will tend towards the notion of international law as the historically conditioned outcome of an evolving state system within which individual members seek some common ground that allows them to coexist. The fragmented nature of such a society has made for a body of law that, compared with the municipal variety at least, is much fragmented too. On the other hand, a *structuralist* view of the way the world is organised will see law as securing the interests of those who dominate the capitalist world economy, that is, the global bourgeoisie. International law defends the coherent material concerns of the dominant world class, disguising the divergence between such concerns and those of other groups and classes. In this latter conception class collusion will condition at every point the pluralistic precepts that are applied to the competitive pursuit of national interest.

World Society and International Law: the Pluralist Paradigm

International law is most commonly discussed in terms of a world of states, and the peculiar constraints and opportunities this world provides. The Treaty of Westphalia in 1648 first endorsed the formal European concept of territorial sovereignty, a concept subsequently imposed upon the political patterns of the global populace at large. The peoples involved in the original process had long traditions of social trade, and could appeal to a large historical stock of ideas about how a system of this sort might best be organised. The notion of a world of legally discrete and equal states, defending that fact and enjoining the mutual recognition of the perimeters of national authority, was the fundamental premiss upon which they proceeded. Given such an approach the 'basic norm' of international law became one that countenanced custom: that 'states ought to behave as they have customarily behaved' (in Europe at least, and in European dominated domains).[7] In this sense it is one of the most intriguing aspects of contemporary world society that we all live now under the general terms of a three-hundred-year-old compromise that was used to effect a European peace. No alternative notion of a law that might structure that society, however cogent, has overwhelmed it. Hence it is no accident that so much of international law is state-centric and assumes the central significance of this unit of behaviour, reinforcing human expectations about where we should turn to donate our dutiful allegiance and claim rights. Statesmen further the rules upon which their own roles are predicated, and their stylised routines define the distance between the entities they represent. Beyond this there is a plethora of principles, the result of specific treaties or of conventional practice, which help render the global arena less arbitrary in its influence upon any individual member. These decree (in statist terms) who can go to war and roughly when and under what conditions, that formal agreements be duly acknowledged and observed, that those who represent states in the interests of their own autonomous domains do not reach into other countries without the latter's permission, and that they seek to co-ordinate their diverse polities whenever mutual advantage might be served thereby. All such premises ease joint enterprise when there is no war, which for most states is much of the time. Governments need not, and indeed do not, relate in an anarchic fashion just because there is no commanding authority to prevent them playing chaos.

Within this plural social context international law has been depicted spanning the spectrum of control strategies from the coercive to the culturally diffuse, though pluralists themselves cluster at the pole of 'command'. This majority position is most clearly represented by those who argue that law is strictly construed only in terms of what can be enforced as law by physical means. It is very much in the mode of John Austin, whose influential statements on the subject reflect his own social status as 'a Victorian *paterfamilias* whose disciplinarian authoritarianism and egocentricity were only emphasised by his experience in the army'.[8] Since a plural world society possesses no generally authorised instrument for deciding what is to be 'the law', or for disciplining the disobedient, the global legal system is seen as something of a sham, as an elaborate set of forms without real substance that devolves in the end upon individual initiative alone to uphold what is set aside by those who choose to do so. The negative comparison with what is possible in a domestic context is only too apparent.

Not all who look at international law in coercive terms are so pessimistic, however. Wilhelm Wundt has argued that law need not be predicated upon the state at all; that we require only 'an association or society . . . capable of producing a collective will because of [a] correspondence of ideas and interests'.[9] Hans Kelsen has gone on to depict domestic and international law as constituting essentially the same sort of *imperium*; both, that is, posit sets of norms providing for socially organised sanctions against those who violate them.[10] Their crucial difference lies, he argues, in the degree of centralisation they display, international law having to cope with a comparatively dispersed social constituency, a fact that directly determines how it is derived (by custom and treaty rather than legislation) and the indirect way in which it must be applied. Each nominally independent state retains the ultimate capacity to affirm its ordinances. The international society must rely on its subjects to carry out, interpret, adapt, legitimise and defend them. Kelsen considers a social order as law 'even if it establishes only a decentralized force monopoly of the community constituted by the order, that is, if the principle of self-help still prevails'.[11] It is still possible, he maintains, to distinguish in such cases between the legal and illegal use of force, however 'primitive' the self-help, self-defence sort of system may seem. Even centralised orders are not able to dispense with this crude sanction altogether. Domestic law may seem more effective in that, once established, a monopoly of force can be used to create and impose an ordered state that is more readily maintained, less arbitrary, and less liable to neglect. Nevertheless it is an empirical fact that for the most part the international law that has prevailed for three centuries or so has been followed with unfailing care by those who subscribe to it. Which is not to say that there have not been disasters, or attempts to legislate the sort of behaviour some states or all of them will not abide. Too many people have too much in common, however, and too much to gain from a regulated environment for there not to be referential rules of some kind. 'Law gives to society that element of fixity and regularity and continuity without which no coherent life is possible,'[12] and the fact that there *are* collective sanctions, even though they take the form of 'reprisals and war' rather than 'punishment and civil execution',[13] suggests that international law does deserve the name. Though 'reprisals and war' are not always, or even usually, used to defend the integrity of the international system, they do exist for that purpose and though they may mostly occur in pursuing other than legal ends, rarely is there no appeal at all to the legality of the moves made. What referential rules exist are wilfully misinterpreted, or spuriously endorsed to defend political claims, but not with impunity. The accounting process is limited and imperfect and radically compromised, but it does exist. And the fact that considerable human enterprise is committed to the articulation and the adjudication of referential rules *as if* they were laws, and not only orders supported by a sense of menace or value imperatives or good global manners, has positivistic consequences that cannot be ignored.

If we admit more than the notion of law as the creature of will, politics and power, but as one conveying norms and reasons too; if law is more than the generalised description of what is done in its name and is recognised as a vehicle for moral rules about what *ought* to be done as well; then we admit a more subtle realm that moves towards the communalistic end of the spectrum of social control. Laws may be 'morally quite indifferent',[14] finding a social place simply because of the need for at least something of the sort regardless of ethical decree. Indeed, the moral merits or the cultural consequences of *domestic* laws are commonly ignored in practice, and debates about their legality are conducted as often as not in terms of what can be established from prior ordinance and the judgements of authorities on the same or similar decrees. The same applies to international law. But this cannot explain why they are finally obeyed where obedience is in fact forthcoming.

Law, we may remember, 'is regarded as binding because it represents the sense of right of the community: it is an instrument of the common good'. Enforced by the 'strong arm of authority' law 'can be, and often is, oppressive . . .[15] [but] Law, like politics, is a meeting place for ethics and power'.[16] We need the double dimension to explain its effects (though what is 'binding' may be a product ultimately of what is thought to be, spoken of, and functions as such.)[17] To be construed as *law* there must be somewhere in the background the concept of a clear and certain obligation; the heightened likelihood that such dictates will be obeyed; the impending sense, that is, of a kick in the pants where they are not. As an artifact of a society of states, however, international law will confirm whatever sentiments enable such a society to cohere. It will never be the *same* as moral or cultural values since it cannot and does not appeal to conscience alone, but the link between law and justice will always implicate values of some sort, reflecting the moral outlook of the society in which these values persist. International law may well play a less significant part than the analogous strategy in the domestic context, but it cannot be understood as something separable from its cultural and moral loading. That loading will be biased in favour of particular social fractions or particularistic national concerns, but there is nothing peculiar to global principles in that. Pluralists portray international values and norms as necessarily group-bound,[18]mostly emphasising 'reasons of state' and remaining resolutely unimpressed by the moral content of international law. A common stock of globalised values will depend, they say, directly upon what the most influential global entities choose to impose, and by international law we simply mean the 'footprints of power passed'.[19] But this goes too far. It underestimates the extent to which the contemporary system has managed to establish, however susceptible to both divergent translation[20] and daily abuse, a common code for a community of all states.[21] The society within which modern international law has evolved has changed markedly over the centuries. 'In a society in which power is the overriding consideration', the basic purpose of law has remained its capacity 'to assist in maintaining the supremacy of force and the hierarchies established on the basis of power'.[22] The defence of state sovereignty furthers this *status quo*, thus vindicating the position of the power-pole pluralists. Values remain relevant none the less though, and we cannot rely upon the judgement of those committed to a definition in 'command' terms alone.

The 'state', to recapitulate, was a European invention, a socio-cultural form the whole world has come by fair means or foul to accept and to work within. Attempting to move against it would be to push up-hill against pointed sticks, or in less metaphorical language, to resist a large and powerful part of the global population that is already organised in such a way and committed to the concept's physical and analytical defence. Nor would it seem particularly desirable to do so either. 'States', however ridiculous they may seem, do lend a measure of much-needed precision to world affairs, 'hence the value of the maze of trip-wires which divides the surface of the globe (and labels its inhabitants) in silly patterns. We need frontiers too badly to let them become quickly obsolete.'[23]

The idea of the 'state' is imbued with a number of basic European values, however, and since it has been used for so long to focus international law, the latter now amounts to an explicit defence of them. In the most general sense, Western legal thought embodies a 'logical rationalism' that is both substantive (internally consistent and consistent with Western society) and procedural. Max Weber considered this the original expression of European culture alone. A totally logical and rational legal system would be impossible of course. It would not be human. Furthermore, other cultures than the Western one have displayed something of this feature. In Weberian terms, however, it is the European tradition that has carried such a process to its present pitch. As one might expect of a people whose developed philosophies have made so much of the subject-object dichotomy, it is to general rules established by reasons (and not revelation or divination or reflex emotion or intuition) that Westerners tend to turn.[24] Emphasis falls upon explicit principles and procedures, which as far as it is possible do not appeal to mystical, religious, political, ethical or sensual preferences for their inspiration or interpretation or the way they are applied. Whatever its origins (and though not a necessary precursor of it, such an approach was highly compatible with capitalism and rose to prominence as part of that socio-economic package) it has become a global possession, and one so pervasive and fundamental it is often completely missed. Perhaps, even though they may resent its failures to embody their own preferred values, it is this very ethos of 'objectification' which has made it possible for diverse global groups to accept European laws. Whatever the case, the most obvious contribution the contemporary international legal system has made is to confirm and defend the value of the pluralist prescription itself, portraying discrete states competing for power as the 'supreme normative principle of the political organisation of mankind . . . the fundamental or constitutional principle of world politics in the present era'.[25]

In more particular terms the doctrine of national equality, for example, a fundamental tenet of the original body of international law, is a transparent fiction that has helped to defend the highly unequal character of world affairs. Appropriate enough among those countries that first secured the terms of interstate intercourse, it has become progressively less so as the society of them has spread. New states have found the rhetoric of sovereign equality useful in winning a voice in the world and asserting their autonomy and independence, a voice that would otherwise have remained subordinate and largely unheard. Among other things, however, this has only served to obscure global patterns of class inequality. These patterns are revealed once we peel back the panoply of legal forms that support the local hegemony of ruling elites to reveal the links that define, for example, the global bourgeoisie. The preoccupation with sovereign equality and co-operation and the language and practice of law itself conceals the extent to which the contemporary *status quo* serves the material interest of nation-states, and the extent to which support for such equality and co-operation by the leaders of new 'nations' is predicated upon their sharing, as often as not to the detriment of local peoples at large, as much as possible of this material largesse. Hence with very few exceptions it is the evolving world society that has accommodated international law and not the other way around. I shall return to this argument later.

The leaders of new states have been far from compliant, one should add. Ruling what for the most part were once colonies, they have been heir to unequal treaties and averse to accepting the responsibilities these define. Hence they have chosen not to extend the basic principle that 'promises be kept' to the promises such undertakings contain. Strictures against 'intervention' have been attacked too, in as much as they sanction continued control of peoples denied self-determination. There has been considerable controversy over the sort of compensation offered those who have lost property or control of resources in the process of nationalising indigenous assets, or whether payments of this sort are in order at all.[26] Ordinances protecting foreigners themselves and other of their possessions, delimiting territorial waters, securing sea-bed minerals and the like, have also come under contested scrutiny. The general consensus international law inspires, however, has been much too effective to be seriously disturbed by conflicts like these.[27]

It is possible to maintain that beneath this consensual coating the major world cultures will continue to assert their own legal traditions, 'stressing the primacy of the group, assigning essentially role-playing functions to the individual, and keeping thought subordinate to custom and authority'. Competing conceptions like these would seem much less willing to lift out 'law' as a discrete network of norms, or to countenance 'contract' as a definitive device for ordering human affairs, or to render 'rights and obligation in the language of legal abstractions'.[28] It is difficult to envisage just how significant a difference such traditions could make to the present-day legal system but it would appear, superficially at least, that their effects need not always be dissonant ones.[29] The contemporary precepts of international law are often strikingly similar to those of sub-societies like Islam.[30] Indeed it has been argued that a number of notions implicit in international law were derived from the historical relations between Asian and European 'states' in the first place. The imposition of imperial control 'eclipsed' the contribution of extra-European ideas, which were only rediscovered once the particular subject peoples had been freed.[31] It is simply not the case, then, that we are witnessing a general rejection of international law and international organisation as the representatives of new states find their feet, or that precepts of this sort must find themselves in retreat as normative systems that have never accepted the distinctive European vision of law as a discrete entity in its own right, nor the values embedded in it, begin to assert themselves. International law, as it has been constituted so far, has proven remarkably robust, and not just as a cynic might say because it is ultimately irrelevant, but because it serves socio-economic and political purposes that are universally shared.

When we consider the impact of such ostensibly revisionist regimes as those of the Soviet Union and the People's Republic of China, we find a similar outcome. Soviet analyses originally condemned the corpus of international law as a legacy of bourgeois imperialists and not applicable to a revolutionary socialist society like its own. Recognising its own political and national interest in 'peaceful coexistence', however, they chose in due course to abide by its basic definitions, its key categories and fundamental principles, with due allowance for the sort of emphasis that reflected their particular experience and preferred values. Furthermore, except for the rhetorical acknowledgement (and in the Hungarian and Czechoslovakian cases, the adversary imposition) of 'proletarian solidarity', relations between the Soviet Union and the satellite socialist regimes have been conducted along very traditional lines. There has been a distinct preference at large for obligations defined by treaty and for law by consent rather than the customary kind. The latter was seen to be loaded against them, and is incompatible anyway with the Marxist doctrine of class[32] since no one body of customary international laws could be in principle equally applicable to such divergent states as socialist and capitalist ones. In their own discussion of international law, the relative experience of class contradiction is still given pride of place. International relations, it is argued, are truly inter-national, and the 'basic peculiarities of international law', as they are called, 'arise from the fact that it regulates first and foremost, and primarily, the relations between sovereign states'.[33] The foreign policies of these states express the will of each predominant local class, which in capitalist countries is the ruling one and in the Soviet Union is depicted as that of the 'entire people'.[34] Law itself, including international law, is described 'not as a result of an increase in community among people, but as a result of the division of society into classes and the formation of new class contradictions . . .'[35] Bourgeois law is an exploitative device that conceals its 'true essence' behind the declaration that it serves the common good, and a belief in its fundamental antipathy to the normative basis of 'socialist' law is retained. Thus 'peaceful coexistence' in Soviet parlance does not mean an end to class war. This proceeds out of reach of international law, though, and is manifest on a global scale only indirectly in relations among *states*.

By this latter device Soviet doctrine effects a compromise, and its most prominent proponents have long proclaimed 'that general international law, whose norms regulate relations among all states irrespective of their social systems, exists and the possibilities of its further development are increasing'.[36] The Chinese conception has been similar, if marginally more radical in tone. Where not directly derivative of Soviet assertions, it clearly converges upon like themes.[37] Thus we find international law described as the 'superstructure of a capitalist economic base . . . which . . . reflects exactly the will of the bourgeoisie'.[38] This will is not monolithic. The bourgeoisie all over the world have 'their own countries with their legislative and judicial organs' and while equally hypocritical they have their own divergent 'interests' that reflect their different local situations. What is more, within the bourgeoisie of any one state there are discrete groups representing separate views. Hence contradictions are common and diverse schools of thought have been advanced to account for them. Any contention of this sort is of 'secondary importance' however, since on general strategic objectives the bourgeoisie is agreed; such a range of views only facilitates flexibility. The various schools identified above are characterised as 'natural law', 'positive law', 'middle-of-the-road' (Grotian), 'normative' and 'solidarist' ones,[39] and they form, it has been argued, a historical sequence that corresponds to the rise of the bourgeoisie itself. Thus in those places where we find a record of bourgeois revolt against feudal aristocracy, we also encounter — not coincidentally — appeals to 'reason', 'justice' and 'human nature' as the ultimate source of international law. Casting their own particular concerns in terms of their universal principles, bourgeois radicals were able in the past to oppose monarchic authority and such customs and treaties as had been negotiated by the feudal ruling class.[40] Once in power, they developed the doctrine of positive law as an ideological defence against those who would oppose them. Imperial expansion on the part of the most dynamic powers called forth a more adaptable theory, an opportunistic combination of naturalistic and positivistic tenets that was used to rationalise the process of global aggression involved. The hegemonic designs of the most assertive fractions of this class have culminated, the Chinese say, in one-world philosophies that posit the supremacy of a 'transnational' or world law — if not now then potentially and desirably so. The drive to global domination is dressed up in the normative rhetoric of those who advocate international respect for the individual, and a world government overall. In this sense what was once progressive has become an instrument of capitalist/imperialist oppression, and a profoundly reactionary one. How, one might ask, can the Chinese with their anti-capitalist, anti-class predilections accept such a system? They have certainly debated the issue, as the Soviets have done.[41] In practice, though, they have made the inheritance of international law their own, seeking to infuse the principles of sovereignty, equality and non-intervention — said to have been consistently violated by their original bourgeois proponents — with a superior socialistic ethic of their own. This practice they portray in their own lyric idiom as a question of '"sleeping in the same bed but dreaming different dreams"'.[42]

The Western proponents of 'transnational' law, acutely criticised by the Chinese, may be placed within the present framework at the 'cooperative' end of the pluralist spectrum. Holding aside for the moment any ideological function they may serve as the intellectual agents of an insidious bourgeoisie, analysts like these consider themselves as documenting a profound change taking place in world society, a change which has had tangible effects upon international law. They accept the notion of a world of states, so we may legitimately characterise them as pluralists. However, the competition for power and influence that takes place between states is modified, they argue, by structures of global co-operation. Recognition of a growing number of political, economic, social and ecological issues, of concern to not just one or a few states but all human-kind, makes such modification well-nigh irresistible.

In its most extreme form this leads to the notion of world government, of 'world peace through world law'[43] and the establishment of 'world scale institutions corresponding to those which have been found essential for the maintenance of law and order in local communities and nations'.[44] One body of world law, and particularly a law against war, that could be called down upon any individual citizen of a mass world society who contravened it without governmental sanction, would ostensibly bypass the need as now to hold a whole country to account. This would be useful since force, while it may intimidate individuals, is harder to use on a collective enterprise; the 'point of application' is less obvious and more abstract.[45] The explicit analogy with law and order in localised communities is misleading, however. States are not like human beings. They are less defenceless and hence more capable of persisting in a disorderly environment. What is considered above as 'essential' within states may well not be necessary at the world level at all and may even, it has been argued, be positively undesirable there. And anyway, a world government and world law would not preclude or even inhibit, perhaps, world civil war.[46]

The notion of a domestic imperative in this respect is itself misleading, since human societies have been known to exist with practically no government or law at all in the familiar sense. This is not to suggest that there is no politics either, though it is the pristine image of the legal process and a positive aversion to the comparatively sordid business of political and diplomatic bargaining that often prompts such an idealistic preference. 'Law is the poetry of government; politics is its prose,'[47] and who would not choose one resonant image over a page of mundane words? And yet, it is the political and not the legal process that is so prominent a feature of global affairs, and the creative capacities of this process cannot be ignored.

Apart from those who advocate world government, we find a number of pluralists who draw a more modest lesson from the greatly expanded range of contemporary international law.[48] Independent of the social control of overt conflict and diplomatic exchange, they say, the need has arisen to regulate the proliferating body of functional concerns that most separate states pursue, and to articulate and communicate what has been agreed to meet this need. Beside the 'international law of liberty'[49] then, we find an emerging body of principles that pertain to human welfare and national development. A list of these rules, agreements, conventions and recommendations would include any treaty that defined the terms of technical or material assistance that rich states give to poor ones, the work of diverse quasi-autonomous international organisations like the International Monetary Fund (IMF), the World Bank, and other global or regional credit-granting institutions, the General Agreement on Tariffs and Trade (GATT), the United Nations Council for Trade, Aid and Development (UNCTAD), the formal agreements that are made between private or semi-private commercial and financial groups and state regimes, and the public and ratified conventions that flow from those conferences convened to establish states' rights to the commonweal (like those on the law of the sea), or to renegotiate monetary or commodity arrangements, or to revise ways of implementing development strategies in general. The latter would cover the continuing series of conferences that have been held to attempt to redefine the international economic order, as well as such United Nations Resolutions as No. 3281 (xxix) outlining a Charter of Economic Rights and Duties of States, and ratified by the General Assembly in December 1974. Not all that issues from the above has the status of law. Its content has changed as 'minimalist' guarantees of continued political and functional commerce have been joined by 'maximalist' claims for global justice in the pursuit of economic advance. But as an expression of global social 'co-operation' it grows and does not diminish.

These changes are so profound, it is argued, that international law has entered a state of 'arrested ambiguity' between the traditional forms that fasten upon territorial sovereignty, and those contemporary developments that tend to undermine it.[50] Much that was once held to be in the 'private' domain has now become an explicitly 'public' concern since it is 'states' that form the focus once a system of village-level subsistence is left behind; that must mediate the goods and services desired. The assertion of human rights to personal well-being works to extend and strengthen governmental reach; at the same time such rhetoric universalises a moral purpose that is deeply antipathetic to a society of states. Social and economic development, and the attempt to realise for each individual an improved standard of living wherever he or she lives, has become a general communal issue to be pursued, however nominally, by state governments in the interests of whole nations. With a growing amount of international financial and industrial exchange, with the spread of transnational corporations and increasing competition between them, we find state regimes signing away sovereignty in the material self-interest of both the rulers, and at least ostensibly, the ruled, while at the same time legislating defensive controls over just this sort of erosion of their politico-economic domains. The corporations have learned to work with the need to concede a national interest in their branch subsidiaries, even to take advantage of the participatory arrangements in personnel and equity that local law may require them to make. And state regimes—those of poor ones in particular—are usually too dependent financially and technologically on the assistance they get to resist the deals such powerful private concerns can offer. A goodly amount is invariably made of the subtle conditions of the local investment 'climate' and the desirability of keeping up foreign investor 'confidence'. Any felt need to supplement the paucity of domestic capital with foreign input, to expand employment opportunities and to generate the revenue to pay for educational, medical, agricultural and any other such 'development' plans a government may have is used to foster legal agreements that allow 'reasonable' corporate profits (which is a suitably expansive concept) and their repatriation overseas.[51] The tide runs both ways at once.

It would be specious to assert that any of this, or the functional maintenance of such public utilities and social welfare measures as receive global or near-global support, successfully overshadows the fact of modern nation-states. However, the greater volume of contemporary interactions plus their global scope have had a notable impact on international law, which is called upon furthermore to serve an increasingly revisionist function within world society. As well as an 'essentially negative code . . . of abstention' that defends a strategic *status quo*, we find a growing body of 'positive rules of co-operation',[52] though arriving at such rules may involve as much conflict in fact as co-operation. International conferences that once allowed founding states to accommodate diverging concerns under the auspices of accepted legal understandings have become overtly political events where the disadvantaged and the dispossessed seek to establish the legitimacy of what in the contemporary context are often very radical claims. Beside occasions for confrontation like these we find much smaller groups of countries, plus corporate bodies, negotiating company, copyright and patent agreements, tariff and tax, loan and investment, trade, aid, labour and utility conventions in a 'positive and formative' way. It has become commonplace to argue that world society relies increasingly upon traffic of this sort to secure conditions of peace and ecological stability, and to avoid extensive wars or irretrievable environmental decline.

It remains a difficult area, however. The notion of a universal human interest has been notably absent from contemporary clashes over communal world property and development opportunities. In these cases Grotius has been decisively despatched. It has been evident for some time, in fact, that in the 'enlarged community of nations . . . we find a new majority with new demands about the task of the new community, with new opinions about the aims of the law'. Such an assault tends to be met by 'annoyance', the 'dignified, self-satisfied minority' castigating that 'materialism, mere selfishness, and resentment that forgets the good done and only remembers the evil'. We find the founding fathers talking in dismissive terms about those who behave in so 'ill-mannered, so little civilized' a manner.[53] Over the last two decades this clash has become less rhetorical and more serious; the tone of the debate has become more penetrating. South-world states have sought cogent arguments to advance their sense of dissatisfaction, and contested issues are now joined at a no less political but a much more sophisticated level. Rich North-world countries still accept international law as a valued instrument of social control, so they cannot avoid this assault and the charge that those who built the system in the first place possess unfair advantages within it. Which hardly prevents them resenting the attack and defending themselves.

Returning to the general theoretical debate proves a sterile ploy. It is

equally well argued either that the Western nations are entitled to and should be trusted with the further development of international law, for the common good of the world community, or that the whole of international law must be discarded because it is tainted with its past acceptance, and indeed legitimization, of colonial conquest.[54]

One central fact persists. There is no global authority with the capacity to realise what is 'just' about poor-state claims unless the sanctions involved serve the interests of some particularly potent state (or states) and the latter decides to act. All of which bears witness to a more divergen and limited body of law overall than is variously supposed. Those treaties, precepts and conventions that do pertain to co-operative law must be scrutinised closely for what effect they really have upon the society of states.[55] The chance that 'all states will contract with one another with respect to all subjects'[56] is a practical impossibility that points up the heterogeneous and piecemeal way in which the web of law and law-like obligations has been developed. The optimistic ideal of a comprehensi world law, whatever its source, is predicated upon a degree of human solidarity that does not as yet exist. Given the pervasive quality of con-

temporary state-binding forces, it remains one of those 'great intuitions
... those "civilising ideas"'[57] that may well make for a revised social,
strategic and politico-economic order in the end, but whose progress is
invariably difficult to secure and notoriously uncertain in its effects.

International law emerges from this view, then, as a more limited and
practical tool of global social control, though no less significant perhaps.
To demonstrate its importance we only have to wish it away. It may
over-state the case, but we can say that without such precepts:

> there would be no security of nations or stability of governments;
> territory and airspace would not be respected; vessels could navigate
> only at their constant peril; property . . . would be subject to arbitrary
> seizure; persons would have no protection of law or of diplomacy;
> agreements would not be made or observed; diplomatic relations
> would end; international trade would cease; international organ-
> isations and arrangements would disappear.[58]

It remains as state-bound, however, as the society it helps define and
discipline. Those who want to belong to that society accept the principles
of public world conduct it purveys. No people has successfully denied
the ideology of state and nation formation on which it is constructed,
even where they might choose to do otherwise.

Behaving towards others as one would have them behave towards oneself depends upon a sense of enlightened self-interest. As we reach
beyond this to consolidate our commitments in ways that feel more
solemn and secure, we foster a 'sense' of law[59] and the values it articulates
and defends. Society's fundaments are material ones too, however, since:
'any authority guaranteeing a legal order depends, in some way, upon
the consensual action of the constitutive social groups, and the formation
of social groups depends, to a large extent, upon constellations of
material interest.'[60] The latter are served within the contemporary world
economy by a market system that relies upon complex agreements that
'work', that are legally effective and, '*calculable* . . . in accordance with
rational rules'.[61] How can we account for efficiency like this in the
absence of one formally coercive global power? We must look not only
to the shared interests of competing state regimes but to some other
entity that is in a position to regulate the appropriate rules to predictable effect. A pluralist outlook alone is insufficient to describe and
explain the collusive power of those involved.

World Society and World Law: the Structuralist Paradigm

The prime contender, in *structuralist* parlance, is the global bourgeoisie, and a class-based analysis looks to the world society of bourgeois modernising elites—both capitalist and socialist—for the common interests that generate a world law. The most obvious source of an analysis of this sort, the theoretical statements made by the Soviets and the Chinese, has proved quite inadequate. Neither of them has done more than sketch a vulgar Marxist caricature of a structuralist perspective. Tunkin, for example, decrees that: 'The economic structure of society is the primary base which defines in the final analysis the international legal position of a state in its primary features.'[62] Between the economic structure of individual states and their international legal posture, however, lies such superstructural determinants as 'ideology, national law, [and] international legal doctrine', and these too must be taken into account. International economic relations, he continues, whilst increasingly important as a source of international law, are a secondary concern. Class is seen to be the social form through which a state's international legal will is expressed, but we find nothing more precise than a blanket dispensation to this effect.

The Chinese establish the same relationship of superstructure to base, but they make more of the difference between capitalism and socialism, and the competing fractions within the capitalist economic camp. 'World law', they ask 'is the superstructure of which economic base? What type of economic development does it reflect?'[63] They find most compelling the post-war expansion of American influence and the 'neo-colonial' plunder of diverse Asian, African and Latin American states: a '"world law" which reflects this type of economic unification can only express the interest and will of the American monopolistic bourgeoisie'.[64] 'Universalism' is but a verbal device to deceive the victims of American infiltration and control.

Rather than implicate the Americans alone, however, we might extend this sort of analysis to account for the interest any modern-minded bourgeoisie shares in maintaining and extending the global market system wherever they live—even in China. This does not exclude the idea of competing state regimes; it suggests a complementary concept of a society inhabited by those with like outlooks on the industrial mode of production and the capitalistic system of world exchange, whose behaviour is variously conditioned by this synoptic economy and the way it changes and the world law that it requires. It is not necessary to confirm this position or the pluralist one as the ultimate determinant in world affairs. We might realistically expect either one or the other to prevail or to remain a conditioning influence depending upon circumstances and the particular place and time. It does, however, require us to take a structuralist perspective more seriously than is usually the case.

What is the content of 'structural' world law? There is more to it than mere 'transnationalism'. Transnational treaties and agreements, however, are one place where we might seek the empirical content of structuralist precepts—there, and in the partial or general attempts by those who own and control the world's productive capacities to secure free commerce and trade. As a capitalistic system the world economy is imbued with classical liberal notions of comparative advantage—a vision of a world market without barriers, regulated by supply and demand and equally advantageous to all who might choose to take part. Though they are frequently prompted by socio-political concerns to protect their state domains, often to stringent mercantilist effect, the bourgeois beneficiaries of this system are obliged at some point to defend these basic values or go out of business. They also, it seems, purvey a much more subtle process that Marxists call 'commodification'. Under capitalism, products become 'commodities', individuals become 'citizens', and peoples become 'states'. This logic is a fundamental part of the capitalist propensity to render all things in formal, abstract terms. Qualitatively discrete entities are rendered quantitatively equivalent, thus disguising the sense of their difference or needs, and disguising the class *in*equalities that actually prevail:

> just as the commodity form 'replaces' use-value and concrete labour with the abstractions of exchange-value and undifferentiated labor-power, the legal form 'replaces' the multiplicity of concrete needs and interests with the abstractions of 'will' and 'rights' . . . the socially differentiated individual with the abstraction of the *juridical subject* or the legal person,[65]

and the culturally or socially defined collectivity with the abstraction of the sovereign state. Any community assembled from such entities will be as illusory as the reified blocks from which it is built. A capitalist world market is a particularistic one anyway, and under conditions like these law becomes a 'fetish', an order appearing 'not as an object or national choice undertaken by autonomous subjects, but rather as an autonomous subject itself'.[66] It will dominate those who make it; the creature prevailing over its creators and confirming the power of capitalism to alienate and command.

We can explain the structuralist content of international law quite well short of this, however. We can simply compare the functions a state must perform to secure a capitalist market system *within* its boundaries with the conditions that must be met to sustain the same sort of system world-wide. Robin Murray has catalogued a number of the former —protecting property rights, establishing conditions for free, competitive exchange (that is, the free movement of goods, money and people, plus standardised currencies, commercial principles, and weights and measures), regulating business cycles, securing such basic ingredients of the productive process as labour, land, capital, technology and public utilities, and intervening where necessary to control the anti-social effects of pollution, poor conditions of work, and misleading conditions of sale.[67] We find — not surprisingly — that the fundamental 'standards' of international economic law[68] perform precisely these functions. These are, for example, minimal standards, widely endorsed, protecting those who effect global commerce, and their property. 'Most-favoured-nation' arrangements give all interested parties in principle the same rights that a state regime unilaterally grants another. There is also the dictum that states observe, as well as possible, an 'open door' in economic matters, and where they cannot do so to close that door an equal amount to all. No national component of the global bourgeoisie implements such standards in practical detail, and those who do so confine their support to particular issue-areas only. They remain, however, a potent aspiration for all those who would commodify capital and labour and maximise profits on a world scale. The first of them might be said to be a prerequisite for any international economic activity at all. The *quality* of protection, however, such as the amount of compensation that might be sought in the event of the local national take-over of a foreign firm, is meant to establish the legitimacy of international enterprise, and it is a shared belief in that legitimacy as much as any possible punitive sanctions other states might bring to bear that prompts national elites to pay the sort of price often required. The other two standards are compromised by an abundance of preferential agreements, but not radically so. As precepts they recommend the broadest possible access to world commerce, and indeed without the idea of equal opportunity a common cause in an international system of this sort would be impossible to sustain. An expanding range of commercial agreements supports the general freedom that marketing requires. These are buttressed by currency stabilising institutions like the IMF[69] and trading arrangements that militate against commercial discrimination and help keep state barriers down,[70] by profit repatriation schemes, by planned attempts to pre-empt

the global propensity to bust and boom, by international labour regulations, anti-pollution measures, and so on down Murray's list.

For the freedom of the market, for capitalist commodification and
the pursuit of profit to prevail, so must 'equality before the law', which
in the global context is a concept closely supported by that of 'sovereignty'.[71] The fact that class inequality, 'neo-imperialism' and 'dependence'
may be a direct consequence of such an ostensibly neutral system simply
reflects the persistence of pernicious divisions of labour and the capacity
of those who own and control the means of production on a world scale
to appropriate much of what surplus is produced. Market 'freedom'
turns out to be false not in the sense that it is subject to the sort of
direct regulation states are able to make, but in the way it binds those it
formally but unfairly treats as equals who in reality are not. 'Most-
favoured-nation' clauses favour in fact the stronger industrialised states,
who in receiving reciprocal benefits they hardly really need negate the
spirit of judicial equality. The GATT, though it allows for poor-state
preferences, treats them as marginal to the greater body of world trade,
which of course they are. Poor-state power to effect retaliatory measures
remains minimal and so does the influence of the Treaty in this respect.
Contracts across state boundaries, regardless of the public or private
capacities of the parties involved, become one way of negotiating a
dominance/dependence relationship in disguise. While free agreement
between equal entities who meet in a market to exchange goods is quite
possible in principle, in a world as unequal as our own an ideology of
this sort and the law that it generates serves 'not the rational regulation
of power relationships but the irrational legitimation of unjustified inequalities'.[72] We might quibble about our index of 'justification', but
the general point is clear enough.

The world economy is notable for its discontinuities, for the divide
between rich states and poor states and the rich and poor within them.
In so far as international law vindicates such an economy, those who
create it will further the sort of social structures it serves to reproduce;
most obviously here, the various state fractions of the global bourgeoisie,
but also the managerial regimes that control the transnational corporations. Businesses of this size

> live symbiotically with governments in a very strange way . . . [They]
> sometimes need the law, and for that they need governments. But
> they are too big to be ruled by governments . . . Conversely, no oil
> company or fruit company could by any stretch of the imagination
> become a state.

So they coexist, each helping co-ordinate the complex interplay of what is a truly 'extraordinary mixture of free market, ologopolistic competition, political manoeuvre, and direct hierarchical command'.[73]

The original liberal intention to maintain a 'free' market for capitalistic enterprise has never been realised to any notable extent, domestically or globally. It remains limited despite the fact that as production is progressively internationalised the market grows more diverse. Transnationals, for example, further subvert any one country's ability to control the world traffic in money and goods. By buying and selling, producing and consuming within the same enterprise, the inhibiting effects of territorial boundaries are diminished and the independent capacity to influence world economic affairs proliferates. There is a concomitant centralisation and concentration process, however, which may be channelled in due course into regional pools fixed on Europe, the United States, Japan and the Soviet Union, each arena with its own legalised defences. Whether global liberalism will survive and revive as South-world industries spread and other centres of manufacture seek to compete with those of the hegemonic world powers remains to be seen.

Only one thing is reasonably certain, that we will not find any redistribution of global resources by institutional means to those who need them most, nor a world law that reflects a widely shared political will to that effect. Attempts at a nominal redistribution through those international agreements with at least a textual commitment to raising standards of living, promoting real income, ensuring 'high' or 'full' employment, and expanding production and exchange[74] have failed to redress the bias towards the rich states and the 'Wall Street diplomacy' that brought these particular organisations into being.[75] Alternative platforms like those of UNCTAD, or the United Nations itself, have not on the whole functioned as law-creating bodies in any tangible sense, but rather as public sounding boards for poor-state complaints and the appeal to world opinion at large. This North-South conflict, conducted by a numerous and heterogeneous group of states, has not only been ineffective, it obscures the collusive aspects of the world market system and the extent to which, for even the most disaffected and radical poor-state regimes, it has been business as usual and as much as they can get.

The dramatic growth over the last 150 years in the number and the integrity of national polities and in global production and exchange has generated, we may conclude, a very broad body of practical conventions and negotiated accords. We can extract from this collection those general principles that define contemporary interests and values and the world society these reflect, a world society both state-centric and class-bound. From the *pluralist* perspective, the fact that 'sovereignty' and 'national interest' and the inequalities of power make for an uncertain and contingent legal system does not obscure the sheer volume of ordinary everyday transactions that states perform, and the general conventions they observe in the performance. The global acceptance of the sort of bureaucratic methods already discussed has been an important factor in making this possible. It would not have occurred, however, without the universalised belief that it is state-based procedures which are the legitimate and authoritative ones, and that human-kind has more collectively to gain than to lose from diversified territorial jurisdictions and the way this engenders reciprocal respect. *Structuralists* seek the puppeteers, the principal performers, the global privileged who move at will behind the clutter of national masks. They find them since they seek them, and they direct our attention to the way the world entertains much less than all its audience. The bourgeois consensus on the basic rules of the game does not preclude competition, however. Indeed in striving to protect and promote state 'private' property and international 'free' enterprise they actively promote it. Political sovereignty predisposes economic sovereignty. Both are conditioned by the world society of modernising elites and the world market that helps sustain them. International law, however, while it is significantly more than the strategic tool of disparate sovereign powers, is still significantly less than the house code of a monolithic socio-economic cabal.

Notes

1. P. Sites, *Control: the Basis of Social Order* (Dunellan, New York, 1973), esp. Ch. 6, 'Classification of Control Strategies and Tactics'.

2. It was F. Tönnies, *Community and Association* (Gemeinschaft and Gesellschaft), trans. C. Loomis (Routledge and Kegan Paul, London, 1955) who gave this dichotomy particular credence. G. Schwarzenberger has used it to characterise three ideal types of law in, for example, *The Frontiers of International Law* (Stevens and Sons, London, 1962), Part One; *The Dynamics of International Law* (Professional Books, 1976), Ch. 7. I find the use here of the term 'society' to oppose that of 'community' a misleading one, however, hence the formulation in the text.

3. understood in its full purport, sociology of law would have to comprise an investigation into the relationship between *all* legal and all other social phenomena. It should thus concern itself first of all with the question of why law, in the sense of a politically organised enforcement of a social order, has arisen at all; how the enforcement machinery can be organised and how it operates; to what extent it is effective, and by what factors the varying degrees of its effectiveness are determined; what factors influence the content of those rules of social conduct which are legally enforced;

why, how, and in which ways the content of these rules is changed with changing social conditions; which factors determine which fields of human conduct are under given circumstances to be subject to legal control; which are to be subject to ethical, religious, conventional, or other forms of social control, and which are to be left free of all social control altogether (M. Rheinstein (ed.), *Max Weber on Law in Economy and Society* (Harvard University Press, Cambridge, Mass., 1954), p. xlvii).

Also E. Ehrlich, *Fundamental Principles of the Sociology of Law* (Harvard University Press, Cambridge, Mass., 1936); C. Reasons and R. Rich (eds.), *The Sociology of Law: a Conflict Perspective* (Butterworths, Toronto, 1978).

4. R. Pound, 'Sociology of Law' in W. Moore and G. Gurvitch (eds.), *Twentieth Century Sociology* (The Philosophical Library, New York, 1945), p. 300.

5. This corresponds to Schwarzenberger's Law of Power ('brutal domination') and Law of Coordination ('saintly self-negation') alluded to above in note 2. See *The Frontiers of International Law*, pp. 11-16. His third ideal type (Law of Reciprocity) is what I have termed, following Sites, as 'exchange'. He has nothing equivalent to the other categories. Note in this connection S. Diamond, 'The Rule of Law versus the Order of Custom' in Reasons and Rich, *The Sociology of Law*, who argues that customary and legal orders are basically contradictory; they are related historically but not logically (p. 241). The latter emerges with 'civilisation' and the state, and is the 'autonym' of order, not its synonym (pp. 257, 259). He concludes:

> The progressive reduction of society to a series of technical and legal signals, the consequent diminution of culture, i.e., of reciprocal, symbolic meanings, are perhaps the primary reasons why our civilisation is the one least likely to serve as a guide to 'the unshapeable basis of human society' (p. 259),

which has not prevented it attempting to do so.

6. E.H. Carr uses a similar construction, *The Twenty Years' Crisis* (Macmillan, London, 1962), p. 179.

7. H. Kelsen, *Principles of International Law*, 2nd. edn (Holt, Rinehart and Winston, New York, 1966), pp. 5, 564. See the critique of the need to posit any such 'basic norm' in H.L.A. Hart, *The Concept of Law* (Oxford University Press, Oxford, 1961), pp. 228-9. He calls this an empty repetition of the mere fact that the society concerned (whether of individuals or states) observes certain standards of conduct as obligatory rules; that those who accept certain rules must also observe a rule that the rules ought to be observed. I am not sure myself this can be written off, as Hart does, so readily as a 'mere' reduplication. It seems to me particularly important that a set of rules *are* generally observed by states, a fact that bears restatement in Kelsenian terms.

8. L. Green, *Law and Society* (A.W. Sijthoff, Leiden, 1975), p. 2.

9. Quoted in Pound, 'Sociology of Law', p. 330.

10. Kelsen, *Principles of International Law*, p. 551.

11. Ibid., p. 15.

12. Carr, *The Twenty Years' Crisis*, p. 179.

13. Kelsen, *Principles of International Law*, p. 551.

14. Hart, *The Concept of Law*, p. 223.

15. Carr, *The Twenty Years' Crisis*, p. 177.

16. Ibid., p. 178.

17. Hart, *The Concept of Law*, p. 226.

18. See J.D.B. Miller, 'Morality, Interests and Rationalisation' in R. Pettman

(ed.), *Moral Claims in World Affairs* (Croom Helm, London, 1979).

19. J.D.B. Miller, personal communication.

20. A. Bozeman, *The Future of Law in a Multicultural World* (Princeton University Press, New Jersey, 1971).

21. Discernible here is a perennial debate that is normally posed in terms of 'naturalists' versus 'positivists'; the former attempting to relate international law to universal values, the latter grounded in the concept of self-interest and in the present context, that of nation-states.

22. Schwarzenberger, *The Frontiers of International Law*, p. 25.

23. W.J.M. Mackenzie, *Politics and Social Science* (Penguin, Harmondsworth, 1967), p. 364.

24. Rheinstein, *Max Weber on Law*, p. xviii. Also D. Trubek, 'Max Weber on Law and the Rise of Capitalism', *Wisconsin Law Review*, no. 3 (1972), pp. 720-53. Weber saw European law as 'more "rational" than the legal systems of other civilisations, that is, it was more highly differentiated (or autonomous), consciously constructed, general, and universal' (p. 724). Indeed, it was uniquely so, and it played a 'necessary, or at least highly conclusive' part in the development of European capitalism. A capitalist system, to work effectively, requires a predictable normative environment that can contain and regulate the sort of egoistic behaviour upon which it is based. Law alone was sufficient to this purpose, Weber argued. It served in turn to legitimise capitalist class rule. Since this analysis was tied to the notion of a competitive market in which no one member predominates, it is less relevant today for explaining the economic role of law within states. Given the global situation, however, it translates well to any attempt to describe what pertains *between* them.

25. H. Bull, *The Anarchical Society* (Macmillan, London, 1977), p. 140.

26. See K. Carlston, *Law and Organisation in World Society* (University of Illinois Press, Urbana, Illinois, 1962), for a general discussion of nationalisation.

27. S. Sinha, *New Nations and the Law of Nations* (A.W. Sijthoff, Leyden, 1967); F. Okoye, *International Law and the New African States* (Sweet and Maxwell, London, 1972); J. Stone, 'Afro-Asian Nations and International Law' in Stone, *Of Law and Nations* (Wilhelm Hein, New York, 1974); L.C. Green, 'The Impact of New States on International Law', in Stone, *Of Law and Nations*; A. El-Erian, 'International Law and the Developing Countries' in W. Friedmann *et al.* (eds.), *Transnational Law in a Changing Society* (Columbia University Press, New York, 1972).

28. Bozeman, *The Future of Law*, pp. 162-3.

29. A. Fatouros, 'The Participation of "New" States in the International Legal Order' in R. Falk and C. Black (eds.), *The Future of the International Legal Order*, vol. 1 (Princeton University Press, New Jersey, 1969).

30. M. Talaat Al Ghunaimi, *The Muslim Conception of International Law and the Western Approach* (Martinus Nijhoff, The Hague, 1968), p. 222.

31. C. Alexandrowicz, *Introduction to the History of the Law of Nations in the East Indies in the 16th, 17th and 18th Centuries* (Oxford University Press, Oxford, 1967); R.P. Anand (ed.), *Asian States and the Development of Universal International Law* (Vikas, Delhi, 1972).

32. R. Erikson, *International Law and the Revolutionary State: a Case Study of the Soviet Union and Customary International Law* (A.W. Sijthoff, Leiden, 1972).

33. G. Tunkin, *Theory of International Law* (Harvard University Press, Cambridge, Mass., 1974), p. 241.

34. Ibid., p. 211.

35. Ibid., p. 27.

36. Ibid., p. 34., cf.:

> Although International Law, like any other branch of law, has a class character and pertains to the superstructure it cannot express the will of the ruling class of any particular State. It is the expression of the agreed will of a number of States in the form of an international agreement or custom which has grown up over a long period. The purpose of present-day International Law is to promote peaceful coexistence and cooperation between all States regardless of their social systems (Academy of Sciences of the USSR, *International Law* (Foreign Languages Publishing House, Moscow, 1960?).

37. J. Cohen and H. Chiu, *People's China and International Law: a Documentary Study* (Princeton University Press, New Jersey, 1974); H. Chiu, 'Communist China's Attitude towards International Law', *The American Journal of International Law*, vol. 60 (1966), pp. 245-67.

38. Ying Tao, 'Recognize the True Face of Bourgeois International Law from a Few Basic Concepts' in Cohen and Chiu, *People's China*, p. 41.

39. Ibid., pp. 38-40.

40. Ibid., p. 39.

41. Korovin was the leading proponent of the view that socialist and capitalist societies inhabited divergent realms of discourse and international law could not be used to bridge the gap.

42. Chiu, 'Communist China's Attitude towards International Law', p. 253.

43. G. Clark and L. Sohn, *World Peace through World Law*, 3rd edn (Harvard University Press, Cambridge, Mass., 1966).

44. Ibid., p. xi.

45. R. Fisher, 'Bringing Law to Bear on Governments' in R. Falk and W. Hanrieder (eds.), *International Law and Organisation* (J.B. Lippincott, Philadelphia, 1968).

46. See the critique of the world law approach in I. Claude, *Power and International Relations* (Random House, New York, 1962), pp. 260-5.

47. Ibid., p. 263.

48. J. Nye and R. Keohane (eds.), *Transational Relations and World Politics* (Harvard University Press, Cambridge, Mass., 1972); W. Friedmann, *The Changing Structure of International Law* (Stevens and Sons, London, 1964). We may note here Friedmann's distinction between the international law of 'coexistence' and that of 'co-operation'.

49. B. Röling, *International Law in an Expanded World* (Djambatan, Amsterdam, 1960), p. xv.

50. W. Coplin, 'International Law and Assumptions about the State System', *World Politics*, vol. 17, no. 4 (1964), pp. 615-35; S. Hoffmann, 'International Systems and International Law' in K. Knorr and S. Verba (eds.), *The International System* (Princeton University Press, New Jersey, 1961).

51. Very evident in many empirical cases. See Ch. 5.

52. Friedmann, *Changing Structure*, p. 82.

53. Röling, *International Law*, p. 68. See the Third United Nations Conference on the Law of the Sea (1973-7) that by 1974 involved 137 countries and has been described as the 'first formal law making conference operating at this level of size and complexity' (E. Miles, 'Introduction' to the special issue of *International Organisation*, vol. 31, no. 2 (Spring 1977) on 'Restructuring Ocean Regimes: Implications of the Third United Nations Conference on the Law of the Sea', p. 157). Driven by the confrontation between global North and South, this was foremost 'a fight to redistribute ownership and control over world ocean resources'. Also R. Friedheim, 'The "Satisfied" and "Dissatisfied" States Negotiate International

Law: a Case-Study', *World Politics*, vol. 18, no. 1 (1965), pp. 20-42.

54. Fatouros, 'Participation of "New" States', p. 349.

55. J. Stone, 'A Common Law for Mankind?' in Stone, *Of Law and Nations*, p. 49.

56. Fatouros, 'Participation of "New" States', p. 362.

57. C. De Visscher, *Theory and Reality in Public International Law* (Princeton University Press, New Jersey, 1957), p. 99.

58. L. Henken, *How Nations Behave* (Pall Mall Press, London, 1968), pp. 22-3.

59. Ibid., p. 94. Also M. McDougal *et al.*, 'The World Constitutive Process of Authoritative Decision' in Falk and Black, *Future of the International Legal Order*, p. 95; 'Fundamentally, international law is a process by which the peoples of the world clarify and implement their common interests in the shaping and sharing of values.'

60. M. Weber in Rheinstein, *Max Weber on Law*, p. 37.

61. Ibid., p. 40.

62. Tunkin, *Theory of International Law*, p. 236.

63. Chiang Yang, 'The Reactionary Thought of "Universalism" in American Jurisprudence' in Cohen and Chiu, *People's China*, p. 42.

64. Ibid., p. 43.

65. I. Balbus, 'Commodity Form and Legal Form; an essay on the "Relative Autonomy" of the Law' in Reasons and Rich, *The Sociology of Law*, p. 78.

66. Ibid., p. 84.

67. R. Murray, 'The Internationalization of Capital and the Nation State', *New Left Review*, no. 67 (May-June 1971), pp. 84-109. Note here, too, the correspondence with the 'capital logic' school of the Free University of Berlin (whose case is summarised and criticised in B. Jessop, 'Recent Theories of the Capitalist State', *Cambridge Journal of Economics*, vol. 1, no. 4 (December 1977), pp. 361-4. This approach attempts 'to derive the general form of the capitalist state, as well as its principal functions, from the pure capitalist mode of production and its conditions of existence'. The state must realise those

> legal and monetary systems necessary to facilitate the production and exchange of commodities (including labour-power), as well as the development of legal apparatuses able to adjudicate and enforce these rights. The state must also establish a monetary system that facilitates exchange and permits rational economic calculation. The state is also required to secure the reproduction of wage labour to the extent that this cannot be done through market forces and to ensure its subordination to capital in the labour process (p. 362).

In its more rigid form, the argument is ultimately reductionist, and cannot account 'for the origins of the capitalist state nor explain how it can function *as if* it were an ideal collective capitalist'; and it is assumed 'that the interests of capital are always realised in the final analysis' (p. 364). Used in a more flexible fashion, however, this approach is very revealing at both the domestic *and* the international levels – the latter being the one most relevant here. At the very least, it helps specify the 'broad limits' within which variations can occur 'without fundamentally threatening the process of capital accumulation'.

68. Schwarzenberger, *The Frontiers of International Law*, pp. 219-21. Not all of his list is relevant under contemporary circumstances. Also F. Garcia-Amador, 'Universalism and Regionalism in International Economic and Trade Law: the Experience of Latin America' in C. Schmitthoff and K. Simmonds (eds.), *International Economic and Trade Law* (A.W. Sijthoff, Leyden, 1976).

69. M. Shuster, *The Public International Law of Money* (Oxford University

Press, Oxford, 1973), who notes (p. 3) an 'extensive network of international agreements . . . concluded by States establishing monetary rules of varying scope and impact . . . more far-reaching and elaborate than is generally realised', and a 'more general and ever-continuing post-war movement towards the establishment of a more rational, legally-orientated, international monetary system' (p. 318). He cites as evidence the 'near non-existence not only of any regulating devices of a legal nature, but of any other form of international monetary cooperation during the inter-war period'. He observes:

> Contemporary international monetary law has, through a network of multi-lateral (both global and regional) and bilateral treaties, subjected to a relatively rigorous legal regime two of the three principal corrective devices which States resort to when confronted with a deteriorating payments situation – namely exchange rate alteration and direct commercial and financial controls (p. 315).

For a more sceptical discussion in the light of contemporary developments see F. Block, *The Origins of International Economic Disorder: a Study of United States International Monetary Policy from World War II to the Present* (University of California Press, California, 1977); C.F. Bergsten and L. Krause (eds.), *World Politics and International Economics* (Brookings Institution, Washington, 1975); J. Spero, *The Politics of International Economic Relations* (George Allen and Unwin, London, 1977).

70. K. Dam, *The GATT; Law and International Economic Organisation* (University of Chicago Press, Chicago, 1970).

71. S. Picciotto, 'The Multi-National Firm and the Nation-State' in J. Zorn and P. Bayne (eds.), *Foreign Investment, International Law and National Development* (Butterworths, Sydney, 1975).

72. Ibid., p. 59. Also K. Renner, *The Institutions of Private Law* (Routledge and Kegan Paul, London, 1949), p. 39; 'Introduction' by O. Kahn-Freund.

73. Mackenzie, *Politics and Social Science*, pp. 375-6.

74. GATT, 'Preamble'; IMF, Article I, 'Purposes'.

75. B. Gosłovic, *UNCTAD: Conflict and Compromise* (A.W. Sijthoff, Leiden, 1972).

8 THE SOCIOLOGY OF WORLD CONFLICT

'Conflict' denotes opposition and struggle. 'Competition', its less dramatic cousin on the conceptual continuum, assumes opposition too, in the sense of an opponent, a competitor.[1] We generally think of the latter as a less troubled process though, and while the struggle for superiority *may* lead to conflict it does not itself involve the overt clash of interests or ideas. Conflict is distinguished by a moment of conscious irreconcilability, however brief or however protracted that moment might be; by the dashing together of what has come to diverge, and the mutual awareness on the part of those concerned that this is what is taking place: 'Implicit in the sociological conceptualisation of conflict is some theory of cost. Conflict arises when there are incompatible or mutually exclusive goals or aims or values'[2] that are regarded as such by the antagonists involved.

When applied to human society, conflict is used to describe a wide range of activities, from psychic anxiety to world war. As such it is a fundamental quality of human behaviour, and one so general as to seem synonymous with life itself. Few human beings not obviously psychotic achieve that state of personal grace and spiritual harmony where inner strife has been transcended and mental peace becomes a permanent possession. Certainly no society has ever done so. A comprehensive explanation of a phenomenon so pervasive would amount to a general theory of human nature and human association itself. Not many have turned their hand to such a task, and I am not about to do so here.

Nevertheless, a considerable amount is known about human conflict and because the phenomenon *is* so pervasive each discipline has attempted its own specialised understanding of it; psychology, economics, politics, anthropology, social biology and sociology, all ask and variously answer their own particular questions about the human propensity consciously to contend in a pacific or violent way. Successfully combining what is known under one coherent theoretical umbrella is another matter again though.

Rather than attempt what may well be impossible anyway, I would like to conclude in this chapter with a discussion of the way social conflict is generated by particular social structures,[3] and more especially, how the pluralist and structuralist perspectives depict conflict within world society: mainly, why this arises, but also where it goes, how it is handled, and what are its effects. Though this means entering the global arena at the level of the social collectivities of state and class, whatever is said cannot both begin and end there since insights derived from other analytic strata will bear upon what we seek to explain, and to decide that the sociological approach is wholly sufficient is to legislate in advance where our most pertinent conclusions will be found. Given the synergistic quality of human interactions, however, the entry point is well chosen none the less. The analysis will inevitably be biased by working from the top down rather than starting, for example, with the socio-psychological attributes of individuals and proceeding from there to society at large. But it is a bias that seems justified in terms of its explanatory range.

World Society and World Conflict: the Pluralist Paradigm

The traditional image of world politics as a group-bound affair, states and other more or less autonomous entities colluding and colliding, rolling about the global billiard table, rising from the fertile felt or falling off the edge into oblivion, has been a most productive one in terms of our understanding of contemporary world conflict. Those who have attempted to move beyond this to formulate a 'systems' approach almost invariably characterise the world as one where the 'sub-systems' (states and corporations predominantly) are determinative. They recast notions of power and power-balancing in a technical language that does no more than re-state policy-making in the light of a larger calculus, and leaves policy-makers looking considerably less purposeful and less capable of realising their own objectives than in practice they are.[4]

Systems do not, with the exception of John Burton and his 'cobweb' model and Kenneth Waltz with his 'systemic' approach, move much beyond a familiar pluralistic conception of the world. Burton's notion of it in terms of global networks, try as he might to locate states in the context of larger transactional systems that the importance of territorial boundaries tends to obscure, did not dispute their central significance. 'World society', he concluded, 'is best analysed by considering systems first, and then the role of States, which is the reverse of a traditional approach.'[5] The latter remains the paradigmatic focus of concern that the traditionalists have always espoused, and Burton himself has never made much of the border-crossing networks that he considers so significant. 'Trade flows, letters exchanged, tourist movements, aircraft flights, population movements and transactions in ideas, cultures, languages and religions'[6] may all be suggestive of independent institutions, but in reality they are heavily conditioned by national borders and what these borders represent. To my mind the only 'system' of any truly transnational quality is that of the world's modernising elites—the bourgeois promoters of the virtues of industrial production—and even these may be riven at any moment by the effect of national rivalries.

Kenneth Waltz is the exception in this regard. He has drawn attention to the regular outcome of state-based decisions made under circumstances of self-help, and the balance of power that as a systemic principle invariably recurs to constrain and dispose particular foreign policies. Competition is the natural plight of an anarchical society like the one in which we live, and all others that bear a historical similarity to it. Wherever we find the perception of irreconcilable differences and the sense by one party that the other is moving to exclude it from realising its own ends or attempting to pre-empt it from doing so, contention is imminent. Once translated into active policies, we have the familiar situation of international impasse.

Short of these systemic structures, a plurality of states will provide ample opportunities for conflict, some very imprecise. The 'defense of democracy', or of 'proletariat solidarity', for example, are very diffuse aspirations, though no less productive of dissensus perhaps than arguments over where to place a border marker or how much tax a transnational company should pay. Interests and values can be more or less central to a social collectivity's cognitive scheme, and hence more or less readily and intensely defended. They can also overlap, and what might seem a marginal source of contention or quite misperceived can become a symbol for much more profound antagonism that has little to do with the immediate source of difference, and is consequently much less amenable to management or resolution. More particularly, conflict arises where the representatives of a state or corporation or movement seek to protect or extend the physical integrity, the fundamental ideas, or the productive capacity and income of their domain at the expense of that of others. It may also arise as a flow-on from domestic contention, from a generalised sense of injustice or grievance perhaps, or the interplay of institutions inadequate to their tasks, from social assertiveness, deep cultural or ethnic or racial enmities, sheer accident or, as Waltz would see it, from the uncertainties that attend a life led by bargaining and alliance and the threat that force must be the ultimate arbiter in an 'ungoverned' world.

Force denotes 'power' and the comparative possession of it and the fact that to defend and promote their interests and values states (and corporations and global movements) must garner the means to make convincing threats or carry them out. A notoriously difficult concept to pin down, 'power' in the sense of the capacity to effect action (that of the power-holder or that of the power-impressed) can range from the subtlest intellectual influence to violence outright. Likewise conflict can occur in terms of contending authority or the clash of military might. Some would argue that the former is becoming more prominent now; the 'struggle for power' being matched by a struggle for the 'shaping of perceptions . . . for the privilege of defining reality . . . International politics in the past was often an arena of coercion without persuasion; it is tending to become an arena of persuasion more or less coercive.'[7]

Convincing others, where this implies more than mere indoctrination, assumes a capacity for rational response. There is a considerable literature debating the degree to which this is possible given the non-rational side of ourselves and the ways in which we may be biologically or physiologically predisposed towards patterns of behaviour that have contentious consequences.[8] To the extent that conflict is a rational process, conscious strategies of threat and appeasement can be applied and ideas like those of deterrence and *détente* become the currency of analytic exchange.[9] To the extent that it is not, theories of bargaining and 'independent decision' are conditional, and indeed, may actually mislead. This is especially so where psychological images and attitudes are a prominent influence — stereotyping for example, or a belief that the antagonist possesses undesirable national or racial or ideological characteristics; the 'intolerance of ambiguity'; 'cognitive dissonance'; conformity and aggression and misperception of many and varied kinds.[10] (In this context it is worth noting, as Geoffrey Blainey puts it, that 'the idea that the human race has an innate love of fighting cannot be carried far as an explanation of war . . . Since war and peace mark fluctuations in the relations between nations, they are more likely to be explained by factors which themselves fluctuate than by factors which are "innate".'[11]) At the societal level psychological or biological properties may emerge in some aggregate form, though precisely how mass 'moods' or mind states effect conflict remains ambiguous, and even in seemingly obvious cases it is not easy to establish the connection with any degree of clarity.

It is more useful, perhaps, to focus upon decision-making processes, their capacity to routinise change, and why they fail. How well leaders cope in this respect has been called 'the vital point in the chain of events that determines peace or conflict'[12] and the concept of 'controlled communication' was devised specifically to meet the point where it breaks down. Assuming states as 'not in themselves a cause of conflict, aggressive or power motivated', and that given 'perfect knowledge' of how others might

respond they would not engage in conflicts 'more costly' than other
ways of doing what they want to, there is a case, Burton has argued, for
establishing the institutional means to allow them to 'reperceive' what
they are doing and to learn about the interests and aspirations of their
erstwhile opponents.[13] To the extent that conflicts occur over interests
and aspirations that *are* actually irreconcilable, however, no amount of
re-perception on the part of decision-makers will prevent them contest-
ing the issue and indeed, misperceptions may have the effect of actually
inhibiting conflicts that would otherwise prove more intense.

Related to the above are models of cybernetic stress that suggest how
conflict can arise because of the inability of organisations and institutions
as self-steering communications networks to handle the environmental
demands placed upon them. Thus Karl Deutsch has argued:

> An impending conflict would . . . be reckoned to be the more serious
> the greater the amount of expectable changes that . . . conflict, if it
> were joined, would impose upon the structures of one or both of the
> acting systems; and, also, the greater the changes that would be re-
> quired in one or both of these systems if this conflict were to be
> avoided . . . In the case of governments, the costs of physical, social,
> or psychological change may appear even higher; and it may seem
> less 'unrealistic' to political decision-makers to let their countries run
> into war . . . rather than to take the risks of the changes in policy,
> and internal programs and structure, that might still avoid the col-
> lision.[14]

In cybernetic language this could arise from 'amplifying feedback'
behaviour, for example, that reduces any reciprocal sense of advantage
and drives the spiral of competitive interaction higher and higher. The
most constructive governmental response under the circumstances would
be a commitment to social learning, and a readiness to meet global
challenge by openly seeking information, avoiding the 'intoxication of
success' or the 'worship of ephemeral practices and institutions',
encouraging criticism, and allowing dissenting opinion into the decisional
arena and using it to a consciously integrative end.[15] This is not as easy
as it may sound though since

> any network whose operating rules can be modified by feedback
> processes is subject to *internal conflict* between its established work-
> ing preferences and the impact of new information . . . The more
> complex, relatively, the . . . networks involved, the richer the pos-

sibilities of choice, the more prolonged may be the period of indecision

or domestic strife,[16] and the more hazardous the business of learning and change.

In global terms the most important socio-psychological process is that of group inclusion and group exclusion.[17] Conflict, it has been argued, is a 'form of sociation' itself — a positively unifying factor in its own right.[18] George Simmel's vision, cited here, is a holistic, almost mystical one. After acknowledging the 'common view' of life as dualistic, as the counter-position, that is, of happiness and suffering, virtue and vice, strength and inadequacy, success and failure, he posits a 'higher conception' that considers

> all these polar differentiations as one life; we must sense the pulse of a central vitality even in that which, if seen from the standpoint of a particular idea, ought not to be at all and is merely something negative; we must allow the total meaning of our existence to grow out of both parties.

This approach is 'all the more necessary . . . in respect to the sociological phenomenon of conflict, because conflict impresses us with its socially destructive force as with an apparently indisputable fact'.[19] What between individual human beings is a negative and damaging process may have integrative consequences for the larger society to which they belong, helping preserve social boundaries (those who benefit most from the system may deliberately further hostile patterns of behaviour to defend the desired *status quo*) and helping individuals define their social place (which serves to legitimise the society as a whole and the sense of security that comes from accepting it).

The same mechanism works at a world level, though in positing that fact we must remain wary of talking in terms of 'function' or 'dysfunction', a device that not only shifts our attention from the traditional realities of 'power, domination and conflict of interests' to a 'non-reality' — that of a system's 'adaptation'[20] but is also tautologous, defining functional conflict in terms of a society's capacity to persist, and persistence as proof that conflicts are functional. Given a concept of conflict predicated upon a plurality of groups that possess irreconcilable outlooks or interests and competing for influence or power, there is no way of deciding in advance what sort of behaviour is socially benign and likely to conserve the well-being of the whole, and what is not. War, for example, is an outcome of a world where the leaders of each global group are in the ultimate resort the arbiters of interest and responsible for defending them, by diplomacy and sharp political or economic practice if possible, and by violence if not. To construe war as functional is to ask a well-nigh meaningless question.[21] The contrary point of view is well satirised by the *Report from Iron Mountain* where war is seen to serve many beneficial purposes that are basic and unique. In the terms of this Report:

> War is not primarily an instrument of policy utilized by nations to extend or defend their expressed political values or their economic interests. On the contrary, it is itself the principal basis of organisation on which all modern societies are constructed . . . [and] at the root of all ostensible differences of national interest lie the dynamic requirements of the war system itself for periodic armed conflict.[22]

War maintains ordered life, and in a neat reversal of common sense, it is peace that is seen to breed disorder. That this is only a short step from more serious analysis of the subject is well illustrated by Simmel's assertion (made in 1908) that in the modern age of focused states 'war . . . no matter how destructive and expensive . . . results in a better overall balance than do the incessant small conflicts and frictions characteristic of periods during which governments are less strongly centralized.'[23]

Avoiding the worst excesses of a self-fulfilling functionalism, inter-state conflict can still be sensibly construed defining in-group/out-group boundaries in political and territorial terms and serving individual desires for civic identification. It allows the expression of frustration, and as such pre-empts the desire to withdraw from the world and forgo the process of interaction altogether.

> If we did not even have the power and the right to rebel against tyranny, arbitrariness, moodiness, tactlessness, we could not bear to have any relations to people[s] from whose characters we thus suffer . . . Not only because of the fact . . . that oppression usually increases if it is suffered calmly and without protest, but also because opposition gives us inner satisfaction, distraction, relief.[24]

The immediate cause of such identification, and the enmity against others that attends it, can be quite trivial in fact. One is reminded of Gulliver's travels, and the wars between Lilliput and the land of Blefuscu over the evocative issue of which end one should break eggs.[25] Indeed, the ephemeral quality of proximate causes can be misleading, since they are usually only excuses that allow latent tensions to manifest themselves. Where these tensions occur between those who share more basic values, subsequent conflict, however bitter it may be, is likely to proceed with some reference at least to that underlying social 'consensus', and to be resolved by compromise. Where the objective differences are thoroughgoing ones conflict proceeds without it, and mitigation is that much more difficult to achieve. This is particularly serious if those in conflict are not affiliated in other ways that complicate their relationship, inhibiting the advent of a situation of polar opposed that allows of no ambiguities, and where hostility becomes absolute.

Levels of 'consensus' are hard to define and measure as such, particularly on a global scale. Nominal solidarity exists on the iniquitous nature of world poverty and the need in principle to realise a more just and equitable world. Wealth is something that is made and traded for, however. If a country does not command a raw material in high demand, it remains at a global disadvantage as long as it lacks the productive capacity to manufacture modern goods and generate an agricultural surplus. Common knowledge of this fact may prove frustrating to those peoples who aspire to the industrial status that is denied them, or where industrialisation proceeds without the social changes that would disseminate what is earned to the mass. Consensus then gives way to conflict: industrial culture at variance with more traditional values, generating social alienation and ecological crisis; indirect competition for the means of productive advance leading to more overt forms of contention where these are monopolised on in short supply. There is also a broad political consensus on the value of sovereignty and the heinous nature of policies that promote, for example, racial discrimination. The terms are very loose and are readily distorted for nationalistic ends, but 'deviant' behaviour does exist on this issue, and there are states within the world society pursuing socially repugnant practices that most of the rest find it safe to stigmatise (while ignoring the strictures against global *harijans* to allow investment or trade or strategic alliance). South Africa, for example, has achieved something of this sociological pariah status, though the hypocrisy of those who decry apartheid is often glaringly apparent, and in fastening upon this one issue in this one country as safe for everyone else to hate we may distract from other policies in other places equally if not more inhumane. The uniform desire to ostracise and discipline the disvalued regime is evidence none the less of some sort of aggregate social sense.

Dissensus throws society into relief as it were, as what is the 'figure',

in *gestalt* terms, immediately defines what is 'ground'. It is not necessary
to posit this as a functional need to find in it one way the members of
such a society affirm what they share, the very contrast consolidating
the value of conscious association itself and making solid in that instance
what may otherwise be quite diffuse. It is the notion of nominally sovereign interests and attitudes, however, that remains central to the pluralist
approach and pluralist perceptions of conflict. Groups contend within
themselves or with each other and the subjective appreciation of their
interest prompts them to do so. The 'groups' are mostly 'states', conflicts within them assuming their most dramatic form as revolution or
civil war, and between them as armed skirmish or total assault. It is one
index of how important the ideology of the state has become that so
much of world conflict, and war in particular, should be conducted by
'sovereign' regimes. War is now a legitimate prospect for governments
alone, or at least for those recognised by a majority of the members of
the global society as such. 'Private' war has been decreed an anachronism,
as the very use of the term 'private' as opposed to 'public' implies, and
where a dissident group like the Palestinians instigates a campaign of
organised and persistent violence, it will invariably characterise itself as
a frustrated national entity fighting for a sovereign territorial frame.

Accepting this change, much work has been done of a quantitative
kind trying to find in state-engendered conflicts heuristic correlations
that would suggest a common cause. One such study found that the
occurrence of domestic conflict, for example, had very little to do with
the incidence of external strife, and that the familiar ideas about leaders
resorting to threatening others and waging war to distract the populace
from internal dissension, or foreign adventures inducing ructions at home,
were false.[26] A subsequent discussion did, however, detect a statistically
significant if fairly modest link between governments (particularly those
of a 'centrist' and 'polyarchic' sort) facing internal upheaval, and foreign
contention and war,[27] as other empirical and theoretical work suggests
there must be.[28] State levels of economic development, indices of
social stress and strain (such as unemployment, population density,
degree of urbanisation, industrialisation, homicide rates, alcoholism and
suicide), state 'power', official values, the number of borders a country
possesses, its 'heterogeneity', its voting patterns in the United Nations,
the number of co-operative arrangements it has, and the volume of its
communications with the wider world; all have been treated as possibly
co-variant with foreign conflict and war, though generally to inconclusive
effect. Assessing these attributes *comparatively*, for the differences and
similarities they display, gives similarly arid or confused results,[29] which

is hardly surprising given the problems associated with the 'macro-quantitative' approach, problems that some would say prohibit their receiving any serious consideration at all.[30]

One such analyst has ventured 'racial distance' as 'the most important characteristic distinguishing between peace and conflict in international systems'.[31] This is a rather opaque statement, but its extreme character does serve to point up the neglect of the 'ethnic' factor in world affairs. The subjugation of various pigmented peoples by off-whites in recent world history, and the consequent coincidence of racial divisions and socio-economic ones, suggests an important focus for global dissensus.[32] 'Race' is the most irrelevant and at the same time the most potent of all modes of human discrimination. The technological edge that various Caucasian groups used to establish global dominion over more colourful peoples in other lands was inevitably taken, by the conquerors in particular, as symbolic of an intrinsic cultural and physiological superiority, and they purveyed to their inferior subjects this quaint belief. Many of the latter, impressed by such capacities, accepted the assignation. They are less likely to do so now and 'white' supremacy, though it remains part of the pattern of the global hierarchy and the confrontation this portends, is much less of a factor than it was once. The prized teachings of the Western world's own science have reinforced the liberal belief that the potential for achievement is a species-specific one, and not the province of any physically distinct fraction of human-kind alone. The end of the great empires has meant the pursuit of predominance by less blatant and more ambiguous ploys like 'neo-imperialism', and the capacity to create new knowledge and to convince others of its worth. More and more of the 'natives' themselves have rejected the assumptions upon which white 'destiny' was based, and generated their own brands of racist discrimination too. And though racial difference remains a direct cause of domestic, particularly urban, conflict (as poor-state non-white populations find their way into the cities of the rich) as a transcendent source of inter-state contention it remains of considerably lesser importance than nationalism, or a sense of being 'modern' and middle-class.

If we move from the in-group/out-group perspective we encounter a systemic perspective once more, and the notion that the particular configuration of global groups at any one time may be itself a cause of conflict and war. Certainly no single such configuration has preserved social integrity for very long, though it could well be that 'multi-polarity' is more harmonious overall than 'bipolarity', and the universal hegemony of one group over the others would be the most peace-prone system of all. As between multipolarity and bipolarity the choice, even if there were one, could well prove fruitless if, as Michael Hass has concluded, the former simply harbours the more violent and wider wars while the latter makes them longer.[33] There is also a certain socio-psychological logic to *arms races* that might, it is felt, predispose confrontation. In a perverse way these may actually *prevent* dissensus, allowing the sublimation of rivalry and suspicion and fear. Spiralling military preparedness and the finely judged capacity for deterrence can act as a surrogate, stalling the desire to test the substance of what is being signalled back and forth in this way.[34] Arms races do break down, of course, and more than one theorist has argued that: 'Wars usually begin when two nations disagree on their relative strength, and . . . usually cease when . . . [they] agree.'[35] Thus: 'Any factor which increases the likelihood that nations will agree on their relative power is a potential cause of peace. One powerful cause of peace is a decisive war, for war provides the most widely accepted measure of power.'[36] Other such measures involve, from a lengthy list of possible subjective assessments, the competitive appreciation of national military and economic strength, the use of strategic incidents to test resolve and the quality of response, other general impressions of a potential opponents's patterns of behaviour and civil solidarity, and memories of previous campaigns.[37]

Social conflict as such never 'ends', and given its importance as a positive as well as negative factor in the dialectic that reconciles human concerns, never will. Conflicts, particularly violent ones, are readily deplored. They may also be accorded due recognition as part of the process of social change, not to be resolved or managed in a single-minded way, but actively sought and sustained where the consequences can be constructive ones. War itself, where no alternative mechanism exists, is the only means available on occasion to challenge and revise a repressive *status quo.* Not that non-war always stultifies and violent conflict inevitably promotes 'progress'; not that what constitutes 'progress' and a non-'repressive' global regime could ever be given an agreed definition; not to ignore the potentially terminal quality of contemporary weaponry or the disastrous nature of a nuclear victory whose fruits would lie, as President Kennedy once remarked, like ashes in our mouth;[38] but where force is the only machinery left to effect change and those involved perceive advantage in its employ, force will be used, and we cannot exclude from debate the possibility that the using might be to beneficial effect. Conflict stimulation[39] has much to recommend it as an instrument of social renewal on a world scale, where the costs of conflict 'management' may involve sanctioning social structures that are pernicious in the extreme. It is also in the global context a most fraught undertaking that will commonly produce quite the opposite outcome to any of those planned. But then, so is conflict 'resolution', where to win the degree of agreement or submission required the pursuit of the possible may well be lost and war ensue regardless.

From a pluralist perspective conflict occurs at so many levels, over so many different sorts of issues, engaging state values and interests in such diverse ways, that no single principle for responding to the process of dissensus, except that of self-help, could possibly apply to all. It may not be necessary anyway, since complex entities like world society are prone to 'alternation', which is one cost of being so complex, and the resurgence of harmony and order is quite as sure as its eventual collapse.[40] This 'covert-overt' pattern, this 'almost regular cycle' is seen to be typical of world affairs, where diplomacy gives way to war and war to diplomacy in a rhythm analogous to that of market boom and bust. We only have to wait, it seems, and strife will pass as readily as it came.

This picture of cyclical passage does not disallow voluntarism though, and the notion of 'interests', nationally conceived, confirms that voluntarist instinct. They are defined in practice by those in power, and where such interests are subject to definition, in whole or at least in part, by military institutions with their own reasons for keeping images of conflict vivid and imminent, there will be a perennial bias towards scenarios of a world in constant travail. The pluralist notion of interests also tends to be a 'subjectivist' one. It construes them as *'given . . .* random i.e., as unstructured by the form of social organisation as a whole'.[41] There *is* an alternative conception that locates groups, and especially here, states, in their objective systemic context, and reads from that the extent to which their opportunities and choices are determined, or at least constrained or predisposed, by the logic of the balance of power. On the whole, the idea of a plurality of interests is identified with the several states, however, and the majority sense is that of global power as diffused, a circumstance that is felt must maximise state freedom while constraining conflict. Pluralism also detaches the idea of the 'public interest' from those of any particular country or countries, and makes it a rather empty and artificial one. World society can display no moral aspiration more exalted than that of competing groups as they help themselves. Countervailing influence is exerted by cross-cutting interests — where a state's economic ties, for example, generate concerns at odds with its political or ideological or cultural ones. But the better organised and more determined groups usually predominate, and in world society any need that is not so supported is not relevant. Where state survival and state gain are the ultimate criteria, groups that fail to organise in their own defence will tend to lose.

Global inequalities, and the neglect of those not aware of the need to defend themselves or not able to do so, are the inevitable outcome, and these are justified by their beneficiaries because a doctrine of state gain is compatible with that of sovereignty and the workings of the capitalist world market within which the doctrine evolved. There is not a little social Darwinism about such a point of view and, indeed, the notion of separate nations whose own interests come first in the competition for survival and influence has always drawn heavily upon the analogy of biological conflict and a sense of the world as anarchic and possessed of no comprehensive communal institutions to discipline individual states.

The simplest solution to this sort of conflict would be to give each and every people its own global patch and to keep them, where feasible, from interacting at all. In a world of territorial contiguity this is not possible, and there is no authority to do the 'giving' anyway. Uninhabitable zones like rivers, mountains and deserts may help distinguish borders and separate states from each other, but modern technology has made it possible to leap such divisions in a single bound. So 'distance' becomes an idea that inhabitants are socialised to accept by the preservation or the encouragement of a national identity and by differentiating this from that of others. Those in power enforce such socialisation by means that range from 'ridicule' to 'execution for treason',[42] and transgressions are met by anything from border patrols, radio-jamming, and compulsory haircuts for long-haired male tourists, to war. Bringing states together in various forms of global association or alliance is the alternative stratagem, though group identification and nationalism, whether intrinsic or induced, makes for only temporary and contingent accommodation, and where this breaks down for 'distance' again. For any one state the preferred socio-political interval will vary widely, depending upon who it is at the other end. The gap will also change, and along more than one scale. Preserving those international spaces that prevent war depends on all the familiar devices that sovereignty provides. It also depends on the ability to deter the unruly, an ability that relies in turn upon threat and counter-threat.[43] Where the latter are 'implicit and impersonal, somewhat symmetrical, credible without continual protestation of credibility, and . . . have a tradition of success', they provide a workable way of sustaining a *status quo*, which as far as confrontation between the great powers is concerned is very welcome. Between great powers and the rest, deterrence is a function of hegemony, and though this may likewise prevent overt violence it is more likely to do so at the expense of 'structural' violence and feudal social arrangements that per-petuate social injustice, and to fatal effect.[44]

As a general proposition one structural source of social conflict lies in any such situation of assymmetrical authority between those who rule and those who do not. To the extent that this assymmetry cor-responds to another one, that is, between those with an objective interest in the *status quo* and those who would be better served by its revision; where the opposing parties have become conscious of this fact; potential conflict will likely become actual. This applies to the hierarchy of *states*. It also applies to the division of world society into *classes*, a focus that deserves our separate concern.

World Society and World Conflict: the Structuralist Paradigm

'All societies are differentiated along class lines, communal lines, or both. (Class divisions refer to objective group differences in wealth, income, and occupation. Communal divisions refer to ascriptive criteria, including racial, tribal, religious, linguistic and ethnic differences.)'[45] Adding nationalism to the communal list, this statement applies as readily to the world as a whole as it does to smaller groups.

There are classes of states, to be sure, and attempts have been made to derive a cause of global conflict from the 'rank disequilibrium' that particular countries may suffer because they are 'top dogs' on one scale and at the same time 'underdogs' on others.[46] The greater the number of such states the more disturbed, it is said, the society of them will be. This does not necessarily generate grievance, conflict or war — the leaders of afflicted states may become apathetic rather than self-righteous, or feel inadequate to the task of making for change, or they may feel com-pensated by the fact that their state is high in some areas, though low elsewhere.[47] It can be a causal factor, however, where permissive con-ditions exist, like a general propensity for violence where this has been employed before, and where other means of status promotion have failed. Similarly placed states tend to interact most with each other, which creates a feudal global situation dominated by top-rankers. Low-rankers are disassociated among themselves, and connected upwards to those in the class above them. Should low-rankers actually begin to come together, a global situation of state classes in opposition to each other could arise. Where this is ideologically polarised as well, as between East and West, a higher level of interaction that is both 'positive' and 'less dependent on rank' is indicated if conflict and war are not to fol-low.[48] In Wallerstein's view, where it is the emerging world economy that is the key unit of analysis, classes of states can accept not only a central or peripheral position, but also a semi-peripheral one. It is the semi-peripheral group that most effectively defuses global confrontation between North and South, he argues, as middle-classes do in domestic society. Down-turn in the world economy works to the advantage of semi-peripheral states, when core countries will seek wider markets, but semi-peripheral regimes may still choose a more independent strategy, denying these markets to the core and provoking conflict rather than de-fusing it.[49]

If we take class formation not in this pluralistic sense however, but as the advent of antagonistic social entities *within* states, and particularly in the case of a modernising bourgeoisie, also *across* them, a different picture begins to emerge. I have discussed such a perspective in some detail above and here would only point up those aspects of it that pertain to our understanding of conflict.

Classes congeal as those who belong to similar sorts of financial or professional aggregates become aware of that fact and begin to assert their collective concerns in opposition to those of other social groups. At this point we find potential interests becoming more immediate and tangible ones. This is not to attribute an illusory character to those that remain latent, since the particular ways in which a society is organised *can* shape human opportunities, whether those affected perceive the fact or not. Groups constrained by such means can be said to share interests even if in reality they are oblivious to them. Indeed, groups served by this state of ignorance, who can dictate what the dominant values and concepts of a society should be and who control the means of disseminating them, will invariably do so. They are helped in this task by the human propensity not only for obedience to external con-straint, but also for internalising norms. Hence the relevance of cultural and institutional factors, and the need not to succumb to sociological reductionism. Where the interests of the ignorant become conscious ones (however that transformation is achieved), and where they are seen to be irreconcilable with those of another class or classes, then we confront a possible explanation for certain social conflicts, and where conflict does not produce impasse, of social change.[50]

Marx saw this in terms of a grand dichotomy between the custodians of capital and the labouring mass, a dichotomy that he used to structure his understanding of the social consequence of industrialisation by private and pecuniary means. He said:

We have seen that the constant tendency, the law of development of the capitalist mode of production, is to separate the means of product-

ion increasingly from labour, and to concentrate the scattered means
of production more and more into larger aggregates, thereby transforming labour into wage-labour and the means of production into
capital. There corresponds to this tendency, in a different sphere,
the independent separation of landed property from capital and
labour, or the transformation of all landed property into a form
which corresponds with the capitalist mode of production.[51]

Marx further maintained:

> that particular individuals are not 'always' influenced in their
> attitude by the class to which they belong, but this has . . . little
> effect upon the class struggle . . . [upon] *whole classes* which are
> based upon *economic* conditions independent of their will, and as
> as a result of these conditions are placed in a relation of material
> antagonism.[52]

Dichotomisation has been stalled in the West by a growing middle
class and by greater affluence in general.[53] Revolution has been more
common in predominantly agrarian countries where peasants, led by
radical intellectuals, have occasionally sustained sufficient resolve to replace traditional or foreign elites. Class conflict, even violence on
occasions, has remained the common experience of industrialised states
however. In global terms: 'The relations between different nations
depend upon the extent to which each has developed its production
forces, the division of labour, and international intercourse.'[54] Conflict
between centres of capital tends to be resolved as capital achieves a
greater and greater concentration and as those who control the productive process choose, regardless of their nationalistic preferences, to consolidate their common concerns. Other classes are put at a distance by
both social and spatial means. Capital cannot dispense with labour and
the labouring force needs to be a physically accessible one, but with
contemporary modes of management and efficient communications and
transportation they can be held at both a social and physical distance,
hence the use of foreign labour by particular centres of capital that find
incentive and profit in offering transnational employment.[55]
    This is the global version in fact of Ralf Dahrendorf's argument that
class conflict is reduced where the bourgeoisie and the proletariat who
confront each other on industrial issues no longer do so on political
grounds as well. Regardless of whether this judgement applies domestically
or not, it is a significant trend on a global scale where a nascent modern-

ising bourgeoisie stands over a highly fragmented set of under-classes, but the political factor of nationalism intervenes to prevent transnational polarisation. The mitigating influence of the transnational trade union movement and the case, for example, of Swedish workers striking on behalf of their beleaguered brethren employed by a Brazilian division of the same transnational corporation, has remained marginal.[56] International capital may have created the opportunity for an international response on the part of the trade union movement, but competition between centres of capital is still mirrored by a similar disparity between the national fractions of the global labouring force.

The contemporary world market as a capitalistic construction (or what is a different but related notion, as one dominated by capitalist states) requires for its efficient performance commercial responses that are regular and predictable ones, which is one explanation for the strain overall towards a global order that can fix around nationalistic self-interest a framework of predictable constraints and secure the stability of the system overall. Regardless of the above, however, the global arena remains comparatively irregular in the way it proceeds, and 'conflict formations' continue to prevail.[57] An interdependent 'grid' of capitalist metropoles confronts both more and less actively a number of socialist ones, while retaining its historical ascendancy over the global 'underdeveloped' through diverse more or less client elites. Each formation in turn is hardly a monolithic affair; capitalist centres compete among themselves (a process that Lenin declared the cause of war, with imperialistic powers fighting for advantageous shares of the exploitable areas of the world), socialist states at loggerheads, and the underdeveloped (broadly conceived) resisting imperial exploitation while at the same time bound by neo-colonial penetration and divided too.

In class terms all this is comprehensible as a consequence of industrialisation, and more particularly, its 'combined' and 'uneven' effects. Overt conflict itself must await the subjective appreciation of a divergence of interests by the collectivities involved, which is not much different from a vision of the world as a 'single plural society, animated by Western conceptions of justice, the presence of vast economic and social disparity . . . unleash[ing] ideological assault against the privileged'.[58] In reality, several modes of production persist within any particular social formation, at different stages of development. Each stage within each mode shapes contemporary classes, such that

at any moment within a social formation there is likely to be (i) antagonistic relations between modes of production, (ii) antagonistic relations between classes within phases of the development of the dominant mode of production as well as (iii) competition between class factions within the dominant and subordinate class.[59]

This is a rich field for conflict, and a generous harvest for those who would gather it in.

In Communist parlance, a world where the logic of mounting antagonism has ultimately despatched capitalism and classes altogether will be one without war. Such conflicts as then arise — between individual self-interest and that of the collective, for example — will be resolved short of war by the 'mechanism of socialism'. Where this does not work 'as it should', one could always argue that conflict persists because the socialist system is distorted by a power elite that has co-opted the public interest to serve its own.[60] This circular and self-justifying logic is defeated in practice by other social forces, however. 'Socialism' could only be perfected in a perfectible world and there is much about this one, and its inhabitants, that will continue to resist the attempt. Whether 'classes' in the Marxist sense can ever be overthrown by revolutionary violence, or reformed away, conflict will persist, and with it, the potential for war.

Notes

1. For a detailed discussion of the differences, see C. Fink, 'Some Conceptual Difficulties in the Theory of Social Conflict', *Journal of Conflict Resolution*, vol 12, no. 4 (December 1968), pp. 440-53.

2. J. Bernard, 'The Sociological Study of Conflict' in *The Nature of Conflict: Studies on the Sociological Aspects of International Tensions* (UNESCO, 1957), p. 38; she distinguishes social psychological, sociological and semanticist sorts. Also L. Kriesberg, *The Sociology of Social Conflicts* (Prentice-Hall, New Jersey, 1973), pp. 4-5, 61:

> For social conflicts to emerge three major aspects of awareness are needed. First, the groups or parties to the conflict must be conscious of themselves as collective entities, separate from each other. Second, one or more groups must be dissatisfied with their position relative to another group. Finally, they must think they can reduce their dissatisfaction by the *other* group acting or being different; that is, they must have aims which involve the other group yielding what it would not otherwise yield.

3. R. Dahrendorf, 'Toward a Theory of Social Conflict', *Journal of Conflict Resolution*, vol. 2, no. 2 (1958), pp. 170-83. Fink, 'Some Conceptual Difficulties', is still the best introduction to the conceptual and terminological confusion that surrounds the subject as a whole.

4. This literature is reviewed in R. Pettman, *Human Behaviour and World Politics* (Macmillan, London, 1975), pp. 135-46.

5. J. Burton, *Systems, States, Diplomacy and Rules* (Cambridge University

Press, Cambridge, 1968), p. 10; K. Waltz, *Theory of International Politics* (Addison-Wesley, Reading, 1979).

6. Ibid., p. 8. Also J. Burton, *World Society* (Cambridge University Press, Cambridge, 1972), pp. 35-45.

7. S. Hoffman, 'Perceptions, Reality and the Franco-American Conflict' in J. Farrell and A. Smith (eds.), *Image and Reality* (Columbia University Press, New York, 1967), pp. 57-9. From a structuralist perspective power is a product of the relationship that pertains between classes; organisations and institutions like the state and the corporation being the dynamic expression of class relationships and the conduits of dominant class rule. R. Hill, 'Urbanism and the State: a Debate', *International Journal of Urban and Regional Research*, vol. 1, no. 1 (March 1977), pp. 37-44.

8. Pettman, *Human Behaviour*, Chapters 7 and 8.

9. T. Schelling, *The Strategy of Conflict* (Harvard University Press, Cambridge, Mass., 1960); A. Rapoport, *Fights, Games and Debates* (University of Michigan, Ann Arbor, 1960); M. Kaplan, 'The Sociology of Strategic Thinking' in A. Lepawsky *et al.* (eds.), *The Search for World Order* (Appleton-Century-Crofts, New York, 1971).

10. Pettman, *Human Behaviour*, Chapter 9.

11. G. Blainey, *The Causes of War* (Macmillan, London, 1973), p. 248. See also Q. Wright, 'The Causes of War' in *A Study of War* (University of Chicago Press, Chicago, 1942).

12. J. Burton, 'Conflict as a Function of Change' in A. de Reuck and J. Knight (eds.), *Conflict in Society* (J. and A. Churchill, London, 1966), p. 400.

13. J. Burton, *Conflict and Communication* (Macmillan, London, 1969).

14. K. Deutsch, *The Nerves of Government* (Free Press, New York, 1966), p. 113.

15. Ibid., pp. 193, 243.

16. Ibid., p. 95.

17. G. de Vos, 'Conflict, Dominance and Exploitation in Human Systems of Social Segregation' in de Reuck and Knight, *Conflict in Society*; R. LeVine and D. Campbell, *Ethnocentrism: Theories of Conflict, Ethnic Attitudes and Group Behavior* (John Wiley, New York, 1972); G. Simmel, *Conflict* (Free Press, Illinois, 1955); L. Coser, *The Functions of Social Conflict* (Routledge and Kegan Paul, London, 1956).

18. Simmel, *Conflict*, p. 18.

19. Ibid., p. 16, fn 4.

20. I. Zeitlin, *Rethinking Sociology* (Prentice-Hall, New Jersey, 1973), p. 106.

21. K. Waltz, *Man, the State and War* (Columbia University Press, New York, 1954), p. 1.

22. *Report from Iron Mountain (on the Possibility and Desirability of Peace)* (Penguin, Harmondsworth, 1966), p. 111.

23. Simmel, *Conflict*, p. 90.

24. Ibid., p. 19.

25. J. Swift, *Gulliver's Travels* (Collins, London, 1952), p. 456.

26. The original study was by R. Rummel, 'The Relationship between National Attributes and Foreign Conflict Behavior' in J. Singer (ed.), *Quantitative International Relations* (Free Press, New York, 1968). For a general review see Pettman, *Human Behaviour*, pp. 243-55.

27. J. Wilkenfeld, 'Domestic and Foreign Conflict Behavior of Nations', *Journal of Peace Research*, vol. 5 (1968), pp. 56-9; *Conflict Behavior and Linkage Politics* (David McKay, New York, 1973).

28. Cf. Blainey, *The Causes of War*, p. 248. Proposition 27: 'The evidence of past wars does not support the scapegoat theory and its assumption that rulers

facing internal troubles often started a foreign war in the hope that a victory would promote peace at home.'

29. A typically vague observation is as follows: 'differential rates of population growth in combination with differential rates of technological growth contribute to international competition and sometimes to conflict, insofar as competing nations have differential – grossly unequal – access to resources and capabilities,' relationships that are neither 'direct' nor 'simplistic'. N. Choucri and R. North, 'Dynamics of International Conflict: Some Policy Implications of Population, Resources, and Technology', *World Politics*, vol. 24 (1972), pp. 83-4.

30. A. Mack, 'Numbers are not Enough', *Comparative Politics*, vol. 7 (1975), pp. 597-618, who has described Rummel's work, and that of those who have followed his lead, as 'brute, mechanistic and negative inductivism which proves absolutely nothing'. 'The positive and negative relationships between foreign and domestic conflict . . . tend to be self-cancelling in aggregate analysis' and those who then turned to

> smaller samples of 'types' of nations . . . found that the sample sizes were too small. To get out of this difficulty they turned to 'time series' analysis in which a few indicators are tapped over many time intervals, instead of many indicators being measured with one time period. Introducing the idea of time lags in causal relationships, they become hopelessly confused,

and more and more remote from the real world. Furthermore:

> The 'events' data which were used, were suspect, there was no theoretical elaboration at all, unwarrantable assumptions were drawn from the statistical techniques employed and the whole endeavour was marked by an extra-ordinarily crude behaviourist bias,

that measured what seemed measurable and avoided, to invalidating or trivialising effect, what was not. 'Review article: World Politics and the Behavioural Revolution', *Politics*, vol. 12, no. 1 (May 1977), p. 174.

31. R. Rummel, 'Some Empirical Findings on Nations and their Behavior', *World Politics*, vol. 21, no. 2 (January 1969), p. 239.

32. H. Tinker, *Race, Conflict and International Order: from Empire to United Nations* (Macmillan, London, 1977).

33. M. Haas, 'International Subsystems: Stability and Polarity', *American Political Science Review*, vol. 64, no. 1 (March 1970), p. 1211.

34. Blainey, *The Causes of War*, pp. 111, 248.

35. Ibid., p. 246. 'Indeed one can almost suggest that war is usually the outcome of a diplomatic crisis which cannot be solved because both sides have conflicting estimates of their bargaining power . . . War is a dispute about the measurement of power. War marks the choice of a new set of weights and measures' (p. 114). Also Ch. 8, 'The Abacus of Power', particularly pp. 122-4.

36. Ibid., p. 247.

37. Many mental mechanisms can perpetuate a specific conflict once it is actually in train. See R. White, *Nobody Wanted War* (Doubleday, New York, 1970).

38. I am reminded here of Dan O'Neill's comment that the complement of the strategist's 'overkill' is 'underbury'; with the entire human race blown away, no one is stuck with the tedium of clean-up and reconstruction. As O'Neill then observes: 'If it wasn't for good old hysteria, I wouldn't be able to make it through the day' (D. O'Neill, *The Collective Unconscience of Odd Bodkins* (Glide Publications San Francisco, 1973). Or perhaps we should choose Leunig's Dictum: 'The man who

laughs has not yet heard the terrible news.'

39. J. Galtung, 'Peace Thinking' in Lepawsky *et al.*, *The Search for World Order*, p. 134, who uses the concept of conflict 'creation' to avoid 'too heavy a burden of political bias in favour of top-dogs of all kinds', and to promote 'the idea of peace through increased conflict'.

40. K. Boulding, *Conflict and Defense* (Harper and Row, New York, 1962), p. 40.

41. I. Balbus, 'The Concept of Interest in Pluralist and Marxist Analysis', *Politics and Society*, vol. 1, no. 2 (February 1971), p. 155.

42. J. Galtung, 'Peace Thinking' in Lepawsky *et al.*, *The Search for World Order*, pp. 136, 137.

43. T. Schelling, 'War Without Pain and Other Models', *World Politics*, vol. 15, no. 3 (April 1963), pp. 486-7; *Arms and Influence* (Yale University Press, New Haven, 1966).

44. The structure seems to survive very well . . . And we may well suspect that even the 'permanent revolution' — presumably intended to keep the Sisyphos stone on the summit of egaltitarianism and to prevent it from ever falling again into the abyss of feudalism — will develop its high priests and its experts, its 'old boys' who know how to do it, its chains of command (J. Galtung, 'Peace Thinking' in Lepawsky *et al.*, *The Search for World Order*, p. 148.)

45. E. Nordlinger, *Conflict Regulation in Divided Societies* (Harvard Center for International Affairs, Cambridge, Mass., 1972), p. 6.

46. J. Galtung, 'A Structural Theory of Aggression', *Journal of Peace Research*, vol. 1 (1964), pp. 95-119.

47. Kriesberg, *The Sociology of Social Conflicts*, p. 74.

48. J. Galtung, 'East-West Interaction Patterns', *Journal of Peace Research*, vol. 3 (1966), p. 172.

49. I. Wallerstein, *Old Problems and New Syntheses: The Relation of Revolutionary Ideas and Practice* (University of Saskatchewan, Saskatchewan, 1975), pp. 24-5.

50. Balbus, 'The Concept of Interest'.

51. T. Bottomore and M. Rubel (eds.), *Karl Marx: Selected Writings in Sociology and Social Philosophy* (Penguin, Harmondsworth, 1963), p. 186.

52. Ibid., p. 208.

53. M. Mann, *Consciousness and Action and the Western Working Class* (Macmillan, London, 1973), pp. 68, 71:

> Marx was surely right in observing that the major contradictions of capitalist society was between the individual interests of capitalists and the collective interest of the working and consuming population. He was also correct in pointing out the Western class's inherent drive toward collective identity and organisation. Yet these two trends need not converge in a proletarian revolution. If the working class and its organisations accept as the framework for part of their activities an economism that does not challenge the structure of capitalism, then their collectivism does not escalate into an aggressive societal force but turns in upon itself (pp. 71-2).

54. Bottomore and Rubel, *Selected Writings*, p. 111.

55. This can apply within states, as the South African regime has found, which by apartheid is 'only practising on a larger scale the principle of residential segregation according to social class that today is found in almost all cities in the world' (J. Galtung, 'Peace Thinking' in Lepawsky *et al.*, *The Search for World Order*, p. 138.)

56. W. Olle and W. Schoeller, 'World Market Competition and Restrictions upon International Trade Union Policies', *Capital and Class*, no. 2 (Summer 1977), pp. 56-75.

57. D. Senghaas, 'Conflict Formations in Contemporary International Society', *Journal of Peace Research*, no. 3 (1973), pp. 163-84; J. Spero, *The Politics of International Economic Relations* (George Allen and Unwin, London, 1977).

58. J. Chapman, 'The Political Theory of Pluralism' in J. Pennock and J. Chapman (eds.), *Nomos XI: Voluntary Associations* (Atherton Press, New York, 1969), pp. 113-14.

59. Hill, 'Urbanism and the State', p. 39.

60. K. Kára, 'On the Marxist Theory of War and Peace', *Journal of Peace Research*, no. 1 (1968), p. 18.

CONCLUSION

'. . . and what is the use of a book', thought
Alice, 'without pictures or conversations?' —
Alice in Wonderland (Everymans, 1929), p. 3

> There is, upon the whole, nothing more important in life than to find
> out the right point of view from which things should be looked at
> and judged of . . . for we can only apprehend the mass of events in
> their unity from *one* standpoint; and it is only the keeping to one
> point of view that guards us from inconsistency.[1]

Sound though such advice might be, world society can only be understood, I would argue, in terms of *two* perspectives — a *pluralist* and a
structuralist one; each of which has the analytic consequences described
above.

The very notion of a 'standpoint', however, presumes a human capacity to observe the 'mass of events' in a relatively detached fashion,
which is predicated in turn upon the capacity to choose one's mental
outlook on the world in a way that is not predetermined by other influences. A relatively objective outlook gives rise to a 'scientific' mode
of consciousness; one that is conducive to objective discourse and
imbued with something other than a sense of continuity with the environment. This approach to analysis has now become common global property
— an integral aspect of 'modernisation' and the industrial milieu. World
society is built upon it, bearing the mark of its intellectual origins and
the mark of its moral predilections too. This is not, I might add, to
demean or ignore the cultural diversity we find in practice, and the quite
genuine differences that flow from other premises about the world and
about how human relations should be conducted. Culturally distinctive
groups may still interact, even though they understand the process of
interaction from wholly discrete, even incompatible perspectives; this
'cognitive non-sharing' is a feature of all interpersonal discourse.[2] Though
I fasten here upon the ideas and values that are held in common and
consider these the more significant in defining world society, I remain
mindful of what such a point of view downplays.

World politics are most commonly analysed in terms of a combination
of anarchy and hierarchy[3] — two organising principles that generate their
own characteristic patterns of interaction; the former one of self-help,

and the latter one where the constituent units tend to become more specialised. While a necessary precursor to a precise understanding of the balance of power, for example, an approach of this sort cannot account for more than recurrent patterns of state behaviour of a survivalist sort. It tells us very clearly how the system is maintained and how it recovers its familiar form if this has been destroyed. It cannot explain, however, the system-creating influence of changes in modes of production. For that we need to fasten upon social formations and the development and dissemination of values. We need, in other words a notion not only of *system*, but also of *society*.

Within the *world* society there are two fundamental processes at work, that of state formation and that of class formation, and by fastening upon one or the other we define two different realms of discourse with their own precepts and analytic preoccupations. Reality is indivisible, though. We may turn from the pluralist projection of it to a structuralist one and back again, but these remain partial representations of a singular phenomenon that can only be understood in anything like its entirety by bringing them together in a more comprehensive way – the 'one view' Clausewitz recommends. A combination of this kind has been tried by both structuralist and pluralist theorists, each in their own terms. Both tend to over-emphasise, however, the part played by 'social practices'. Structuralists talk of human behaviour as determined by the logic of an emerging world capitalist market or a scientific-technological revolution;[4] of the 'articulated unity' of the economic and social forces that derive from these basic forms.[5] Their pluralist counterparts look to the 'tyranny of small decisions'[6] generating 'big changes' at the systemic level, and the way the anarchic nature of the whole constrains the behaviour of the constituent corporations and states, disposing similar responses that recur throughout history as the 'balance of power' regardless of the individual attributes of the agents involved. Both tend to exaggerate the autonomy of the 'systemic' as a causative force. They are ultimately reductionist, albeit from a more exalted perspective than those who sum the values and interests of global groups or classes.

In fastening upon social formations I have remained myself within the tradition that attempts to explain world affairs in terms of the fundamental actors we find there, and the manifold interrelations they display. Though I acknowledge the power of the pluralist theory of the logic of the system, enough has now been written on the subject to establish its limitations. Most debilitating is its incapacity to explain the 'modernisation' of the contemporary world. I have discussed the global formula of the structuralists and the logic of world market capitalism and again what it can and does not accommodate should be clear. In particular, no structuralist analysis adequately accounts for the balance of power.[7] Which leaves one the task of understanding just who does what to whom and why, in a way that employs both perspectives at the same time. As far as it makes sense to do so, the foregoing is one such attempt.

The central thread of the analysis, and the dominant feature of the contemporary world society, is that of industrialisation, a process I consider to be a very general one indeed.[8] At some point any assessment of who is winning in the world must be referred to that process, or it will fail to make sense. There is one task I have not undertaken in this respect, and that is to ask: who are they that generally make this attempt, and just whose interests do their understandings serve? A sociology of global sociologists is implicit in my argument, as is the means to categorise those who dot the field with their endeavours. As their ranks thicken it will be a worthwhile task providing a comprehensive answer to questions like these, but not yet.

Nothing has been concluded, of course. The debate does not end. I would only say that it is a certain voluntarism that renews the means. Voluntarism can take the most pernicious forms and both ends of the political spectrum share many points of reference in this respect.[9] But those who despair altogether do the human enterprise a similar disservice. If we cultivate a concept of existence and of our knowledge of that process as to some extent undertaken and not just imposed, then we will recognise that to survive we must try to survive; we have to 'intend' it, and the quality of our trying determines the quality of our lives.[10]

Notes

1. Carl von Clausewitz, *On War* (Penguin, Harmondsworth, 1968), p. 404.

2. James Fox, 'Moral Order and their Cultural Forms', a paper delivered to a seminar on *Moral Claims in World Affairs*, the Department of International Relations, the Australian National University (1976), p. 7.

3. K. Waltz, *Theory of International Politics* (Addison-Wesley, Reading, Pa., 1979), esp. Ch. 6, 'Anarchic Structures and Balance of Power'.

4. For one Marxist perspective see E. Hoffmann, 'Soviet Views of "The Scientific-Technological Revolution"', *World Politics*, vol. 30, no. 4 (July 1978), pp. 615-44.

5. C. Pickvance, 'Marxist Approaches to the Study of Urban Politics', *International Journal of Urban and Regional Research*, vol. 1, no. 2 (June 1977), p. 227.

6. Waltz, *Theory of International Politics*, quoting Alfred Kahn, see Ch. 6.

7. In the discussion of theories of economic development and the world market system, Joan Spero, *The Politics of International Economic Relations* (George

Allen and Unwin, London, 1977), discriminates between a liberal, a Marxist and a structuralist school (pp. 121-5). Her 'liberals' correspond to what my 'pluralists' would have to say. As to the 'structuralists' and 'Marxists', as she points out herself, they share similar analyses of how the system works, and diverge only on their assessments of the capacity of international capitalism for reform. The former are *optimists*, who see industrialisation as ultimately decisive in creating development. The latter tend to be *pessimists* who look to a much more radical transformation for development to occur, and to the advent of world socialism. Because of the similarities in their understanding of market mechanics I prefer to keep the two under one rubric, discriminating different emphases *within* the general paradigm they define rather than between them.

8. I do not subscribe to a single-factor theory of social change, nor would I appeal to an eclectic and indiscriminate multi-causal one. Some causal factors are more important than others, and in the contemporary world those technological, economic and cultural ones that cluster around the concepts of industrialisation, and more broadly, modernisation, are to my mind significant in this regard. Cf. P. Cohen, *Modern Social Theory* (Heinemann, London, 1968).

9. See O. Holsti, *The Study of International Politics Makes Strange Bedfellows: Theories of the 'Old Right' and the 'New Left'*, Centre for Advanced Study in the Behavioral Sciences (1972).

10. J. Shotter, *Images of Man in Psychological Research* (Methuen, London, 1976), p. 89.

INDEX

achievement 183, 204
agriculture 189
alienation 34, 36-8
anarchy 263
arms race 251

balance of power 51, 55, 265
basic needs 95, 97n9
behaviourism 19
bourgeoisie 142-4, 151, 169, 178n104,
    184; fractions of 129, 154, 233;
    global 48, 53, 76, 92, 128, 163-4,
    169, 230
bureaucracy 34, 35, 46, 95; and
    bourgeoisie 130; and the 'new
    class' 156; co-operative 206; in
    developing areas 212n92; Marxist
    concept of 205
bureaucratic collectivism 175n63
bureaucratisation 181, 200-7; and
    industrialism 204

capital 58, 144, 160, 178n104, 190;
    accumulation 46, and the state
    149, patterns of 158; finance
    148-9, 150-1; industrial 149, 151;
    internationalisation of 153-5;
    merchant 148-9
capitalism 22, 26, 36, 54, 81, 143,
    160, 162, 169; and imperialism
    149-50, 161; and law 237n24;
    and nationalism 125; and the
    formation of the state 178n107;
    and world society 92; as the mode
    of production of the world econ-
    omy 166; definition of 178n104,
    183; industrial 152, 158, 183;
    merchant 158; monopoly 149
capitalist: mode of production 255-6,
    as 'fair' 91
capital-logic 239n67
cargo cults 23
centre: capitalist 155; capital move-
    ments into 58; global 22, 23-4,
    166; social formations in 155-7;
    socialist 155
choice 20
Christianity 22

cities: and industry 194, 195; on the
    periphery 196
civil hegemony 133
civil society 130
class 13, 24, 52, 54, 172n11,n12,
    242; and class conflict 131, 141,
    168, 256; and state 130-2, 139,
    169; comprador 158; consciousness
    142, 153, 156, 169; definition of
    139-42; formation 52, 65, 141,
    154, 164, 168, 255; political 162;
    ruling 24, 132; structure in capital-
    ist and socialist states 156; trans-
    national corporate 154
class system: global 53-4, 59, 62
commodification 165, 183, 186,
    231, 233
commodity: labour as 93
common good 114; global 59, 78,
    227-8
community 214
conflict 241, 258n2; and capital 256;
    and class 257-8; and cybernetic
    stress 245; as a form of sociation
    246; international, statistical
    analyses of 249-50, 260n30;
    in world society; pluralist para-
    digm of 242-54, structuralist
    paradigm of 254-8; manage-
    ment 251; resolution 252; stim-
    ulation 251
consciousness 13, 18-20, 25, 66;
    class 142, 153, 156; political 133;
    scientific 26, 263; traditional 26
consensus: global 248
control strategies 214
convergence: of capitalism and
    socialism 205
core *see* centre
corporations 153-5, 226-7, 233-4; and
    the nation-state 154-5
culture 13, 17-18, 20-2, 25, 29, 166;
    and cultural penetration 24; and
    cultural Westernisation 47;
    industrial 26, 94, 127; Marxist
    concept of 24; oral 32; scientific
    29; world 25, 26, 34-41, 72, 96;
    written 32